THE EVERYTHING
Meals on a Budget Cookbook

Dear Reader,

It's hard to believe now, but when I first got married, my husband and I lived on $800 a month. That included the $300 rent on a one–bedroom apartment, utilities, insurance, clothes, and food. By relying on many of the recipes in this book, I made our budget work.

Some of my secret weapons included Dressed–Up Macaroni and Cheese, Tex–Mex Pizza, and 28¢ Split Pea Potage (at the time, it was 10¢ Split Pea Potage!). By using fresh food and not letting food go to waste, we ate very well. I made bread, pies, cakes, and desserts from scratch, and never bought any prepared food.

Now, as everyone is concerned about where our food is made and the safety of the food chain, many people are turning to old–fashioned recipes and cooking from scratch. Gardens are more popular than ever, and farmer's markets are crowded every weekend during the spring and summer. Not only does fresh food taste better, it's better for you and it's less expensive!

Food is the most fluid part of most household budgets. By following the precepts in this book, clipping coupons, making lists, and watching for sale items, you can feed your family well for less money. And you'll be feeding them better too, by turning away from fast food and take–out restaurants.

All but seven recipes in this book cost less than $2.00 per serving. I decided the number of servings for each recipe by the calorie count. All of the recipes in this book have between 200 and 600 calories per serving. Entrées have more and salads and breads less.

I hope you enjoy these simple and easy recipes and enjoy watching your budget balance as you feed your family delicious food.

Linda Larsen

Welcome to the EVERYTHING® Series!

These handy, accessible books give you all you need to tackle a difficult project, gain a new hobby, comprehend a fascinating topic, prepare for an exam, or even brush up on something you learned back in school but have since forgotten.

You can choose to read an *Everything*® book from cover to cover or just pick out the information you want from our four useful boxes: e-questions, e-facts, e-alerts, e-ssentials. We give you everything you need to know on the subject, but throw in a lot of fun stuff along the way, too.

We now have more than 400 *Everything*® books in print, spanning such wide-ranging categories as weddings, pregnancy, cooking, music instruction, foreign language, crafts, pets, New Age, and so much more. When you're done reading them all, you can finally say you know *Everything*®!

QUESTIONS?
Answers to
common questions

FACTS
Important snippets
of information

ALERTS!
Urgent
warnings

ESSENTIALS
Quick
handy tips

DIRECTOR OF INNOVATION Paula Munier

EDITORIAL DIRECTOR Laura M. Daly

EXECUTIVE EDITOR, SERIES BOOKS Brielle K. Matson

ASSOCIATE COPY CHIEF Sheila Zwiebel

ACQUISITIONS EDITOR Kerry Smith

DEVELOPMENT EDITOR Brett Palana-Shanahan

PRODUCTION EDITOR Casey Ebert

THE EVERYTHING MEALS on a BUDGET COOKBOOK

High-flavor, low-cost meals your family will love

Linda Larsen
The About.com Guide for Busy Cooks

avon, massachusetts

To my sweet Doug, again
and always.

An Everything® Series Book.
Everything® and everything.com® are registered trademarks
of F+W Publications, Inc.

Published by Adams Media, an F+W Publications Company
57 Littlefield Street, Avon, MA 02322 U.S.A.
www.adamsmedia.com

ISBN 10: 1-59869-508-8
ISBN 13: 978-1-59869-508-3

Printed in the United States of America.

J I H G F E D C B A

Library of Congress Cataloging-in-Publication Data
is available from the publisher.

This publication is designed to provide accurate and authoritative information
with regard to the subject matter covered. It is sold with the understanding that
the publisher is not engaged in rendering legal, accounting, or other professional advice. If legal advice or other expert assistance is required, the services
of a competent professional person should be sought.
—From a *Declaration of Principles* jointly adopted by a Committee of the
American Bar Association and a Committee of Publishers and Associations

Many of the designations used by manufacturers and sellers to distinguish their
products are claimed as trademarks. Where those designations appear in this
book and Adams Media was aware of a trademark claim, the designations have
been printed with initial capital letters.

This book is available at quantity
discounts for bulk purchases.
For information, please call
1-800-289-0963.

Contents

Introduction

ow many times have you gone to the store just to pick up a few items, only to end up paying $40.00 at the checkout, and for only one bag of food? Read on and you'll learn how to shop in a grocery store, plan meals, write lists so you won't run out of food unexpectedly, and make a few meals out of practically nothing.

Some thrifty cookbooks offer recipes for entrées that cost less than 50 cents a portion. While it is possible to feed your family on that, or less, look closely at some of the recipes. Many have calorie counts for main dishes that are 200 or 100 calories or less per serving. It's very difficult to feed a family, especially growing children, on that number of calories; children simply will not be satisfied. They'll come looking for snacks an hour after dinner, and there goes your plan and your budget.

The price per serving in this book, for all but seven recipes, is less than $2.00; many cost less than $1.00 per serving. Recent issues of popular magazines offered budget meals with a cost per serving of $2.50 or less, and a popular fast–food restaurant is bragging that you can feed your family for less than $4.00 a person. These meals are a deal! And each entrée recipe has at least 300 to 600 calories per serving, so you know your family won't be hungry again a few hours after dinner is over.

To cook successfully on a budget, you must follow a few rules. Making and abiding by a grocery list is one of the most important. Having a list in hand helps reduce temptation, and will keep you focused on your goal. When you're busy comparing the prices of two kinds of chopped canned tomatoes, you'll be less likely to think about the freshly made chocolate chip cookies beckoning you from the bakery.

In this book, you'll find tips on how to avoid the traps that grocery store designers set for you. (Look high and low on the shelves because the most expensive products are placed at eye level.) And you'll learn how to get the best value for your money with a little secret called unit pricing.

The Leftovers chapter is very special. Remember that each of those recipes can be used as a template for almost any leftover food. Make a quiche with leftover cooked chicken and broccoli one week, then an omelet with some cooked ground beef and Cheddar cheese the next. That's one of the secrets to efficient budget–minded cooking: using your imagination and having fun in the kitchen once you learn basic recipes.

The cost for each recipe was figured using NutriBase Clinical Version 7.0. To get the best representative cost for each ingredient, price lists at SimonDelivers.com, YourGrocery.com, and Peapod.com were used. Sale prices, discounts, and coupons were not included in the calculations, so you may find that prices in your area are higher or lower than those stated here. Every cook is different and so is every kitchen. These recipes were developed with cost savings in mind. Each recipe has the cost per serving, and many have a note to make the recipe more special and expensive if you want to splurge. Let's cook!

▸ CHAPTER 1 ◂

Cooking On a Budget

Doesn't it seem that every time you turn around, prices are going up? Changing weather conditions and natural disasters, strikes, inflation, recalls, and the price of oil and transportation all factor into grocery prices. With our busy lifestyles, it's usually easier to just stop at a fast–food joint, call up the local pizza place, or buy completely prepared foods that just need reheating at home. And your budget feels it. But you can control your budget—and still eat very well, for very little—as long as you learn some new habits and follow a few simple rules.

Start with a Plan

Everything should start with a plan, whether you're building a house, searching for a job, or trying to feed your family on less money. Writing lists, planning menus, and cutting coupons all take time, but like any worthwhile endeavor, will save you money in the end.

Here's the most important rule: you're automatically going to save money if you cook at home rather than eat out. The more work you do, the more money you will save. This may sound daunting, but once you get into the habit of cooking it will take you less and less time. By choosing to make your own food, you are controlling nutrition and are keeping your family healthy, which will save even more money in doctor's bills.

Did you know that it's cheaper to eat breakfast and lunch, rather than dinner, in a fancy restaurant? It can be the same at home! Breakfast recipes or lunch recipes for dinner are just as satisfying as traditional dinner food, and much less expensive. In addition, French toast, scrambled eggs, and grilled sandwiches are easier to make than most dinner recipes.

Plan every meal. Plan for snacks and for the occasional evening out. Plan to use leftovers, and budget for special occasions. This may feel rigid, but you will realize that when you have meals planned for the week, you will have the food you need in the house. Then you can relax and think about something other than what you're going to make for dinner every night.

The Indispensable List

To get started, go through your pantry, fridge, and freezer. For two weeks make a list of the staples your family uses. For instance, every week you may buy milk, bread, cereal, ground beef, carrots, tomatoes, and rice. Use these foods to create a master list to save time. Then post that master list on the refrigerator, and when you run out of a food make a note on the list.

The rest of your list should come from ingredients you need for your planned meals. Note the amounts you'll need and any specifics on the list. When you go shopping, abide by the list. But at the same time, be open to change! You may find that there are in–store specials on certain foods, especially meats, that might change your meal plan. Be flexible when you see something is a good buy.

Cutting Coupons

Coupons can save you a significant amount of money. But be sure to use coupons only for those products you know you will use. Sometimes manufacturers offer coupons for a free sample; that's a good way to try a product to see whether you and your family like it. If they do, look for more coupons!

There are many coupon sites on the Internet that offer free, printable coupons, like smartsource.com and thegrocerygame.com. Browse the sites, and if they offer coupons for the things you actually use and like, sign up for their mailing lists. Then each week you'll be reminded to check those sites for new coupons.

Be organized when you use coupons. Use a small folder or expandable notebook to keep your coupons organized by type of food. And be sure to review your coupons regularly, making sure you use them before they expire, and discarding those that are out of date.

Run the Grocery Store Gauntlet

Did you know that grocery stores are planned to keep you in the store for a longer period of time and to tempt you with the layout? The items people shop for, especially on quick mid–week runs, are located at the back of the store.

Grocery stores are usually laid out so you enter at the produce aisle. The gorgeous fruits and vegetables are a tempting visual feast, and often there are samples of fruits in season, laid out so you'll drop "just a few" into your basket as you walk by. The bakery aisle comes next, with its fabulous aromas and gorgeous loaves of bread, racks of cookies, and beautiful cakes.

After you've made it through these aisles, you'll finally come to the dairy aisle. But the milk, which you originally came in for, is at the end, past the cheeses, prepared meals, deli foods, and yogurts. You pick up the jug of milk and turn to leave. But first you have to pass the meat counter, and the snack food aisle, and oh yes, aren't you out of soda?

Meanwhile, pleasant music is piped throughout the store, and the ends of the aisles (known as "end caps" in the business) are packed with wonderful "bargains" to tempt you.

ALERT!

The only way to learn how much food is at the regular price, and therefore how much you save when it goes on sale, is to keep a running list. A small notebook will do. Take it with you when you shop, and make notes of the prices. After a few weeks you'll see a pattern emerge. So when that round steak goes on sale, you'll know if it's a good buy!

Choose a fixed time to go grocery shopping. For some people, first thing in the morning is an excellent time to shop. For others, late at night, when the stores are empty, shopping can be an efficient and soothing activity. And please, if at all possible, leave the children at home. Not only will they be tempted by special products placed exactly at their eye level, but they will slow you down. And it's too easy to give in and let them have that expensive box of cereal or candy just for some peace.

Always shop at a grocery store that you know well. If you have to search for items, not only will you waste time, but you may become so frustrated that you'll buy things you weren't intending to just because they look good at the moment. You don't have to limit yourself to one store, though! If you learn the layout of two or three stores, you can increase your chances of finding more bargains.

Never shop hungry. Foods that aren't on your list will look very appealing when you get a whiff of them or see them packaged so prettily in that colored wrap. Hunger distorts your judgment and will weaken even the strongest resolve.

When you shop for groceries, you'll notice a small plastic tag on the shelf below all of the products. This contains information about the food, including manufacturer's information and the cost per ounce, called unit pricing. Use this information to compare brands and product sizes to get the best value, and the most food for your money.

And finally, be sure to watch the prices at the checkout. Sometimes coupons aren't scanned properly, and the computer does make mistakes. Whether you are buying generic or have a "buy one get one free" coupon, be sure to check that cash register tape—before you leave the store.

The Biggest Budget Buster

The biggest budget buster isn't that $1.00 candy bar or $4.00 bag of grapes. It's waste! Americans throw away as much as 45 percent of the food they buy. If you spend $500 a month on food, you may be throwing away $225 a month. Whether it's a head of lettuce that languishes in the fridge until it wilts, or a steak imperfectly wrapped so it develops freezer burn, people are experts at wasting food.

FACT

Products that save steps in cooking are called "value–added." They can range from a fully–prepared seafood entrée stuffed with cheese to refrigerated biscuits to a can of tomatoes with garlic and herbs added. These products almost always cost more than the raw ingredients assembled by you. Be sure to compare prices and shop wisely.

Leftovers, even those that are not planned, can make another meal. Be careful to save leftovers, refrigerate food promptly, know what's in your fridge and freezer, and plan your weekly meals with leftovers in mind. In

Chapter 8, you'll find a collection of recipes specifically developed to use common leftovers, and more recipes like those are also sprinkled throughout the book.

Alternative Food Sources

Food co-ops may offer some significant savings. Use your notebook and compare prices. Sometimes, even if a food is more expensive at a co-op, you may purchase it if it has a special attribute, like organic certification or a label showing it's locally grown. Be sure that, before you join a co-op, you have walked through the store several times and are familiar with the foods it carries. Bulk bins in co-ops can be a significant budget saver.

ALERT!

If you have a fisherman or hunter in the family, all the better! But be sure that the food is quickly prepared and refrigerated or frozen. Also be sure that the lakes or ponds that your family member is fishing from are clean and wholesome. Many states post information about water quality and any warnings about eating fish from certain lakes.

In the spring, summer, and fall, farmer's markets can be a good source of inexpensive produce. Be sure you know the supermarket prices of foods, though. Sometimes the prices at these markets are higher than the regular grocery store. But again, there may be mitigating circumstances: you are supporting local farms and farmers, and you are buying the freshest possible produce.

Pick-your-own farms are a great idea, as long as you have the ability and space to process, preserve, and store the food. You'll never taste juicier, sweeter strawberries or crisper apples than those you pick yourself, right off the vine or tree.

Where to Cut Corners

Try to cut down on more expensive ingredients by reducing the amount you use in recipes or make up the difference with less expensive ingredients.

For instance, use just ¾ pound instead of a pound of beef, and add more chopped mushrooms to stretch the beef. Think of using meat as a flavoring instead of as the main ingredient in entrée recipes.

The price per ounce is the best indicator of value. Larger boxes, bottles, and cans may not always be the better buy. If your grocery store doesn't carry unit pricing information, carry a calculator and figure the cost per ounce yourself. Simply divide the price by the number of ounces in the product. Write this down in your price comparison notebook so you only have to do the work once.

Learn what an actual "serving size" is (see **TABLE 1–1**). Over the past twenty years, Americans have become used to "serving sizes" that are two to three times what the body actually needs. This is not only expensive, but is contributing to our expanding waistlines!

Table 1–1: Serving Sizes		
Food	**Serving Size**	**Recommended Servings Per Day**
Meat	2–3 ounces	1–2 servings
Legumes	½ cup	1–2 servings
Vegetables	½ cup cooked	3 or more servings
Fruit	1 medium piece	2 or more servings
Milk	8 ounces	1–2 servings
Cheese	1½ ounces	1–2 servings
Bread	1 ounce slice	3–4 servings
Cereal	1 cup	2–4 servings
Pasta	½ cup	1–3 servings

In restaurants and fast-food outlets, serving sizes, especially for meats, are too large. A person doesn't need ½ or even ¼ of a pound a meat in *every* meal. Your stomach is about the size of your fist. Think about fitting a large restaurant size–meal into something that size! Abide by FDA recommended serving sizes and your family will be healthier and weigh less too.

Think about where the food is going to be used. For instance, extra–virgin olive oil isn't necessary if you're using it primarily for sautéing food.

Regular olive oil is much cheaper. A generic brand of pasta will be just fine in a casserole, but you may want to buy a name brand if you're making Spaghetti Carbonara or another recipe where pasta is the star.

Generics

Generic foods first made an appearance on the American grocery store scene in the 1970s. These "non–brand" foods offer significant savings over brand name items. Is the difference worth it? What about quality?

Most food brands have to advertise in one way or another. Whether the companies choose print ads, television, or radio, the costs of advertising is included in the price of the food. But generic names don't advertise, so they do cost less than brand name products.

Generic foods are usually processed in the same plant as the brand name foods. The appearance may be slightly different, though. For instance, tomatoes with a less than perfect appearance may go into a can of generic stewed tomatoes. But the food quality, nutrition, and safety are the same. You can buy generic products without worrying about quality.

Money-Saving Tips

As with all tips, take these with a grain of salt. You may find bargains that don't follow the rules. Start by being flexible. Be flexible with serving sizes, with the amount of meats you use in recipes, and with what you've planned to eat for the week.

Tips for Not Wasting Food
- Plan meals for the week. All of them. Every week.
- Clean out your fridge every single week, without fail.
- Clean out your freezer every three months.
- Unless you can store it long-term, buy only what you need.
- Don't buy what your family doesn't like, even if it's a good deal.
- If you're tempted to run to a fast-food joint, start cooking; you're bound to finish.

Best Food Values

Generally, the simpler and less–processed the food, the cheaper it will be. Plain chicken breasts are cheaper per pound than boneless or seasoned. Pre–formed hamburger patties can be 30–40 percent more expensive than bulk ground meat.

Pasta, tomato sauce, plain fruits and vegetables, dairy products, and unprocessed meats all take more work on your part to make them into a meal, but you'll save the most money buying them. In addition, you can control what your family eats by reducing or eliminating salt, fat, and preservatives. Consider the time you have to spend and your comfort level using real versus artificial ingredients.

Generally, the closer to the source a food is, the lower its price will be and the fresher it will be. Once again, be sure to know the prices of foods in your area, so you can judge if the food offers good value.

Worst Food Values

The more processed a food is, the higher its price will be. Purchasing a 16-ounce jar of Alfredo sauce, for instance, usually costs around $3.10. But the ingredients to make the same amount of your own Alfredo sauce cost around $2.10.

While meats that have been prepared and are oven–ready, like stuffed chicken breasts and marinated pork roasts, are quick and easy, you are paying for that convenience. The cost of Spinach Stuffed Chicken Breasts (page 141) is $1.85 per serving, while the same dish, frozen and ready for the oven, costs $5.09 for two smaller servings.

You also waste money on excessively packaged foods. If there's shrink–wrap, a cardboard box, plastic dividers, and more plastic wrap around food, not only is that wasting Earth's resources, but it costs you money to throw it away.

The same goes for prepared fruits and vegetables. A package of baby–cut carrots, now the most popular form of carrots in the supermarket, costs around $1.60 for 12 ounces, and a 10–ounce bag of shredded carrots is $1.99, while a bag of regular sized carrots is 99 cents for a pound (16 ounces). You need to decide how much work you want to do if your main concern is your budget.

Don't forget that almost all products you buy are guaranteed. If you buy a product and don't think that the quality is good, tell the company about it instead of just throwing it away. Write to them via their Web site or address on the package. They want you to be happy and will probably send you a coupon to try another one of their products. The store you shop at may also have a generous return policy. But don't abuse this privilege!

Ground meats, like ground beef, pork, sausages, ground turkey, and chicken vary greatly in price. Ground turkey and chicken are generally more expensive, so compare prices. You may get a better deal by buying boneless meat and grinding it yourself in the food processor or food mill. Ground beef is more difficult to make at home, so buy it after carefully checking the unit price.

Actual Yield

One issue rarely addressed in budget cookbooks is the issue of yield (see **TABLE 1–2**). Sure, the price of boneless pork chops is $1.00 more per pound than the bone–in variety, but what are you really spending for actual yield?

Table 1–2: Meat Prices Per Ounce of Cooked Meat				
Meat	Type	Price Raw/ Pound	Cooked Yield	Price Cooked/ Ounce
Ground Beef	73% lean	$2.60	11.68 ounces	22 cents
Ground Beef	80% lean	$3.00	12.80 ounces	23 cents
Ground Beef	85% lean	$3.99	13.60 ounces	29 cents
Ground Beef	93% lean	$4.99	14.88 ounces	33 cents
Chicken Breasts	Boneless	$5.28	15.52 ounces	34 cents
Chicken Breasts	Bone–In	$2.72	7.76 ounces	35 cents
Pork Chops	Boneless	$6.85	12.80 ounces	54 cents
Pork Chops	Bone–In	$5.70	8.80 ounces	65 cents

If you calculate three ounces of cooked beef per serving, the best buy is 80 percent lean ground beef. You are getting four three-ounce servings per pound, which is the standard USDA recommended amount, and there is less waste in fat and gristle than with the 73 percent lean beef. Also, the leaner types of ground beef are usually made from a more expensive cut of meat, accounting for the different fat amounts and the price difference.

Bone-in, skin-on chicken breasts cost around 17 cents per ounce, while boneless, skinless breasts cost about 34 cents per ounce. That's a no brainer, right? Nope! Only about half of the bone-in, skin-on chicken is edible, so they average out to about the same cost. However, you can use the skin, bones, and leftover meat on the bone–in, skin–on breasts to make chicken stock for practically no cost so in this way you can stretch your budget.

Boneless pork chops are a better buy than bone-in chops because the yield is so much higher. But bone-in meat can have more flavor than boneless, especially if it's slow–cooked. The choice is yours.

More Ways to Save Money

Saving money and cutting corners will become second nature. You'll discover more ways to save money and feed your family better than ever before. The way you handle, store, and cook food will lower your grocery costs.

Save Money Growing Food

Even if you don't have a backyard or a small area of land to grow food, you can supplement your budget by growing food. Many plants grow very well in pots, as long as they are well cared for. One tomato plant can yield up to thirty pounds of fresh tomatoes over a growing season. Choose fruits, vegetables, and herbs that can be frozen or dried to preserve your harvest.

If you garden, one way to recycle food scraps and even food that has spoiled is to start a compost pile. Don't include meat, dairy products (except crushed eggshells), or high-fat foods like salad dressings.

You can have a few small pots with some herbs growing on a sunny windowsill in your kitchen. Fresh herbs are one of the most expensive items in the grocery store, and they add fabulous flavor and aroma to foods. Grow them at home!

Save Money Storing Food

Remember to clean out your fridge once a week and your freezer once every three months. Rotate foods, using the oldest first, making sure to mark the dates food was purchased, stored, or frozen. You might want to think about posting a list of the leftovers on your fridge so you don't forget about that bit of cooked chicken or broiled salmon. To wrap foods properly, first be sure they are completely cool. Cool food, unwrapped, in the refrigerator. Then layer waxed paper or plastic wrap on top of foil and either cover the food tightly, or wrap it completely, being sure there are no exposed parts of the food. Squeeze out any excess air, and seal with freezer tape. Be sure to label those packages!

In the freezer, wrap foods properly. Freezer burn is caused by dehydration, which is caused by improper wrapping. The freezer is a very dry place, and unless food is stored in freezer bags or containers, well wrapped (not just the end tucked into a package), it will dry out. Food with freezer burn isn't dangerous, but it is unpalatable.

In your pantry, make sure that you can see all of the food stored there. Wire baskets and shelves will help separate foods so you can see what's on hand. Group the same types of foods together and use older foods first. And again, mark the purchase date on the product and follow use–by dates to the letter.

Save Money Cooking

Undercooked or overcooked food is wasted as much as food that is allowed to go bad in your refrigerator. Be sure that you understand "doneness." For instance, meats have specific temperatures at which they are safe to eat (see **TABLE 1–3**). A meat thermometer is a good investment that will help you prevent waste.

Table 1–3: Meat Doneness Temperatures		
Meat	**Doneness**	**Internal Temperature**
Ground Meats	Well Done	165°F
Beef	Rare	140°F
Beef	Medium	145°F
Beef	Well Done	160°F
Chicken Light Meat	Well Done	165°F
Chicken Dark Meat	Well Done	170°F
Whole Chicken	Well Done	180°F
Pork	Medium Well	155°F

Learn the difference between "crisp" and "tender" when cooking vegetables and train yourself to recognize when pasta and rice are perfectly cooked. These skills come with experience; when you're beginning, rely on cooking times in recipes.

Watch foods carefully when they are sautéing, broiling, baking, or grilling. Set your timer for a few minutes short of the shortest cooking time in a recipe so baked goods won't burn.

There are many places to save money on purchasing appliances. From eBay to exchange sites like freecycle.com, you can find good deals on slow cookers, pressure cookers, toaster ovens, and kitchen utensils.

ALERT!

Used appliances can be a great deal and save you a lot of money, but you should be cautious buying and using them. If you buy a used electric or gas appliance, be sure to have it inspected by a qualified technician to make sure it is safe to use. Also, gas appliances, especially, should be installed by a professional.

You can also save money with the appliances you choose to use. Slow cookers, pressure cookers, toaster ovens, and microwaves operate for just pennies. Think about the amount you're cooking when you preheat an appliance. If you only need to toast a few nuts, use your toaster oven or microwave rather than using your large regular oven. Only preheat your oven when necessary. For example, recipes that will cook in the oven for longer than one hour don't need any preheating time.

Save Money with Leftovers

Refrigerate leftovers promptly so they can be used. Remember, any perishable food (that includes meat and dairy) that is left out more than two hours at room temperature MUST be discarded because it can develop bacteria and toxins that will make you sick.

Collect recipes that use small amounts of leftovers. For instance, if at the end of the week you have a cup of ground beef, ½ cup of cooked carrots, some mashed potatoes, and grated cheese left over, combine those for a filling that you stuff into pizza dough to make calzones. A quick stir-fry (just to heat up cooked ingredients) is also an excellent way to use bits and pieces of leftover food.

Plan leftovers too. If you're cooking chicken breasts, cook one or two extra and refrigerate promptly. Then use the cooked chicken later that week in a sandwich spread or in chicken noodle soup. If you're splurging and serving salmon fillets, cook one more and save it to toss with spaghetti, chopped tomatoes, and pesto to make another entire meal.

What's in Season?

Back in the twentieth century, many products used to be available only during the growing seasons. Strawberries, raspberries, asparagus, apples, and most other fruits and vegetables, were harvested in the spring, summer, and fall in the United States, and that is when they appeared in the grocery stores.

Now, because many foods are imported from other countries, you can eat strawberries and raspberries in the dead of winter, and apples in early spring. The prices will fluctuate with the seasons, however, and that's where you can pocket some significant savings.

The seasons also affect frozen and processed foods. At the beginning of the growing season you can find frozen fruits and vegetables at significant savings because manufacturers and distributors want to move goods before the new crop is harvested and processed.

Preserving Food

If you choose to can food, be sure to keep safety in mind. Get information about safe canning methods from your state university extension office. Call the university in your state and ask for information about home food preservation. They'll connect you to the correct department. There is also lots of information online from extension services. Go to *www.csrees.usda .gov/Extension* and click on your state in the map to be connected to the extension program in your area. Extension services also offer information about buying supplies and timing charts for processing.

Drying foods is a good way to preserve them. Food dehydrators work well and may be a good investment if you prefer to preserve food with this method. Herbs, especially, are a good bargain if you grow and dry them yourself.

If you want to freeze food, there are many sources of good information. *The Everything® Meals for a Month Cookbook* has complete information about preparing, wrapping, freezing, thawing, and reheating foods.

The Food Chain and You

Eating lower on the food chain will help you save money. For instance, in the price of a steak, costs include the grain fed to cattle, which is grown on huge amounts of land, using lots of labor and energy. Then the shipping, producing, inspecting, and processing costs combine to make the cost of a steak around $6.00 a pound.

If, instead, you eat lower on the food chain you will save more money. Vegetarian meals can be very inexpensive, but you must be sure that you combine foods (grains and legumes, or grains and nuts or seeds) to ensure meals have complete protein for the best health.

Simple Splurges

Butter is so superior to margarine in flavor that it's difficult to substitute margarine for it in many recipes. In recipes where the fat is used for structure but not flavor, margarine will work well; but don't use reduced–fat or tub margarines, which contain a lot of water. Use butter when necessary to add flavor to a recipe and use only as much as a recipe calls for. Butter freezes well so buy a pound when it's on sale, especially during the holiday season, then label and freeze it.

Cheeses can add a lot of flavor to your cooking, and if you choose highly flavored varieties, a little can go a long way. A quarter–cup of feta cheese can flavor four sandwiches, and one cup of extra–sharp Cheddar cheese mixed with bread crumbs will create a wonderful topping on a ground beef casserole that will serve 6 to 8.

QUESTION?

Should I use imitation or real extracts?
It depends on what you're making. If it's a cookie with many ingredients including chocolate and nuts, imitation vanilla is just fine. It's about 10 percent of the cost of real vanilla. But a simple shortbread cookie may demand the real thing. In a recent taste test, a panel of home economists liked the foods made with imitation vanilla more than those made with real vanilla. Have a taste test yourself and decide.

Use more expensive ingredients as garnishes. A cup of shrimp is an excellent garnish on grilled fish fillets topped with chopped tomato and herbs, and it will finish six servings for just a little money. Macadamia nuts, chopped and sprinkled over a cup of soup, add great flavor as well as eye appeal for a small cost.

Any special food that your family really loves is a worthwhile splurge. Save up to buy that pound of shrimp or smoked salmon to celebrate a special occasion. There's no point in working so hard to save money if you can't splurge once in a while.

Basic Ingredients

With the ingredients listed here on hand all of the time, you will be able to make several complete meals without having to run to the store. Store these foods safely and abide by use-by dates. And use your imagination when considering how to combine these ingredients.

In the Fridge

Milk is a very inexpensive source of protein. If you'd like to save more money, you can make milk from dried milk powder and water, then combine it with fresh milk and chill thoroughly before serving.

Cheese provides a good source of protein and calcium and can be inexpensive depending on how you prepare it. When shredding cheese you're introducing more surface area for your taste buds to react to, so shredded cheese offers more flavor per ounce than sliced cheese.

Many people are eating lower fat products for their health. Consider that some low-fat products have a different taste than the regular varieties. Low-fat cheeses, especially, have less flavor than regular cheeses, so your family may use more of them to compensate. Figure that into the cost when buying these items.

Eggs are also a cheap source of protein. Recent research has shown that most people can eat one egg per day without fear of increasing their cholesterol level. To stretch eggs even more, scramble them with some milk or sour cream!

In the Pantry

Pasta and rice are staples around the world. If you have been avoiding those foods because of a low-carb diet, try whole-grain versions. Those varieties are a bit more expensive, but they are so much cheaper than serving a big chunk of meat for dinner.

Canned fruits and vegetables can make an inexpensive quick meal with little work. Combine some diced tomatoes with minced green chiles and toss with couscous or pasta, then top with pregrated canned Parmesan cheese and you can serve a healthy dinner in minutes.

In the Freezer

Making your own meals and freezing them is one of the best ways to save money and feed your family well. You don't have to cook large amounts. Just double one or two meals a week and freeze the second batch. Before you know it you'll have several meals ready and waiting for you; it's better than takeout!

When you find a good buy on expensive meats or seafood, purchase extra, then carefully wrap, label, and freeze. Be sure to freeze only those foods that handle the freezing process without losing quality.

Let's Eat!

Now that you understand the basics of shopping, unit pricing, list making, cooking, and storing food, here are the recipes that will feed your family well for less money. The price per serving has been kept to $2.00 or less; in many cases, it is below $1.00. Your savings may be greater if you can apply coupons, sale prices, or other bargains. You can also add splurges, by adding more meat per serving, including more expensive or value-added ingredients, or by increasing the serving size. Remember to enjoy your food, eating with family, and the process of cooking and baking.

CHAPTER 2

Cheap and Easy
Appetizers and Snacks

2

Quick and Easy Salsa

COST PER SERVING
26¢

YIELDS ► 3 CUPS
SERVING SIZE ► ¼ CUP

3 red tomatoes, chopped
1 green bell pepper, chopped
1 jalapeño pepper, minced
½ cup chopped red onion
1 clove garlic, minced
2 tablespoons lemon juice
½ teaspoon salt
⅛ teaspoon cayenne pepper
1 tablespoon olive oil

Salsa is one of the easiest recipes to make, although it can be very expensive to buy. If you have fresh tomatoes from your garden, all the better!

Combine all ingredients in medium bowl and mix gently. Cover and refrigerate up to 8 hours before serving.

Freezing Salsa Salsa will freeze and defrost well, but the consistency will be different. Because tomatoes and pepper are so high in water content, they will be a little mushier (like cooked sauce) when frozen and defrosted. But this texture will still be acceptable to most people.

Spicy Pita Chips

COST PER SERVING
3¢

YIELDS ► 64 CHIPS

4 (4-inch) pita bread rounds
3 tablespoons roasted garlic vinaigrette
3 tablespoons finely grated Cotija cheese
1 teaspoon salt
½ teaspoon cayenne pepper

These inexpensive and flavorful little chips are perfect for dipping; they're sturdier than potato chips so they won't break apart in heavier dips, like Big Batch Guacamole (page 24).

1. Preheat oven to 400°F. Using kitchen scissors or a sharp knife, cut the pita rounds in half to make eight rounds. Cut each round into 8 wedges. Arrange wedges on two cookie sheets, rough side up.

2. In small bowl, combine remaining ingredients and mix well. Drizzle this mixture evenly over the pita chips.

3. Bake for 8–13 minutes or until chips are crisp and golden brown. Remove to paper towels to cool. Store in air-tight container.

Creamiest Cheese Dip

COST PER SERVING **37¢**

Adding a bit of butter to a cheese spread really softens the "mouth feel," technical term that means how quickly food softens on your tongue. Try adding it to other dip recipes too.

1. In medium bowl, beat cream cheese with electric mixer until soft and fluffy.

2. Add butter; beat until well blended. Then add remaining ingredients; beat until soft and creamy, about 3 minutes.

3. Serve immediately or cover and refrigerate up to 2 days. For the best texture, let refrigerated dip stand at room temperature for 30 minutes before serving.

> **Softening Cream Cheese**   Cream cheese must be softened before combining with other ingredients, or there will be small lumps of cream cheese throughout the finished product. To soften cream cheese, unwrap it and microwave at 50 percent power for 1–2 minutes, then let stand for 5 minutes. Or let it stand at room temperature for 45 minutes before using.

SERVES ▶ 8

1 (8-ounce) package cream cheese, softened

3 tablespoons butter or margarine, softened

½ cup sour cream

1 teaspoon dried Italian seasoning

⅛ teaspoon white pepper

Yogurt Cheese Veggie Dip

Yogurt cheese takes some time to make, but it lasts for days and is a great substitute for cream cheese. And it's cheaper! For a splurge, use purchased pesto.

SERVES ► 10

2 cups plain yogurt

1 tablespoon olive oil

4 cloves garlic, minced

½ cup shredded carrots

½ cup Spinach Pesto (page 28)

1. The day before, place the yogurt into a strainer or colander that has been lined with a double layer of cheesecloth or a paper coffee filter. Place the strainer over a bowl, cover the whole thing with plastic wrap, cover with a small plate and weight with a 1-pound can, and let stand in the refrigerator for 24 hours.

2. The next day, remove the cheese from the strainer and freeze the whey to use in other recipes.

3. In microwave-safe medium bowl, combine olive oil, garlic, and carrots. Microwave on high for 1 minute, remove and stir, then microwave on high for 30 second intervals until vegetables are tender. Drain well and let cool for 20 minutes. Stir into yogurt cheese along with pesto. Cover and chill for at least 2 hours before serving.

> **Freezing Whey** Whey is full of vitamins and minerals and is a great addition to almost any soup (except clear soups). To freeze it, place it in ice cube trays and freeze until solid. Remove the cubes from the trays, package into freezer bags, label, and freeze up to 3 months. To use, just drop the cubes into the soup and heat.

The Dip Olé!

COST PER SERVING
41¢

Make sure that you thoroughly cook dried beans for best texture. For a splurge, add a layer of Big Batch Guacamole (page 24) between the bean and cream cheese layer.

SERVES ▶ 16

1 cup dried pinto beans

1 onion, chopped

2 tablespoons chili powder

1 (8-ounce) package cream cheese, softened

1 cup sour cream

1 (4-ounce) can diced green chiles, undrained

2 cups chopped iceberg lettuce

1 tomato, chopped

1 cup shredded Cheddar cheese

1. The day before you want to serve the dip, sort the pinto beans, removing any foreign objects. Rinse the beans thoroughly and cover with 10 cups cold water. Cover and let stand overnight. In the morning, drain the beans and place in a 3–4 quart slow cooker with the onion. Add 6 cups water, cover, and cook on low for 8–9 hours until tender.

2. Test to see whether the beans are tender. If necessary, drain the pinto beans, reserving ¼ cup of the cooking liquid. Place the beans and onions in large bowl with the chili powder. Using a potato masher, mash the beans, leaving some whole. Add reserved cooking liquid as needed until a spreading consistency is reached.

3. In another medium bowl, beat cream cheese until softened. Add sour cream and chiles; mix until blended.

4. On a large platter, spread the pinto bean mixture. Top with the sour cream mixture, leaving a 1" border of the bean mixture showing around the edges. Top with lettuce, tomato, and cheese. Serve immediately or cover and chill up to 2 days. Serve with taco or tortilla chips.

Big Batch Guacamole

COST PER SERVING
34¢

SERVES ► 8–10

Lima beans are soft, pillowy, tender, and nutty; a lot like avocados. They're so inexpensive and really stretch expensive avocados in this delicious recipe.

1 cup dried lima beans

½ cup chopped onion

3 tablespoons lemon juice

½ teaspoon salt

1 tablespoon butter, melted

¼ teaspoon cayenne pepper

3 ripe avocados

1 tomato, chopped

1. The day before you want to serve the dip, sort the lima beans, discarding any foreign objects. Rinse thoroughly and drain well. Combine in heavy saucepan with cold water to cover and chopped onion. Cover and refrigerate overnight. The next morning, bring the mixture to a boil, reduce heat, and simmer for 70–80 minutes or until very tender. Drain beans and onions and cool.

2. When you want to serve the dip, combine lemon juice, salt, butter, and cayenne pepper in a food processor. If necessary, drain the bean mixture; add the cooled bean and onion mixture to the lemon juice mixture and process until smooth. Then peel and slice the avocados; add to processor and process again until smooth. Stir in the chopped tomato. Serve immediately, or cover and refrigerate up to 8 hours before serving.

How to Store Guacamole When storing guacamole, be sure to press waxed paper or plastic wrap directly on the surface (don't use aluminum foil). When avocados are cut, enzymes in the cells react with air and turn brown. Keep air away from guacamole, and it won't turn brown! Lemon juice or other acid also helps delay this chemical reaction.

Faux Gras *(Almost the Real Thing)*

COST PER SERVING 84¢

Real foie gras is incredibly expensive, and very controversial because the geese are force-fed to fatten them up. This recipe uses inexpensive chicken livers and a few other ingredients to duplicate the taste and texture of the real thing.

SERVES ▶ 8

1-½ pounds chicken livers

4 slices bacon

¼ cup butter

1 cup finely chopped onion

1 egg

½ teaspoon dried thyme leaves

½ cup soft white bread crumbs

½ cup whipping cream, divided

1. Carefully trim the chicken livers, removing any membranes and tubes. Set aside. In heavy skillet, partially cook bacon until some of the fat is rendered out but the bacon is still pliable. Set bacon aside.

2. Add butter to skillet with bacon drippings. Add onions and cook over medium heat until onions are golden brown, stirring frequently, about 8–10 minutes. Add chicken livers. Cook and stir over medium heat until livers are light brown outside but still pink inside. Remove chicken liver mixture to bowl of food processor and let cool for 30 minutes. Meanwhile, combine egg, thyme, bread crumbs, and ¼ cup whipping cream in small bowl; stir to blend and let stand.

3. Process chicken liver mixture until smooth; add egg mixture and process again until smooth. In small bowl, beat ¼ cup whipping cream until stiff peaks form. Fold into chicken liver mixture.

4. Preheat oven to 350°F. Line bottom and sides of a 9" x 5" loaf pan with the partially cooked bacon. Carefully spoon liver mixture into pan. Cover tightly with foil and bake for 55–65 minutes or until bacon is cooked and pate is set. Uncover and cool on wire rack for one hour, then cover and chill until serving time. Remove from pan and slice thinly to serve.

Cowboy Caviar

*Real caviar can cost up to $200 a pound! This fun recipe
uses black beans to resemble caviar.*

SERVES ► 8–10

2 (15-ounce) cans black beans

1 (15-ounce) can stewed whole
tomatoes, drained

1 jalapeño pepper, minced

½ cup zesty Italian salad dressing

¼ cup olive oil

2 tablespoons red wine vinegar

1 tablespoon Dijon mustard

2 cloves garlic, minced

⅛ teaspoon pepper

⅛ teaspoon cayenne pepper

½ teaspoon salt

¼ cup chopped fresh cilantro

1. Rinse and drain the beans in a colander. Chop the tomatoes and
   add to the beans along with the pepper and salad dressing.

2. In bowl, combine olive oil, vinegar, mustard, garlic, pepper, cayenne pepper, salt, and cilantro and mix well. Add to bean mixture
   and stir gently. Cover and refrigerate for at least 8 hours before
   serving so the beans have time to absorb the liquid and flavors.

> *About Vinegars* White distilled, or plain, vinegar is the cheapest
> but it can have a harsh taste. Apple cider vinegar is milder and smooth,
> and only a bit more expensive. Red and white wine vinegars are more
> expensive but have more flavor. And delicious aged balsamic vinegar can
> cost up to $30.00 a cup!

Crabby Dip

*Imitation crab legs, or surimi, is made from mild white fish,
colored and flavored so it tastes like crab.*

SERVES ► 8–10

1 tablespoon olive oil

½ cup chopped onion

1 green bell pepper, chopped

1 (8-ounce) package cream cheese,
softened

¼ cup mayonnaise

½ cup seafood cocktail sauce,
divided

2 tablespoons mustard

1 (8-ounce) package frozen surimi,
thawed

½ cup grated Parmesan cheese

1. Preheat oven to 350°F. In small saucepan, combine olive oil,
   onion, and green pepper over medium heat. Cook and stir until
   vegetables are crisp-tender, about 4 minutes. Remove from heat
   and let stand for 15 minutes.

2. Meanwhile, in medium bowl combine cream cheese with mayonnaise. Beat until smooth, then stir in ¼ cup cocktail sauce,
   the mustard, and all but 2 tablespoons Parmesan cheese.

3. Cut the surimi into bite-sized pieces and fold into cream cheese mixture along with onions and green pepper; mix well. Place in 8" glass
   baking dish and sprinkle with remaining Parmesan cheese. Bake for
   15–25 minutes or until dip bubbles around the edges and the cheese
   melts. Drizzle with remaining cocktail sauce and serve.

"Lobster" Egg Rolls

COST PER SERVING
61¢

Cod is similar to lobster's fine texture and dense consistency. Cooking it in apple juice adds lobster's characteristic sweetness. These fabulous little appetizers are perfect for a fancy dinner.

YIELDS ► 12 EGG ROLLS

1 cup apple juice

½ pound cod fillets

2 tablespoons butter

2 cloves garlic, minced

½ cup finely chopped onion

½ cup finely chopped carrot

1 tablespoon lemon juice

¼ teaspoon Old Bay Seasoning

12 (6-inch) egg roll wrappers

1 egg, beaten

2 tablespoons water

2 cups peanut oil

1. In heavy saucepan, bring apple juice to a simmer. Add fish, cover, and simmer for 3–5 minutes or until fish flakes when tested with fork. Remove fish from apple juice and place in medium bowl; discard apple juice, wipe out pan, and add butter, garlic, onion, and carrot. Cook and stir over medium heat for 4–5 minutes, then pour over fish in bowl; sprinkle with lemon juice and Old Bay Seasoning. Using a fork, flake fish and blend ingredients together; set aside.

2. Open egg roll wrappers; dampen a dish towel and lay over the wrappers. In a small bowl, combine egg and water; beat until combined. Working with the wrappers one at a time, lay out wrappers with point toward you. Place about ¼ cup of the filling in the center. Roll up once, fold in ends, and roll to close. Use egg mixture to seal edges. Repeat with remaining wrappers and filling.

3. Heat peanut oil in large heavy saucepan until it reaches 375°F. Fry egg rolls, two to three at a time, until golden brown, turning once, about 4–6 minutes. Drain on paper towels, cut in half, and serve.

Old Bay Seasoning Old Bay Seasoning is the classic blend of spices used for cooking seafood. You can make your own mix; it's cheaper and it's fun. Combine 1 tablespoon celery salt, ½ teaspoon paprika, ⅛ teaspoon dry mustard, ⅛ teaspoon each white and cayenne peppers, and ⅛ teaspoon allspice.

Spinach Pesto

COST PER SERVING 33¢

Frozen chopped spinach not only reduces the cost of pesto, but it also adds nutrients and fiber. The lemon juice keeps it a nice bright green color.

SERVES ► 16

1 (10-ounce) package frozen spinach, thawed

½ cup fresh basil leaves

1 teaspoon dried basil leaves

2 tablespoons lemon juice

½ cup chopped walnuts

½ teaspoon salt

⅛ teaspoon white pepper

⅓ cup grated Parmesan cheese

½ cup virgin olive oil

1. Drain thawed spinach in a colander, pressing with your fingers to remove excess water. Combine in blender or food processor with basil, dried basil, lemon juice, walnuts, salt, pepper, and cheese. Process until finely chopped.

2. While processor is running, slowly add olive oil until a smooth thick sauce forms. Serve immediately or cover and refrigerate up to 3 days. Freeze up to 3 months.

Suave Fruit Salsa

COST PER SERVING 43¢

This delicious salsa can be served with corn or tortilla chips, or used as a sauce on grilled fish or chicken.

SERVES ► 12
SERVING SIZE ► ½ CUP

1 (15-ounce) can pineapple tidbits

1 (16-ounce) can sliced peaches

1 cucumber

¼ cup peach preserves

1 jalapeño pepper, minced

½ cup finely chopped red onion

½ teaspoon salt

⅛ teaspoon cayenne pepper

2 tablespoons lemon juice

1. Drain pineapple, reserving ¼ cup juice. Drain peaches, reserving 2 tablespoons juice. Chop peaches and combine with pineapple in medium bowl.

2. Peel cucumber, cut in half, remove seeds, and chop. Add to bowl with pineapple. In a small bowl, combine reserved juices, preserves, jalapeño, red onion, salt, pepper, and lemon juice and mix well. Pour over pineapple mixture and toss gently. Serve immediately or cover and refrigerate up to 2 days.

Crisp Potato Skins

COST PER SERVING
35¢

Making mashed potatoes from scratch is most cost-effective. What to do with the skins? Make this fabulous appetizer, of course! To splurge, double the bacon.

SERVES ▶ 6–8

1. Preheat oven to 400°F. Cut the potato skin halves in half again to make 24 slices; set aside. In a heavy skillet, cook bacon until crisp, remove from skillet, and drain on paper towels. Crumble and set aside. To drippings remaining in skillet, add butter and garlic. Cook over medium heat until garlic is tender, about 3 minutes.

2. Remove skillet from heat and let stand for 10–15 minutes to cool slightly. Then dip each potato skin slice into the butter mixture and place on ungreased baking sheets. Sprinkle skins with salt and pepper.

3. Bake the potato skins for 10 minutes or until they start turning golden and crisp. Remove from oven and sprinkle with cheese and reserved crumbled bacon. Return to oven and bake for 5–8 minutes longer until potato skins are crisp and cheese is melted. Serve immediately.

12 potato skin halves from Creamy Mashed Potatoes (page 224)

3 slices bacon

¼ cup butter

3 cloves garlic, minced

1 teaspoon salt

¼ teaspoon cayenne pepper

1 cup finely grated Cheddar cheese

Cooking Bacon Bacon can be cooked in several ways. You can place it in a cold pan over medium heat and sauté, turning frequently, until the bacon is crisp. It can also be baked on a broiler pan in a 400°F oven for 15–20 minutes until brown. Broiling bacon works well too. Place it 6" from heat source, turning frequently, until brown and crisp.

Freeze Ahead Cheese Puffs

COST PER SERVING **11¢**

YIELDS ▶ 32 PUFFS

*Leftover bread, cream cheese, Cheddar cheese, and onion
can be used in this wonderful freeze–ahead appetizer recipe.
To splurge, add 1 cup crabmeat to the cheese spread.*

1 (3-ounce) package cream cheese,
softened

1 tablespoon grated onion

½ cup mayonnaise

2 tablespoons chopped cilantro

¼ cup grated Cheddar cheese

8 slices bread

1. In medium bowl, combine cream cheese with onion; beat well.
Add mayonnaise gradually, stirring to mix well. Stir in cilantro
and cheese.

2. Cut bread into 4 triangles each. Spread bread with cheese mixture. Place on baking sheet and freeze until solid; remove and
pack into hard sided freezer containers. Freeze up to 3 months.
To bake immediately, bake at 350°F for 12–15 minutes. To bake
from frozen, bake for 16–20 minutes.

About Your Freezer If you have a garden or make a lot of foods
to freeze, think about investing in a chest freezer. You can find them at
scratch and dent sales and sometimes at garage sales. Have an electri-
cian check it out to make sure it's safe to use, then keep a freezer thermometer in it. The temperature should be 0°F or less.

Cheesy Potato Chips

COST PER SERVING 19¢

*Homemade potato chips are so fun to make, and they taste
so much better than packaged chips. For best results, you must
use the fine, pre–grated Parmesan cheese.*

1. Slice potato into paper thin slices, using a vegetable peeler, the slicing blade on a box grater, or a mandoline. As you work, place the potato slices into a bowl of ice water.

2. In a large deep and heavy pot, heat peanut oil over high heat until it reaches 375°F. Remove a handful of potato slices from the ice water and dry thoroughly on kitchen towels. Carefully drop potato slices into the hot oil. Cook and stir to separate. Fry until golden brown. Remove with a large strainer and place in a single layer on fresh paper towels to cool. Immediately sprinkle with some cheese and salt and toss. Repeat with remaining chips, cheese, and salt. Cool completely, then store in air tight container up to 1 week.

> *Which Parmesan Cheese?* When you're preparing snack or appetizer recipes that aren't going to be refrigerated, like this one or Hot and Spicy Popcorn (page 32), use the finely grated Parmesan cheese in the green container. That cheese is meant to be stored at room temperature and doesn't need refrigeration, and it's much cheaper than freshly grated cheese.

SERVES ▶ 8

2 russet potatoes, peeled or unpeeled

4 cups peanut oil

⅓ cup finely grated shelf-stable Parmesan cheese

1 teaspoon salt

Hot and Spicy Popcorn

SERVES ▶ 12

The cheapest popcorn is the kind you buy in the large glass containers. Pop it in an air popper, or on the stovetop over medium high heat.

4 quarts popped popcorn

½ cup butter, melted

3 tablespoons olive oil

3 tablespoons chili powder

1 teaspoon cumin

2 teaspoons salt

1 teaspoon red pepper flakes

1 cup shelf-stable Parmesan cheese

1. Preheat oven to 300°F. For 4 quarts of popcorn, start with ½ cup unpopped kernels. Place in air popper, or in large stockpot over medium high heat. When kernels start to pop, shake pan constantly over heat. Remove from heat when popping slows down. Remove any unpopped kernels.

2. In medium saucepan, combine butter and olive oil and melt over medium heat. Remove from heat and add chili powder, cumin, salt, and red pepper flakes. Place popcorn in two large baking pans. Drizzle butter mixture over popcorn. Sprinkle each pan with Parmesan cheese; toss to coat.

3. Bake for 15–20 minutes, stirring twice during baking time, until popcorn is crisp and cheese is melted. Serve warm or cool and store in air tight container up to 3 days.

Make Your Own Microwave Popcorn You can make microwave popcorn with the regular popcorn you buy in glass jars. Just pour about ¼ cup of unpopped kernels into a brown paper lunch sack. Fold over the top edge twice, then set upright in the microwave. Cook on high for 2–3 minutes or until popping slows down to a pop every two seconds.

Zorba's Hummus

COST PER SERVING
37¢

*Hummus is usually made with tahini, or sesame seed paste.
It's quite expensive, so peanut butter is an inexpensive alternative;
use the real thing for a splurge.*

1. Sort through the garbanzo beans and rinse well. Cover with cold water and let stand overnight. The next day, drain the beans, rinse well, and place in saucepan with onion, whole garlic cloves, and water. Bring to a boil, reduce heat, cover, and simmer for 1½ to 2 hours until beans are tender.

2. Drain beans. Place beans, onion, and garlic in food processor along with lemon juice, half of the olive oil, peanut butter, salt, and pepper. Process until smooth. Place in serving dish and drizzle with remaining olive oil. Serve with tortilla or pita chips.

SERVES ► 8

¾ cup dried garbanzo beans (chickpeas)

1 onion, chopped

6 cloves garlic

2¼ cups water

3 tablespoons lemon juice

3 tablespoons olive oil

3 tablespoons peanut butter

1 teaspoon salt

¼ teaspoon white pepper

Curry Dip

COST PER SERVING
54¢

*At big box grocery stores, you can often find store brands of
chutney that are just as good as the brand names.*

1. In saucepan, heat olive oil over medium heat. Add onion, curry powder, and garlic; cook and stir until vegetables are tender, about 5 minutes. Remove from heat and place in medium bowl; cool.

2. Stir in remaining ingredients and mix well. Serve immediately or cover and chill up to 3 days.

SERVES ► 8

1 tablespoon olive oil

¼ cup finely chopped onion

1 tablespoon curry powder

4 cloves garlic, minced

1 cup mayonnaise

½ cup sour cream

½ teaspoon salt

⅛ teaspoon white pepper

¼ cup mango chutney

Make Your Own Chutney You can make your own chutney to save money. In a large saucepan, combine 2 peeled and chopped apples with 1 chopped onion, 3 cloves minced garlic, ¼ cup sugar, ¼ cup apple cider vinegar, 1 tablespoon grated ginger root, ½ teaspoon salt, and a pinch of pepper. Simmer for 30–40 minutes until thick. Cool and keep in fridge for up to 1 week.

Crostini

Crostini can be stored for up to a week. Use it for a dipper, or top with Suave Fruit Salsa (page 28) or Big Batch Guacamole (page 24) for colorful appetizers.

YIELDS ▶ 48 CROSTINI

1 loaf Whole Wheat French Bread (page 47)

3 tablespoons olive oil

3 tablespoons butter

3 cloves garlic, minced

½ teaspoon salt

⅛ teaspoon pepper

1. Preheat oven to 325°F. Slice the bread into ¼" slices and set on a baking sheet.

2. In small saucepan, combine olive oil, butter, and garlic. Cook and stir over medium heat until garlic is fragrant, then remove from heat. Using a pastry brush, brush the olive oil mixture on both sides of the bread.

3. Bake for 10 minutes, then turn all the bread slices and bake for 10–15 minutes longer until bread is light golden brown and very crisp. Store covered at room temperature.

Budget Breads

3

Peanut Butter Bread

YIELDS ► 1 LOAF
(OR 16 SLICES)

⅓ cup peanut butter
2 tablespoons butter or margarine
1 cup brown sugar
1 egg
1¾ cups all-purpose flour
1 teaspoon baking soda
¼ teaspoon salt
1 cup buttermilk
¼ cup peanut butter
⅓ cup brown sugar
⅓ cup all-purpose flour

Peanut butter is a high quality and inexpensive form of protein when combined with grains. This hearty loaf is great for breakfast on the run.

1. Preheat oven to 350°F. Grease an 8" x 4" loaf pan with solid shortening and set aside. In large bowl, combine ⅓ cup peanut butter, butter, and 1 cup brown sugar and beat until blended. Add egg and beat well. In small bowl, combine 1¾ cups flour, baking soda, and salt. Add dry ingredients alternately with buttermilk to peanut butter mixture.

2. For streusel topping, in small bowl, combine ¼ cup peanut butter and ⅓ cup brown sugar and blend well. Add ⅓ cup flour and blend until crumbs form. Pour batter into prepared pan and sprinkle streusel over loaf. Bake for 45–55 minutes or until toothpick comes out clean when inserted into loaf. Cool on wire rack.

Freezer Wheat Rolls

COST PER ROLL
12¢

Having your own brown-and-serve rolls in the freezer makes entertaining so easy. These rolls are hearty yet light, perfect served warm with some softened butter.

1. In large mixing bowl, combine yeast and warm water; stir until dissolved. Let stand for 10 minutes, or until yeast starts to bubble. Add sugar, whole wheat flour, salt, egg, and oil and beat with an electric mixer for 2 minutes.

2. By hand, gradually stir in bread flour until the mixture forms a medium soft dough. Turn dough out onto lightly floured surface and knead until smooth and elastic, about 8 minutes. Clean bowl and grease with butter. Place dough in bowl, turning to grease top. Cover and let rise in warm place for 1 hour until double.

3. Grease two cookie sheets with unsalted butter. Punch down dough and divide into 24 pieces. Roll each ball between your hands to form a smooth ball. Place on prepared cookie sheets, cover with a kitchen towel, and let rise for 30–40 minutes until double.

4. Preheat oven to 300°F. Bake rolls for 15–20 minutes, reversing cookie sheets halfway during cooking, until the rolls are puffed and firm to the touch, but not browned. Let rolls cool on cookie sheets for 5 minutes. Remove and place on a wire rack to cool. Place in hard-sided freezer containers and freeze up to 3 months.

5. To serve, let frozen rolls stand at room temperature for 1 hour. Then bake in preheated 400°F oven for 10–15 minutes or until rolls are golden brown and hot. Brush with more butter and serve.

Forming Dinner Rolls You can shape these rolls other ways, if you'd like. Flatten the balls, spread with butter, and then fold over to form Parker House Rolls. Divide each ball into 3 pieces and place in a muffin cup for Cloverleaf Rolls. And for knots, roll each ball into a rope, then tie loosely into a knot and fold ends under. Let rise and bake as directed.

YIELDS ▶ 24 ROLLS

2 (0.25-ounce) packages active dry yeast

½ cup warm water

¼ cup brown sugar

1½ cups whole wheat flour

1 teaspoon salt

1 egg

3 tablespoons oil

2–3 cups bread flour

French Bread Braids

French bread is usually made without egg. This recipe uses eggs for a richer flavor and smoother texture. Use it to make Crisp French Toast (page 59).

YIELDS ► 2 LOAVES
(OR 32 SLICES)

2 (0.25-ounce) packages active dry yeast

¾ cup warm water

2 tablespoons sugar, divided

1 cup milk

½ cup light cream

2 teaspoons salt

3 tablespoons oil

2 eggs, beaten

6½ to 8 cups all-purpose flour

1 tablespoon cornmeal

1. In large mixing bowl, combine yeast, warm water, and 1 teaspoon sugar; stir until creamy. In large saucepan, combine milk, cream, salt, oil, and remaining sugar and heat over low heat until warm; set aside. In a small bowl, beat eggs, reserving 1 tablespoon. Add eggs and milk mixture to yeast mixture; beat well.

2. Stir in 1 cup flour and beat for 5 minutes. Then gradually add enough remaining flour to make a soft dough. Turn out onto floured surface and knead in enough remaining flour until dough is smooth and elastic, about 8 minutes. Place in greased bowl, turning to grease top. Cover and let rise until doubled, about 1 hour.

3. Grease two cookie sheets with solid shortening and sprinkle with cornmeal. Punch down dough and divide in half. Divide each half into thirds and roll each third into a 20" rope. Braid three ropes together, pinching edges to seal. Place on prepared cookie sheets and brush with reserved beaten egg. Cover and let rise 30–45 minutes.

4. Preheat oven to 375°F. Place a 9" pan with 2 cups water on bottom rack. Bake loaves, one at a time, 25–30 minutes or until bread is golden brown and firm. Cool completely on wire rack.

Artisan Whole Wheat Bread

COST PER SLICE **16¢**

It's difficult to make whole wheat bread without using some white flour. This proportion is just about perfect. And the several risings help develop the flavor of the wheat.

1. In a small bowl, combine ¾ cup water with yeast and 1 tablespoon honey; set aside for 10 minutes. In a large bowl, combine oil, 2 cups water, ½ cup honey and salt. Add yeast mixture, then stir in all-purpose flour. Beat for 5 minutes. Cover and let rise for 30 minutes.

2. Stir down dough and gradually add enough whole wheat flour to form a soft dough. Turn out onto floured surface and knead in enough remaining flour until the dough is smooth and elastic, about 5–7 minutes. Place in greased bowl, turning to grease top. Cover and let rise until doubled, about 1 hour.

3. Grease three 9" x 5" loaf pans with solid shortening and set aside. Punch down dough and divide into three parts and roll or pat into 7" x 12" rectangles. Spread each with one third of the butter and tightly roll up, starting with 7" side. Place each in prepared loaf pan. Cover and let rise for about 30–40 minutes until bread has almost doubled. Preheat oven to 350°F. Bake bread for 40–50 minutes or until deep golden brown. Turn out onto wire racks to cool.

> *Kneading Dough* Kneading dough develops the gluten, or protein, in the flour so the bread has a good structure, with fine air holes and even texture. To knead, place the dough on a lightly floured surface. Fold the dough over on itself and push into it with the heel of your hand. Turn the dough ¼ turn and repeat until the dough is smooth and feels elastic.

YIELDS ► **3 LOAVES (OR 48 SLICES)**

¾ cup warm water

2 (0.25-ounce) packages active dry yeast

1 tablespoon honey

⅓ cup vegetable oil

2 cups warm water

1½ teaspoons salt

½ cup honey

4 cups all-purpose flour

4–5 cups whole wheat flour

2 tablespoons butter, softened

Multigrain Crackers

Homemade crackers always taste better than store bought, and they are much cheaper. And these little crisps only have five ingredients!

½ cup butter, softened

1 cup shredded Swiss cheese

1 cup all-purpose flour

1 cup unsweetened crushed multigrain cereal

Coarse salt

1. Preheat oven to 375°F. In medium bowl, combine butter and cheese; beat well until blended. Stir in flour until mixed. Then add the crushed cereal, working with your hands if necessary, until combined.

2. Form dough into 1" balls and place 2" apart on ungreased cookie sheets. Using a drinking glass, flatten each ball to ¼" thickness. Using a fork, make several holes in each cracker to let steam escape as the crackers bake. Sprinkle each with a bit of coarse salt.

3. Bake for 10–14 minutes or until crackers are light brown around edges and are set. Remove crackers from cookie sheets and let cool completely on wire racks. Store in airtight container at room temperature.

Freezing Dough Separate cracker dough into individual amounts before freezing. Roll the dough into 1" balls, then flatten to about ½" thickness. Place on a cookie sheet and freeze until solid, then pack in hard-sided freezer containers. To bake, place on cookie sheets and let stand at room temperature for about 20 minutes, then flatten to ¼" thickness and bake.

Double Corn Bread

COST PER SERVING 21¢

What do you do with all the bags of frozen corn that have about ¼ of a cup rattling around at the bottom? Save them up and use in this fabulous quick bread recipe, of course.

1. Preheat oven to 325°F. Grease a 9" × 9" pan with solid shortening and set aside. Place half of the corn in a blender or food processor and process until as smooth as possible. Mix with whole kernel corn in large mixing bowl. Add remaining ingredients and stir just until combined.

2. Pour batter into greased pan. Bake for 40–50 minutes or until corn bread is golden brown around the edges and a toothpick inserted in the center comes out clean. Serve warm.

Northern Versus Southern Corn Bread There is a great debate brewing over what ingredients should be included in corn bread. In the Southern United States, white cornmeal and no sugar are the rule, and the corn bread must be baked in a cast iron skillet. In the North, yellow cornmeal and sugar are usually used, and the bread is cakier and smoother. Which is better? Depends on which one you ate first!

YIELDS ► ONE 9" × 9" BAKING PAN (OR 9 PIECES)

1 cup frozen corn, thawed

1 cup all-purpose flour

1 cup yellow cornmeal

¼ cup sugar

¼ cup vegetable oil

½ cup sour cream

2 eggs, beaten

½ teaspoon baking powder

½ teaspoon baking soda

½ teaspoon salt

Dark Raisin Walnut Bread

COST PER SERVING 18¢

You can add other flours to this recipe if you'd like. Rye flour would add even more flavor and make a darker bread.

**YIELDS ► 2 LOAVES
(OR 32 SLICES)**

2 (0.25-ounce) packages active dry yeast

½ cup warm water

2 cups water

½ cup dry milk powder

½ cup orange juice

¼ cup butter or margarine

1 teaspoon salt

½ cup brown sugar

2 eggs

⅓ cup ground oatmeal

4 cups whole wheat flour

4–5 cups all-purpose flour

2 cups raisins

1 cup chopped walnuts

1. In a small bowl, combine yeast and warm water and set aside. In medium saucepan, combine water, milk powder, orange juice, butter, salt, and brown sugar. Bring to a boil over high heat, then remove from heat.

2. Pour orange juice mixture into a large bowl and let stand until lukewarm. Then add eggs, ground oatmeal, and yeast mixture and beat well. Stir in whole wheat flour and beat for 2 minutes. Gradually add enough flour to make a stiff dough. Work in the raisins and walnuts.

3. Turn dough onto a floured surface and knead until smooth and elastic, about 8 minutes. Place in greased bowl, turning to grease top. Cover and let rise for 1 hour or until doubled. Punch down dough and place on lightly floured surface.

4. Grease two 9" x 5" loaf pans. Divide dough in half and roll or pat into 7" x 12" rectangles. Starting with 7" side, roll up tightly; sealing edges. Place in prepared pans. Cover and let rise until doubled, about 45 minutes.

5. Preheat oven to 350°F. Bake bread for 35–40 minutes or until bread pulls away from sides of pan and sounds hollow when tapped with fingers. Immediately remove from pans and cool on wire racks.

Banana Bread

COST PER SERVING **21¢**

Cake mix is less expensive than assembling the ingredients yourself, and it's much quicker. This easy quick bread is perfect for breakfast on the run.

1. Preheat oven to 350°F. Spray two 9" x 5" loaf pans with nonstick cooking spray containing flour and set aside.

2. In large bowl, combine first five ingredients. Beat until combined, then beat for 3 minutes at medium speed. Stir in walnuts and pour batter into prepared pans.

3. In small bowl, combine sugar and cinnamon and mix well. Sprinkle over batter in pans. Bake for 30–40 minutes or until bread is golden brown, toothpick inserted in center comes out clean, and bread pulls away from sides of pan. Let cool in pans for 5 minutes, then turn out onto wire racks to finish cooling.

Cake Mixes Cake mixes often go on sale at the grocery store and big box chains. When they do, stock up! They store very well, and should be marked with a "best if used by" date. Still, mark the purchase date on the box with a marker, and be sure to store them so you can rotate the boxes from oldest to newest as you use them.

YIELDS ► 2 LOAVES (OR 24 SLICES)

1 (18-ounce) box spice cake mix

3 eggs

⅓ cup corn oil

1 (6-ounce) jar puréed pears

2 ripe bananas, mashed

1 cup chopped walnuts

3 tablespoons sugar

½ teaspoon cinnamon

Flaky Biscuits

YIELDS ▶ 9 BISCUITS

1¾ cups all-purpose flour

¼ cup whole wheat flour

2 teaspoons brown sugar

2 teaspoons baking powder

1 teaspoon baking soda

½ teaspoon salt

½ cup butter or margarine, chilled

¾ cup buttermilk

1 egg white

¼ teaspoon salt

These biscuits are light and flaky with a fabulous taste, for about half the cost of those tubes of refrigerated dough!

1. Preheat oven to 425°F. In a large bowl, combine all-purpose flour, whole wheat flour, brown sugar, baking powder, baking soda, and ½ teaspoon salt and mix well. Cut butter into small pieces and add to flour mixture. Cut in, with two knives or a pastry blender, until the mixture looks like cornmeal.

2. Stir in buttermilk all at once until a dough forms. Form into a ball and place on floured surface. Pat into an 8" square. Using a sharp knife, cut into 9 square biscuits. Place on ungreased cookie sheet about 2" apart.

3. In small bowl, beat egg white with ¼ teaspoon salt until foamy. Brush over the tops of the biscuits. Bake for 9–15 minutes or until biscuits are golden brown. Serve immediately.

Cutting Biscuits When making baking powder, or quick, biscuits, there are tricks to cutting them. Be sure to cut straight down through the dough, whether you're using a biscuit cutter or a knife, so the biscuits don't have twisted edges when they're baked. Cutting the biscuits into squares instead of circles also uses all the dough, with no waste, since re-rolling toughens the dough.

Potato Rolls

COST PER ROLL **10¢**

Leftover mashed potatoes have been baked into bread from the beginning of time. They add moisture and flavor to these simple dinner rolls.

1. In small bowl, combine yeast and water; let stand. In heavy saucepan, combine milk, potatoes, butter, sugar, and salt and heat over medium heat until butter melts. Pour into large mixing bowl and let stand until lukewarm, about 30 minutes.

2. Beat eggs into milk mixture along with dissolved yeast. Add enough flour to form a soft dough. Turn dough onto floured board and knead in remaining flour as needed, until smooth and elastic, about 6 minutes. Place in greased bowl, turning to grease top. Cover and let rise for 1 hour.

3. Punch down dough. Divide into thirds, then divide each third into 12 balls. Roll balls between hands to smooth. Place on greased cookie sheets; cover, and let rise until doubled, about 30 minutes.

4. Preheat oven to 375°F. Bake rolls for 15–20 minutes until golden brown and set. Cool on wire rack.

> *Rising Yeast Bread* Yeast bread is placed into a greased bowl and turned to grease the top before rising. This not only prevents the dough from sticking to the bowl, but it also makes sure the top of the dough doesn't crack, but stays soft and moist. Use solid shortening, oil, or unsalted butter to grease the dough. Salted butter will make the dough stick.

YIELDS ► 36 ROLLS

2 (0.25-ounce) packages active dry yeast

½ cup warm water

1 cup milk

1 cup leftover Mashed Potatoes (page 224)

½ cup butter

¼ cup sugar

1 teaspoon salt

2 eggs

5 to 6 cups all-purpose flour

Pita Breads

Pita Breads are such fun to make, and the homemade ones are so much more delicious than store–bought. And they freeze beautifully too!

YIELDS ▶ 12 BREADS

1 (0.25-ounce) package active dry yeast

1½ cups warm water

1 tablespoon corn oil

1 tablespoon sugar

1 teaspoon salt

2–3 cups all-purpose flour

1 cup whole wheat flour

1 cup bread flour

1. In large bowl, combine yeast and ¼ cup water; mix and let stand until bubbly. Add remaining warm water, oil, sugar, and salt. Stir in 1 cup all-purpose flour, the whole wheat flour, and bread flour and beat for 3 minutes at medium speed.

2. Gradually add enough all-purpose flour to form a firm dough. On lightly floured surface, knead dough until smooth and elastic, about 6 minutes. Place in greased bowl, turning to grease top. Cover and let rise for 1 hour until doubled.

3. Punch down dough and divide into 12 balls. Preheat oven to 500°F. On floured surface, roll each ball to a 6" circle, dusting with flour and turning occasionally to make sure ball doesn't stick to surface.

4. Using a large spatula, carefully transfer 4 pita breads directly to the oven rack and close door quickly. Bake for 4–7 minutes, watching carefully, until breads puff and begin to form brown spots. Remove from oven and let cool on wire rack. Repeat with remaining dough. To use, cut breads in half to expose the pocket.

Oven Temperature When you're baking breads, especially those which bake in just a few minutes like Pita Bread, accurate oven temperature is very important. To make sure that your oven is properly calibrated, buy an oven thermometer and use it to check the temperature. If the oven temperature is off, call a certified repair person and have it calibrated.

Whole Wheat French Bread

 COST PER SERVING **12¢**

Making a sponge of flour, yeast, and water and letting it rise is an easy way to make bread that has more flavor, since the wheat has time to develop.

1. In large bowl, combine yeast with warm water and let stand for 10 minutes. Add orange juice, sour cream, salt, and brown sugar along with the whole wheat flour and ½ cup all-purpose flour and beat well.

2. Cover this sponge with a towel and let rise in warm place for 2 hours. Then add enough remaining all-purpose flour to make a firm dough. Turn onto floured surface and knead until smooth and elastic, about 5 minutes. Place in greased bowl, turning to grease top. Cover and let rise for 45 minutes.

3. Punch down dough and roll or pat into a 12" x 8" rectangle. Roll up tightly, starting with 12" side. Roll on floured surface to a 14" long cylinder. Place on lightly floured cookie sheet, cover, and let rise for 30 minutes.

4. Preheat oven to 375°F. Carefully cut a few slashes on the top of the loaf. Bake for 25–35 minutes or until bread sounds hollow when tapped with fingers. Cool completely on a wire rack.

YIELDS ▶ 1 LOAF (OR 16 SLICES)

1 (0.25-ounce) package active dry yeast

1¼ cups warm water

¼ cup orange juice

½ cup sour cream

1 teaspoon salt

1 tablespoon brown sugar

1½ cups whole wheat flour

1½ to 2½ cups all-purpose flour

Hearty White Bread

Dry milk powder is not only less expensive than regular milk, but it makes the bread fluffier. Technically, the powder is a "finely divided solid," which improves mouth feel.

**YIELDS ► 4 LOAVES
(OR 40 SLICES)**

½ cup warm water

2 (0.25-ounce) packages active dry yeast

1 tablespoon sugar

4 cups warm water

½ cup sugar

6 cups all-purpose flour

1 cup dry milk powder

3 teaspoons salt

¼ cup oil

5–6 cups all-purpose flour

1. In large mixing bowl, combine ½ cup water with the yeast and 1 tablespoon sugar. Mix well and let stand for 10 minutes, until foamy. Add remaining warm water, ½ cup sugar, 6 cups flour, dry milk powder, salt, and oil and beat until smooth. Cover and let rise for 30 minutes.

2. Stir down batter. Gradually add remaining flour until soft dough forms. Turn out onto lightly floured board and knead until smooth and elastic, about 8 minutes. Place in greased bowl, turning to grease top. Let rise until doubled, about 1½ hours. Punch down again.

3. Grease four 9" x 5" loaf pans with solid shortening and set aside. Divide dough into four parts. On lightly floured surface, pat or roll each part into a 12" x 7" rectangle. Tightly roll up, starting with 7" side. Place in prepared pans; cover and let rise until doubled, about 35–45 minutes. Preheat oven to 350°F. Bake bread for 30–40 minutes or until golden brown. Turn out onto wire racks to cool.

Freezing Bread Making big batches of bread and then freezing the results harkens back to Grandma's day—or maybe great-grandma's! Bread freezes beautifully as long as you follow a few rules. First, let the bread cool completely. Then slice it and package the slices in freezer bags. Label the bags and freeze up to 3 months. To thaw, just toast!

Crescent Rolls

COST PER SERVING
12¢

These buttery and flaky rolls are wonderful for a special dinner, and much better tasting than the commercial variety. Serve warm.

1. In bowl, combine yeast with flour, sugar, and salt. Cut in ½ cup butter until particles are fine. Add milk and eggs and mix well until a dough forms. Cover and chill for 8 hours in refrigerator. The next day, take dough out of refrigerator and divide into three pieces. Melt remaining ¼ cup butter and set aside.

2. On lightly floured surface, roll dough to a 12" circle. Brush with ¼ of the melted butter and cut circle into 10 wedges. Roll up wedges, starting with the wide end, and pinching the point to seal. Place on parchment paper-lined cookie sheets.

3. Brush with remaining butter, cover, and let rise for 1 hour. Meanwhile, preheat oven to 400°F. Uncover rolls and bake for 15 minutes or until rolls are golden brown. Cool on wire rack.

YIELDS ► 30 ROLLS

1 (0.25-ounce) package instant blend dry yeast

4¼ cups all-purpose flour

⅓ cup sugar

1 teaspoon salt

¾ cup butter, divided

2 eggs

¾ cup milk

Popovers

COST PER SERVING
8¢

Popovers are showy and a nice treat, and they're easy to make as long as you follow the recipe carefully. Serve hot with lots of butter.

1. Preheat oven to 425°F. Grease a popover pan or six 6-ounce custard cups very generously with solid shortening or unsalted butter; set aside.

2. In a medium bowl, beat eggs until blended. Place all-purpose flour, bread flour, whole wheat flour, and salt in a sifter. Sift over eggs, add milk, and beat with an eggbeater or wire whisk just until batter is smooth and blended.

3. Divide mixture among prepared popover pans or custard cups. If using custard cups, place on a cookie sheet. Bake for 15 minutes, then reduce oven temperature to 350°F and bake for 20–25 minutes longer until puffed and deep golden brown. Serve immediately.

YIELDS ► 6 POPOVERS

2 eggs

¾ cup all-purpose flour

2 tablespoons bread flour

2 tablespoons whole wheat flour

½ teaspoon salt

1 cup whole milk

Simple Apple Nut Bread

COST PER SERVING 23¢

Applesauce and chopped apples add wonderful flavor and texture to this moist quick bread. As well as being a great breakfast, it makes fabulous Crisp French Toast (page 59).

YIELDS ▶ 1 LOAF
(OR 12 SLICES)

1¼ cups all-purpose flour

¼ cup whole wheat flour

½ cup sugar

½ teaspoon baking powder

¼ teaspoon baking soda

½ teaspoon cinnamon

½ cup brown sugar

1 egg

1 teaspoon vanilla

½ cup applesauce

½ cup chopped peeled apples

½ cup buttermilk

1 cup chopped walnuts

1 tablespoon sugar

¼ teaspoon cinnamon

1. Preheat oven to 350°F. Spray a 9" x 5" loaf pan with nonstick baking spray containing flour and set aside.

2. In large bowl, combine all-purpose flour, whole wheat flour, sugar, baking powder, baking soda, and cinnamon and mix with wire whisk until blended. In medium bowl, combine brown sugar, egg, vanilla, applesauce, apples, and buttermilk and mix well with eggbeater. Pour the egg mixture into the flour mixture and stir just until combined. Fold in nuts.

3. Pour batter into prepared pan. In small bowl, combine 1 tablespoon sugar and ¼ teaspoon cinnamon and mix well. Sprinkle over batter. Bake for 55–70 minutes or until bread is dark golden brown and toothpick inserted in center comes out clean. Cool in pan for 5 minutes, then remove to wire rack to cool completely.

Cranberry–Walnut Loaf

COST PER SERVING 18¢

This hearty loaf has a great texture because of the whole wheat flour, walnuts, and oatmeal. It makes wonderful toast for breakfast.

1. In large bowl, combine yeast and warm water and let stand. In medium saucepan, combine milk, orange juice, butter, sugar, brown sugar, salt, and oatmeal and heat until butter melts. Let stand until lukewarm. Beat in egg, then stir into yeast mixture.

2. Add whole wheat flour and ½ cup all-purpose flour and beat for 2 minutes. Then gradually add enough remaining all-purpose flour to make a firm dough.

3. On floured surface, knead dough until smooth and elastic, about 5 minutes. Work in cranberries and walnuts. Then place in greased bowl, turning to grease top. Cover and let rise for 1 hour.

4. Spray a 9" x 5" loaf pan with nonstick cooking spray. Punch down dough and roll or pat to 7" x 12" rectangle. Roll up, starting with 7" side, and place in prepared pan. Cover and let rise until doubled, about 35 minutes.

5. Preheat oven to 375°F. Bake bread for 25–35 minutes or until deep golden brown and loaf sounds hollow when tapped with fingers. Turn out onto wire rack to cool.

YIELDS ▶ 1 LOAF (OR 16 SLICES)

1 (0.25-ounce) package active dry yeast

¼ cup warm water

½ cup milk

¼ cup orange juice

3 tablespoons butter or margarine

2 tablespoons sugar

2 tablespoons brown sugar

½ teaspoon salt

½ cup quick oatmeal

1 egg

½ cup whole wheat flour

2 to 3 cups all-purpose flour

½ cup chopped cranberries

½ cup chopped walnuts

Honey Banana–Cranberry Bread

COST PER SLICE **19¢**

Tart cranberries add great color and flavor to this marvelous velvety banana bread. It's great for the holidays!

YIELDS ► 1 LOAF
(OR 12 SLICES)

½ cup margarine, softened

½ cup brown sugar

¼ cup honey

1 egg

1 cup mashed banana

2 cups all-purpose flour

¼ cup whole wheat flour

2 teaspoons baking powder

½ teaspoon baking soda

¼ teaspoon salt

½ cup chopped cranberries

1 teaspoon cinnamon

2 tablespoons sugar

½ teaspoon cinnamon

1. Preheat oven to 350°F. Spray a 9" x 5" pan with baking spray containing flour and set aside. In large bowl, combine margarine and brown sugar and beat until fluffy. Add honey, egg, and mashed banana and beat well.

2. In medium bowl combine flour, whole wheat flour, baking powder, baking soda, salt, and 1 teaspoon cinnamon. Add half to banana mixture and beat well. Add remaining flour mixture and beat just until blended. Fold in cranberries and spoon into prepared loaf pan. In small bowl, combine sugar and ½ teaspoon cinnamon and mix well; sprinkle over loaf. Bake for 40–45 minutes or until bread is deep golden brown. Cool on wire rack and store in plastic food bag.

Cranberries Cranberries are cheapest during the winter months, when demand for them spikes for holiday baking. Buy several packages and place in freezer bags; freeze for up to 1 year. To use frozen cranberries, do not thaw; add to the recipe as is. The baking time for cookies and breads stays the same; it's a bit longer for cranberry sauce.

Oatmeal Bread

COST PER SERVING
14¢

*You can add even more chopped walnuts to this delicious
bread if you'd like for more texture.*

1. In large bowl, combine yeast and warm water; stir and let stand
   for 10 minutes until bubbly.

2. Meanwhile, in medium saucepan combine Oatmeal, honey, and
   milk and heat until warm. Remove from heat and beat in eggs,
   salt, and corn oil. Stir into yeast mixture.

3. Add whole wheat flour and beat for 1 minute. Then gradually
   add enough all-purpose flour to make a firm dough. Turn onto
   floured surface and knead until smooth and elastic, about
   5 minutes. Place in greased bowl, turning to grease top. Cover
   with towel and let rise until doubled, about 1 hour.

4. Grease two 9" x 5" loaf pans with unsalted butter. On floured
   surface, divide dough into half and pat into two 7" x 12" rectangles. Roll up, starting with 7" side. Place in loaf pans, cover,
   and let rise until doubled, about 35 minutes.

5. Preheat oven to 350°F. Bake bread for 55–65 minutes, or until
   bread is deep golden brown and sounds hollow when tapped
   with fingers. Remove from pan and let cool on wire rack.

**YIELDS ▶ 2 LOAVES
(OR 32 SLICES)**

2 (0.25-ounce) packages
active dry yeast

½ cup warm water

2 cups leftover Nutty Slow Cooker
Oatmeal (page 57)

½ cup honey

½ cup milk

2 eggs

½ teaspoon salt

2 tablespoons corn oil

2 cups whole wheat flour

3–4 cups all purpose-flour

Brown Bread

COST PER SERVING
14¢

This classic recipe makes a delicious and inexpensive old-fashioned meal when paired with Rich Baked Beans (page 195).

**YIELDS ▶ 1 LOAF
(OR 16 SLICES)**

⅓ cup rolled oatmeal

1½ cups all-purpose flour

1 cup whole wheat flour

1 teaspoon baking powder

1 teaspoon baking soda

¼ cup brown sugar

¼ cup sugar

⅓ cup butter

⅓ cup light molasses

1 egg, beaten

1 cup buttermilk

⅓ cup water

1. Preheat oven to 350°F. Grease a 9" x 5" loaf pan with solid shortening and set aside. Place oatmeal in small saucepan. Toast over medium heat until fragrant, about 3–5 minutes. Cool completely, then grind in food processor or blender.

2. In large bowl, combine oatmeal, all-purpose flour, whole wheat flour, baking powder, baking soda, brown sugar, and sugar and mix well. Cut in butter until particles are fine.

3. In small bowl, combine molasses, egg, buttermilk, and water and mix well. Add to flour mixture all at once, and stir just until combined. Pour batter into prepared pan. Bake for 50–60 minutes until dark brown and firm. Cool completely.

Whole Wheat Flour Store whole wheat flour in the freezer to make it last longer. It is more expensive than all-purpose flour, so take care of it! Decant it into a hard-sided freezer container, label with the date you purchased the product, and freeze for up to 6 months. You can use it straight from the freezer, or let it stand at room temperature for 30 minutes first.

4

Stretch Your Scrambled Eggs

COST PER SERVING **22¢**

Cooking scrambled eggs in a double boiler may seem strange, but it's the best way to get the fluffiest result. It does take a bit more time, but it's worth it.

3 tablespoons butter

14 eggs

½ cup skim milk

¼ cup sour cream

½ teaspoon salt

⅛ teaspoon pepper

1. Place a large saucepan with 1½" of water over medium heat and bring to a simmer. Carefully place slightly smaller saucepan in the water and add butter; let melt. In large bowl, combine eggs, milk, sour cream, salt, and pepper and beat well with eggbeater or wire whisk.

2. Pour egg mixture into melted butter in top saucepan. Cook, stirring occasionally, for about 30–40 minutes or until eggs are set and creamy. Serve immediately. You can also cook the eggs in a skillet directly over medium heat, stirring frequently, for about 5–7 minutes.

How to Cook Eggs Eggs are an excellent source of complete protein and are very inexpensive. Usually they are best cooked over medium-low heat, and cooked quickly. Heat the pan with the fat you're using before you add the eggs to reduce sticking. Try Bread Crumb Frittata (page 110) and yes, Eggs Benedict (page 58) for more inexpensive egg recipes.

Nutty Slow Cooker Oatmeal

Steel-cut oats are the only kind that will not cook to mush in the slow cooker. Toasting them and the nuts brings out the best flavor in this simple recipe.

SERVES ► 6

1. Place oatmeal in large skillet over medium-high heat. Toast, stirring constantly, for 8–9 minutes or until oatmeal is fragrant and begins to brown around the edges. Remove to 3½ quart slow cooker.

2. In same pan, melt butter and add chopped walnuts. Toast over medium heat, stirring constantly, until nuts are toasted. Combine with all remaining ingredients except spices in slow cooker with oatmeal. Cover and cook on low for 7–9 hours, until oatmeal is tender. Stir in spices, cover, and let stand for 10 minutes. Serve topped with a bit of butter, maple syrup, brown sugar, and more chopped nuts.

1½ cups steel-cut oatmeal

2 tablespoons butter

1 cup chopped walnuts

6 cups water

½ cup brown sugar

1 teaspoon salt

½ teaspoon cinnamon

⅛ teaspoon nutmeg

Leftover Oatmeal You can use leftover oatmeal in several recipes. Try Oatmeal Raisin Cookies (page 249). Or stir it into a combination of ground beef and pork to make meatloaf or meatballs (use about ½ cup oatmeal per pound of meat). There's no reason to let anything go to waste!

Yes, Eggs Benedict

SERVES ▶ 8

The expensive parts of Eggs Benedict are the Hollandaise sauce and the Canadian bacon. This recipe solves that by making a "fake" Hollandaise and folding some chopped ham into the scrambled eggs.

4 English muffins

2 tablespoons butter, softened

⅓ cup sour cream

¼ cup mayonnaise

2 tablespoons heavy cream

2 tablespoons lemon juice

2 tablespoons butter, melted

10 eggs

⅓ cup milk

2 tablespoons butter

½ teaspoon salt

⅛ teaspoon white pepper

1 cup chopped ham

1 cup shredded Swiss cheese

1. Preheat broiler. Split English muffins and spread each with a bit of the butter. Place on broiler pan and broil until golden brown; set aside. In blender or food processor, combine mayonnaise, sour cream, cream, lemon juice, and melted butter. Blend or process until smooth. Set aside.

2. In large bowl, combine eggs, milk and salt and pepper and beat until frothy. In large saucepan melt 2 tablespoons butter; add egg mixture and cook over medium heat, stirring frequently, until eggs are creamy but not quite set. Stir in ham and continue cooking until eggs are set.

3. Top each toasted English muffin with some of the cheese, a spoonful of the egg and ham mixture and a spoonful of the sauce. Broil for 2–3 minutes or until heated through; serve immediately.

Egg Safety Did you know that it's not safe to eat poached or fried eggs done "softly set" or "over easy"? Eggs must be fully cooked to be safe. In other words, the yolk must be set and firm. You can use pasteurized eggs and still eat them softly set, but they are very expensive. This recipe solves that problem by making Eggs Benedict with scrambled eggs.

Crisp French Toast

COST PER SERVING
39¢

French toast is easy to make and it's an inexpensive way to stretch bread. Use other breads in this recipe too, including Artisan Whole Wheat Bread (page 39) and Simple Apple Nut Bread (page 50).

1. In shallow bowl, combine eggs, milk, sugar, and cinnamon and beat until smooth. Dip each slice of bread into the egg mixture, letting stand for 1 minute, turn over, and then dip into crushed cereal to coat.

2. In large skillet over medium-high heat, melt butter. When it's melted and foamy, add the coated bread pieces, two to three at a time. Cook on first side for 3–5 minutes until golden brown. Carefully turn and cook on second side for 2–4 minutes until golden brown and crisp. Serve immediately.

> *Freezing Pancakes and French Toast* If you have leftover pancakes and French toast, freeze them for busy mornings. Cool completely, then stack in a hard-sided freezer container with waxed paper separating each one. Freeze up to 3 months. To reheat, microwave each frozen pancake, one at a time, on high power for 1–2 minutes; heat French toast in the toaster oven.

SERVES ▶ 4

8 slices Hearty White Bread (page 48)

2 eggs, beaten

⅓ cup milk

2 tablespoons sugar

½ teaspoon cinnamon

2 cups finely crushed leftover cereal flakes

¼ cup butter

Breakfast Cookies

YIELDS ► 24 COOKIES

When your boxes of cereal get down to the crumbs, save them in the freezer and make these delicious crisp and chewy cookies. You could substitute chocolate chips for the raisins for a treat.

⅓ cup butter, softened

¼ cup applesauce

½ cup brown sugar

¼ cup sugar

1 egg

¾ cup all-purpose flour

¼ cup whole wheat flour

2 tablespoons wheat germ

½ teaspoon baking soda

2 cups leftover cereal flakes

¾ cup raisins

1. Preheat oven to 325°F. In large bowl, combine butter, applesauce, brown sugar, sugar, and egg and beat well. Add flour, whole wheat flour, wheat germ, and baking soda and mix until a dough forms. Stir in cereal flakes (and any crumbs) along with raisins.

2. Drop by tablespoons onto ungreased cookie sheets. Bake for 15–20 minutes or until cookies are set and light golden brown. Cool completely on wire racks. Store covered at room temperature.

Freezing Cookie Dough You can make a batch or double batch of these cookies, then freeze the dough to bake them fresh for breakfast. Drop dough by tablespoons onto waxed paper; freeze until solid. Then package into freezer bags; label, and freeze. To bake, place frozen dough onto cookie sheets; add about 5–7 minutes to the baking time.

Cottage Cheese Oatmeal Pancakes

COST PER SERVING **46¢**

You don't need a blender for these pancakes. Just beat the egg whites separately and fold into the batter just before cooking.

1. In a blender or food processor, grind oatmeal until fine; remove. Add eggs, cottage cheese, and orange juice to blender and blend until mixed. Add oatmeal, flour, baking soda, sugar, and salt and blend just until smooth.

2. Heat a large skillet over medium heat until a drop of water sizzles on it. Add butter and melt; spread evenly. Pour batter by ¼ cup portions onto skillet, four at a time. Cook until edges look dry and bubbles form on surface and begin to break, about 3–4 minutes. Carefully turn with a spatula and cook for 2 minutes on second side. Serve immediately.

SERVES ▶ 4

⅓ cup quick oatmeal

4 eggs

1 cup small curd cottage cheese

2 tablespoons orange juice

¾ cup all-purpose flour

1 teaspoon baking soda

3 tablespoons sugar

¼ teaspoon salt

2 tablespoons butter or margarine

Irish Oatmeal Pancakes

COST PER PANCAKE **16¢**

Pancakes are good breakfast food; filling and healthy at the same time. The combination of quick and rolled oatmeal creates a lovely texture.

1. In mixing bowl, combine buttermilk, both kinds of oatmeal, and brown sugar. Mix well and let stand for 10 minutes. Add flour, whole wheat flour, baking powder, baking soda, and salt and mix well. Blend in eggs and vegetable oil until just mixed.

2. In large skillet or electric skillet, melt 2 tablespoons butter over medium heat. Stir batter; you may need to add more buttermilk. Pour batter onto skillet in ¼ cup portions. Cook until bubbles form and start to break on pancakes, carefully flip and cook for 2–3 minutes on second side. Repeat with remaining batter, adding more butter to skillet if necessary. Serve immediately.

SERVES ▶ 6

2 cups buttermilk

1½ cups quick oatmeal

½ cup rolled oatmeal

¼ cup brown sugar

½ cup all-purpose flour

¼ cup whole wheat flour

1 teaspoon baking powder

1 teaspoon baking soda

½ teaspoon salt

2 eggs, beaten

¼ cup vegetable oil

2–4 tablespoons butter

Whole Grain Granola

Homemade granola is not only better tasting and less expensive than store-bought granola, but you can also control the nutrition.

YIELDS ▶ 12 CUPS

½ cup orange juice

½ cup brown sugar

¼ cup honey

¼ cup vegetable oil

2 teaspoons cinnamon

6 cups rolled oatmeal

2 cups quick-cooking oatmeal

1 cup chopped walnuts

2 cups sunflower seeds

1 cup raisins

1. Preheat oven to 250°F. In bowl, combine orange juice, brown sugar, honey, oil, and cinnamon and mix well. In roasting pan, combine oatmeal, walnuts, and sunflower seeds and mix well.

2. Drizzle orange juice mixture over the oat mixture and stir to coat all dry ingredients; spread into even layer. Bake for 60 minutes, stirring every 15 minutes, until granola is crisp and light golden brown. Stir in raisins, then cool. Store in air-tight container.

Uses for Granola In addition to being a healthy breakfast, granola also makes a great snack. Add more dried fruit and it's perfect to take on a hike. It can also be used as a recipe ingredient, as in Banana Split Shakes (page 68) or stirred into a cookie batter for crunch and flavor.

Breakfast Pizza

If you like, you could add any cooked vegetables such as mushrooms, asparagus, or red bell peppers to these cute pizzas.

SERVES ▶ 4

4 Pita Breads (page 46)

1 (3-ounce) package cream cheese, softened

2 tablespoons butter or margarine

4 eggs, beaten

2 tablespoons milk

¼ teaspoon salt

2 Chicken Sausage Patties (page 142), cooked and chopped

1 cup shredded Cheddar cheese

1. Preheat oven to 400°F. Place Pita Breads on a cookie sheet and spread each with ¼ of the cream cheese; set aside.

2. Heat butter in small skillet over medium heat. In small bowl, combine eggs with milk and salt and beat well. Pour into skillet. Cook and stir until eggs are set but still moist, about 5 minutes. Divide among Pita Breads.

3. Top with chopped Chicken Sausage Patties and cheese. Bake for 10–15 minutes or until pizzas are hot and cheese melts and begins to bubble. Let cool for 5 minutes and serve.

Breakfast Sandwiches

 COST PER SERVING **40¢**

These sandwiches taste like those at your local drive–through, but better. Plus, they're about half the price. If you don't like to eat bell peppers in the morning, leave them out.

1. In large skillet, melt butter over medium heat. Add bell pepper; cook and stir until crisp tender, about 3 minutes. Add potatoes; cook, stirring occasionally, until potatoes are tender and beginning to brown.

2. In medium bowl, combine eggs, milk, salt, and pepper and beat well. Pour into skillet with vegetables. Cook, stirring occasionally, until eggs are scrambled and set. Sprinkle cheese over eggs, remove from heat, cover, and let stand for 3 minutes. Divide egg mixture among pita breads and serve immediately.

Other Breakfast Sandwiches For an easy and inexpensive breakfast on the run, you can make a sandwich out of any cooked egg mixture. Scramble up an egg or two, add some cheese and chopped tomatoes, and wrap it in a corn or flour tortilla. English muffins make great breakfast sandwiches, filled with a fried egg and a bit of crumbled cooked sausage.

SERVES ▶ 6

2 tablespoons butter

1 green bell pepper, chopped

2 cups frozen hash brown potatoes

6 eggs

¼ cup milk

½ teaspoon salt

⅛ teaspoon pepper

1 cup shredded Swiss cheese

3 Pita Breads (page 46), halved

Raspberry Oatmeal Muffins

COST PER SERVING 31¢

Ground oatmeal is the secret ingredient in these muffins; it adds texture and a slightly nutty flavor.

YIELDS ► 12 MUFFINS

1 cup all-purpose flour

½ cup whole wheat flour

½ cup brown sugar

¼ cup ground oatmeal

1 teaspoon cinnamon

2 teaspoons baking powder

½ teaspoon salt

1 cup leftover Nutty Slow Cooker Oatmeal (page 57)

1 egg

¼ cup butter, melted

3 tablespoons vegetable oil

1 cup frozen raspberries

1. Preheat oven to 400°F. Line 12 muffin cups with paper liners; set aside. In large bowl, combine all-purpose flour, whole wheat flour, brown sugar, ground oatmeal, cinnamon, baking powder, and salt and mix well.

2. In small bowl, combine Oatmeal, egg, butter, and vegetable oil and mix well. Add to dry ingredients and stir just until combined. Fold in raspberries. Spoon batter into prepared muffin cups.

3. Bake muffins for 18–23 minutes or until they are set and golden brown. Let stand for 5 minutes, then remove from muffin cups and cool on wire rack. Serve warm.

Americanized Aebleskiver

COST PER SERVING 13¢

Aebleskiver (pronounced AB-el-skiv-er) are like silver dollar pancakes, but are fluffier, with a richer flavor. They're perfect for a leisurely Sunday brunch. For a splurge, buy an Aebleskiver pan!

SERVES ► 4–6

4 eggs, separated

2 tablespoons sugar

1½ cups milk

2 cups all-purpose flour

½ teaspoon salt

1½ teaspoons baking powder

¼ teaspoon baking soda

½ teaspoon nutmeg

2–3 tablespoons butter

1. In large bowl, beat egg whites until frothy; gradually add sugar until stiff peaks form; set aside. In small mixer bowl, combine egg yolks, milk, flour, salt, baking powder, baking soda, and nutmeg and beat until smooth. Stir a dollop of the egg whites into the egg yolk mixture, then fold remaining egg yolk mixture into the egg whites until blended.

2. In large skillet, melt butter until foamy. Drop batter by tablespoon measures into hot butter. Cook until the bubbles start to burst, about 2 minutes, then carefully flip each pancake and cook for 1–2 minutes on the other side. Serve immediately with jam and powdered sugar.

Chocolate Orange Doughnut Balls

Making your own doughnuts is really fun, so make it a family activity! Just be careful with the hot oil.

YIELDS ► 30 DOUGHNUTS

1. In large bowl, combine all-purpose flour, whole wheat flour, sugar, baking powder, baking soda, salt, ½ teaspoon cinnamon and mix well. Add melted butter, milk, orange juice, and egg and combine until well blended.

2. In large heavy saucepan, heat peanut oil over medium heat to 375°F. In small bowl combine powdered sugar and 1 teaspoon cinnamon and mix well; set aside. Rinse a spoon in cold water and scoop up a spoonful of dough. Push three chocolate chips into the center of the dough and smooth over the dough to cover. Drop into the hot oil; fry for 3–4 minutes or until doughnut balls are golden brown. Repeat with remaining dough and chocolate chips.

3. As the doughnut balls are fried, carefully remove from oil with slotted spoon; drop into powdered sugar mixture and roll to coat. Then place on wire rack to cool.

1¾ cups all-purpose flour
¼ cup whole wheat flour
¼ cup sugar
2 teaspoons baking powder
1 teaspoon baking soda
½ teaspoon salt
½ teaspoon cinnamon
¼ cup butter, melted
¼ cup milk
½ cup orange juice
1 egg
½ cup chocolate chips
3 cups peanut oil
½ cup powdered sugar
1 teaspoon cinnamon

Used Cooking Oil If you carefully cool and strain oil used for deep frying, it can be reused up to three times. But consider what was cooked in the oil before. You don't want to use oil that was used to fry fish to cook doughnuts or apple fritters. Be sure to refrigerate the oil after it has been cooled and strained.

Graham Cracker Streusel Muffins

COST PER MUFFIN **21¢**

YIELDS ► 24 MUFFINS

When there are just a few graham crackers in the box, freeze them. When you have enough, process them until the crumbs are fine to use in this muffin recipe.

1 (18-ounce) package spice cake mix

1½ cups finely crushed graham cracker crumbs, divided

3 eggs

¼ cup oil

¾ cup water

¼ cup butter, softened

½ cup brown sugar

½ cup chopped walnuts

1. Preheat oven to 350°F. In large bowl, combine cake mix, ½ cup graham cracker crumbs, eggs, oil, and water. Mix until blended, then beat on medium speed for 2 minutes. In small bowl, combine remaining graham crumbs, butter, brown sugar, and walnuts and mix until crumbly.

2. Line 24 muffin cups with paper liners. Divide cake mix into prepared muffin cups; sprinkle each with some of the walnut mixture. Bake for 18–23 minutes or until muffins are set when touched with finger. Let cool in pans for 5 minutes, then remove to wire racks to cool completely.

Freezing Muffins Muffins freeze beautifully, so when you make a batch, freeze some for breakfast on the run. Freeze muffins individually on a cookie sheet, then wrap each in freezer wrap and package into freezer bags. Label and freeze for up to 3 months. To thaw, unwrap muffins and let stand at room temperature for 30–40 minutes.

Fruity Smoothie

COST PER SERVING $1¹²

With this much fruit, you're actually getting a lot of your daily fruit requirement in one delicious smoothie. For a splurge, top each smoothie with some fresh raspberries.

In blender or food processor, combine all ingredients. Blend or process until mixture is smooth. Serve immediately.

Frozen Fruit Frozen fruit is sold as two types: loose pack and solid pack. For these drinks, you'll want to purchase loose pack fruits without sugar. Loose packs are easier to measure and are of higher quality. You can substitute almost any loose pack frozen fruit for another in any recipe. Do not thaw before using in baking recipes.

SERVES ► 6

2 cups frozen strawberries

1 cup frozen raspberries

1 cup vanilla frozen yogurt

1 cup plain yogurt

1 cup orange juice

Blueberry Yogurt Blend

COST PER SERVING 89¢

Smoothies, those trendy breakfast beverages, are quick and easy to make and can be very healthy. Be sure to use low-fat products and use plenty of fresh fruit and juices.

In blender or food processor, combine all ingredients. Blend or process until smooth and thick. Serve immediately.

SERVES ► 6

2½ cups frozen blueberries

1½ cups orange juice

¼ cup dry milk powder

1 cup vanilla yogurt

1 (8–ounce) can crushed pineapple, undrained

½ teaspoon vanilla

Banana Split Shake

This shake does taste like a banana split in a glass, but it's healthier. If you use frozen bananas, omit the ice cubes.

SERVES ▶ 6

3 bananas, peeled

2 cups vanilla yogurt

⅓ cup chocolate syrup

1 cup canned pitted cherries, drained, reserving juice

½ cup dry milk powder

1 cup ice cubes

1 cup Whole Grain Granola (page 62)

1. Cut bananas into chunks. In blender or food processor, combine bananas, yogurt, chocolate syrup, cherries, dry milk powder, and ¼ cup reserved cherry juice. Cover and blend or process until smooth. Add ice cubes, cover, and blend or process until mixture is smooth and thick.

2. Spoon into six tall glasses and top with the granola. Serve immediately.

> *Leftover Bananas* When your bananas start to become too ripe to eat out of hand, peel them, cut into chunks, and freeze in freezer bags up to three months. Use them in this and other smoothie recipes. Or they can be used in Honey Banana-Cranberry Bread (page 52); just thaw and mash.

Hearty Economy Soups

Gazpacho

4 ripe tomatoes, chopped

½ cup orange juice

2 teaspoons sugar

2 cucumbers

1 (46-ounce) can tomato juice

2 green bell peppers, chopped

1 red onion, chopped

1 teaspoon salt

⅛ teaspoon white pepper

½ teaspoon Tabasco sauce

1 teaspoon dried tarragon leaves

1 cup water

1 cup Hot and Spicy Popcorn (page 32)

¼ cup chopped fresh parsley

Gazpacho is the perfect answer to a garden bursting with ripe tomatoes. Serve it with Lemon Chocolate Pie (page 265) for dessert.

1. In large bowl, mix tomatoes, add orange juice, and sugar and stir. Peel cucumbers, cut in half, remove seeds, and chop. Add to tomato mixture along with tomato juice, bell peppers, and red onion.

2. Add salt, pepper, Tabasco sauce, tarragon, and water and stir gently but thoroughly. Cover and chill soup for at least 2 hours before serving. Top with popcorn and parsley.

Garlic Tomato Bisque

1 tablespoon olive oil

2 tablespoons butter

1 onion, finely chopped

5 cloves garlic, minced

2 (10.75-ounce) cans condensed tomato soup

1 (8-ounce) can tomato sauce

3 cups water

½ teaspoon dried basil leaves

½ cup heavy cream

½ cup milk

Heavy cream is a splurge, but it's necessary for the creamy texture characteristic of bisques. Garnish with some tiny grape tomatoes if you're feeling rich!

1. In large pot, combine olive oil and butter over medium heat. Cook onion and garlic, stirring frequently, until tender, about 5–6 minutes. Add soups, sauce, water, and basil. Bring to a simmer and simmer for 10 minutes.

2. Add cream and milk and stir well. Heat soup through but do not boil. Serve immediately with croutons and a sprinkle of Parmesan cheese.

Simple Oven Stew

COST PER SERVING
62¢

*This easy and wholesome stew bakes in the oven so you can
go about your day without worrying about it. Serve it with a gelatin
salad and some breadsticks for a retro meal that evokes memories
of the 1960s.*

SERVES ▶ 6

1. Brown ground beef in large skillet. Remove meat from skillet with slotted spoon and place in 3-quart baking dish. Drain all but 1 tablespoon of drippings from skillet. Add olive oil, then cook onion and carrots in drippings for 3–4 minutes until glazed. Add to beef in baking dish.

2. Add garlic, soup, and water to skillet and bring to a simmer, scraping any brown bits from the bottom of the skillet. Then pour into baking dish along with remaining ingredients and stir well. Cover tightly with foil and bake at 325°F for 1½ to 2 hours or until vegetables are tender and soup is bubbling.

Soup Science Soup is one of the most forgiving recipes in all of food science. You can add almost anything to it, and leave everything out but the liquid. It's a great way to use leftover vegetables and meats. Just remember, if the ingredients are already cooked, add them at the very end; you just want to reheat them, not overcook them.

1 pound ground beef

1 tablespoon olive oil

2 onions, chopped

4 carrots, sliced

3 cloves garlic, minced

1 (10.75-ounce) can cream of mushroom soup

2 cups water

3 russet potatoes, sliced

2 cups frozen peas

½ teaspoon dried tarragon leaves

½ teaspoon salt

⅛ teaspoon pepper

Vichyssoise

*This classic soup, which sounds so expensive, is just potato
and leek soup, blended until smooth and chilled. Because leeks
are expensive, onions are a good substitute.*

SERVES ▶ 6

2 tablespoons butter

2 onions, finely sliced

3 potatoes, peeled and diced

2 cups Chicken Stock (page 79)

2 cups water

2 cups whole milk

½ teaspoon salt

⅛ teaspoon white pepper

½ cup heavy cream

2 tablespoons minced fresh parsley

1. In large pot, melt butter over medium heat. Add onions; cook and stir until translucent. Add potatoes, stock, and water and bring to a simmer. Cover and cook until potatoes are tender, about 10–15 minutes.

2. Purée the soup either by using an immersion blender, a standard blender, or forcing the soup through a sieve. Return to pot. Add milk, salt, pepper, and cream and heat through. Soup can be served hot with a sprinkling of parsley, or chilled and served cold with some diced fresh chives.

Blending Hot Liquids Hot liquids expand in the blender, so whether you're blending a soup or a sauce, don't fill the blender all the way to the top. Filling it half way and blending in batches is the safest way. Remember to cover the lid with a folded kitchen towel; hold onto the towel to keep the lid down.

Rich Split Pea Soup

COST PER SERVING
64¢

Combining several cans of condensed soup and adding some fresh vegetables is a great way to add flavor and nutrition to canned soup. Look for soups when they're on sale, and stock up.

SERVES ▶ 6

1. In large pot, combine oil and onion over medium heat; cook and stir until onion is tender and starts to brown around the edges, about 10 minutes. Stir in lentils and add water and bouillon cubes. Bring to a boil, cover, reduce heat, and simmer for 20 minutes.

2. Add condensed soups to pot and stir well. Bring back to a simmer; cook for 10 minutes. Then stir in evaporated milk and heat through but do not boil. Serve immediately.

2 tablespoons olive oil

1 onion, chopped

1 cup lentils

5 cups water

2 chicken bouillon cubes

1 (11-ounce) can condensed split pea soup

1 (11-ounce) can condensed cream of potato soup

1 (5-ounce) can evaporated milk

Chicken Bouillon Cubes Some brands of bouillon cubes are better than others. Buy the best brand that you can afford. You can find them at the large container stores and at dollar stores. They're made from concentrated chicken stock and other flavorings. Try to avoid those with MSG added. Buy a lot, because they last for years!

Black Bean Stew

*Combining legumes, such as these black beans, with grains
(the corn and rice) makes a complete protein out of this healthy stew.*

1 tablespoon olive oil

1 onion, chopped

2 (15-ounce) cans black beans, drained

1 (14-ounce) can corn, undrained

1 (10.75-ounce) can condensed tomato soup

1 (14-ounce) can vegetable broth

2 cups water

¼ teaspoon pepper

1 tablespoon chili powder

½ cup brown rice

1. In large pot, heat olive oil over medium heat. Add onion; cook and stir until tender, about 6 minutes. Stir in all remaining ingredients except rice. Bring to a boil, reduce heat, cover, and simmer for 10 minutes.

2. Uncover and stir in rice. Cover and simmer for 30–40 minutes longer until rice is tender and soup is blended.

> *About Canned Foods* Canned foods are totally prepared and ready to eat. They can be higher in sodium than the raw variety of the food. Look for lower sodium types (read labels!). You can also rinse the food before use to reduce the sodium content. Beans and vegetables such as corn and peas especially benefit from rinsing.

Beer Cheese Soup

*This thick and hearty soup is so filling that with a simple salad
it is enough for dinner.*

¼ cup butter or margarine

1 cup shredded carrots

1 cup finely chopped cauliflower

1 onion, chopped

3 cloves garlic, minced

⅓ cup all-purpose flour

½ teaspoon salt

⅛ teaspoon cayenne pepper

1 (12-ounce) bottle beer

3 cups Chicken Stock (page 79)

1½ cups whole milk

½ cup heavy cream

2 cups shredded Cheddar cheese

1 cup shredded Swiss cheese

1. In large stockpot or saucepan, melt butter over medium heat. Add carrots, cauliflower, onion, and garlic and cook and stir until vegetables are tender, about 5–6 minutes. Add flour, salt, and pepper; cook until mixture bubbles, then cook and stir for 2 more minutes.

2. Add beer; cook and stir until mixture thickens. Add stock; cook and stir for 5 minutes. Add milk and cream and cook until mixture is hot. Add cheese, a handful at a time, stirring until cheese melts and soup is blended and thick. Serve immediately.

Minestrone

COST PER SERVING
78¢

This hearty Italian soup was originally made to use up the vegetables of the harvest. It's filling, delicious, and very rich tasting. For a splurge, throw in some cubed ham.

1. In large stockpot, heat olive oil over medium heat. Add onions and garlic; cook and stir for 5 minutes until tender. Add cabbage, carrots, and zucchini; cook and stir for 10 minutes.

2. Add beef bouillon cubes, water, pepper, salt, and marjoram. Bring to a simmer; simmer for 15 minutes. Then stir in potatoes, pasta, beans, and tomatoes. Cook for 15 minutes longer until potatoes and pasta are tender. Serve with grated cheese.

From Your Garden You can throw almost anything you can grow in a garden into soups. Root vegetables such as potatoes and parsnips, delicate foods like tomatoes and squash, and fresh herbs are all wonderful in soups. Just pay attention to cooking times. Hard vegetables like potatoes need longer cooking times than delicate ones like tomatoes and peppers.

SERVES ▶ 8

2 tablespoons olive oil

1 onion, chopped

4 cloves garlic, minced

2 cups shredded cabbage

2 carrots, chopped

1 zucchini, chopped

3 beef bouillon cubes

2 quarts water

¼ teaspoon pepper

1 teaspoon salt

½ teaspoon dried marjoram

1 potato, peeled and diced

1 cup macaroni pasta

2 (15-ounce) cans red kidney beans

1 (14-ounce) can diced tomatoes, undrained

½ cup grated Parmesan cheese

Ribollita

Ribollita means "re-boiled" in Italian. It's a vegetable and bean soup thickened with leftover bread. Made in the slow cooker, it's a cinch.

SERVES ▶ 8

1 pound dried cannelloni beans

4 cups water

4 cups Beef Stock (page 80)

¼ cup olive oil

2 onions, chopped

4 cloves garlic, chopped

2 potatoes, peeled and cubed

1 teaspoon salt

¼ teaspoon pepper

3 cups chopped red cabbage

3 carrots, peeled and sliced

4 stalks celery, chopped

6 Freezer Wheat Rolls (page 37)

3 tablespoons butter

1 (28-ounce) can stewed tomatoes, chopped

½ cup grated Parmesan cheese

1. Sort beans and rinse. Place in large pot and cover with water; bring to a boil. Boil for 2 minutes, then remove from heat, cover, and let stand for 2 hours. Drain well and pour beans into 5–6 quart slow cooker; add water and stock.

2. In heavy saucepan, heat olive oil over medium heat. Add onions and garlic; cook and stir for 3–4 minutes until vegetables start to soften. Add to slow cooker with potatoes, salt, and pepper; stir well.

3. Add cabbage, carrots, and celery to slow cooker. Cover and cook on low for 7–8 hours until vegetables and beans are almost tender. Meanwhile, slice rolls in half and spread cut sides with butter. Place under broiler or in toaster oven; broil or toast until crisp and golden brown. Cut rolls into 1" pieces and stir into soup along with tomatoes. Cover and cook on low for 1–2 hours until bread has softened. Stir the soup well and serve with Parmesan cheese.

Turkey Broth To make turkey broth with a leftover roasted turkey, cover the turkey carcass with water and add a chopped onion and carrot. Bring to a boil, reduce heat, and simmer for 3–4 hours. Strain broth, discard solids, and freeze in ½-cup portions. Use in any soup in place of chicken broth.

Chicken Noodle Soup

COST PER SERVING 41¢

You can make the broth ahead of time. When you're ready to eat, cook the onion and carrots, add the broth, and simmer the egg noodles until tender.

1. Place bones and trimmings from chicken into a large pot and cover with water. Add salt, ginger root, onion, and cloves; bring to a boil. Reduce heat, cover, and simmer for 2 hours. You can also cook this in the slow cooker for 8–9 hours. Strain broth, discarding solids.

2. In large saucepan, combine butter, onion, and carrots; cook until tender, about 6–8 minutes. Add broth; bring to a simmer. Then add egg noodles; bring back to a simmer and cook until noodles are tender, about 8–10 minutes. Stir in lemon juice and serve immediately.

SERVES ▶ 6

Bones from Slow Cooker Simmered Chicken Breasts (page 145)

8 cups water

1 teaspoon salt

3 slices fresh ginger root

1 onion, sliced

2 whole cloves

1 tablespoon butter

1 onion, finely chopped

3 carrots, chopped

2 cups egg noodles

1 tablespoon lemon juice

Leftover Holiday Soup

COST PER SERVING 92¢

A whole turkey is expensive, but what leftovers! Use every bit of the bird, from the sliced juicy white meat to the leftover bones.

1. In pot, heat olive oil over medium heat. Add onion; cook until tender, about 5 minutes. Add carrots, celery, and potatoes; cook and stir for 3 minutes. Add turkey broth and water. Bring to a boil, reduce heat, and simmer for 15 minutes or until vegetables are tender.

2. Stir in remaining ingredients except evaporated milk and bring to a simmer, stirring to dissolve mashed potatoes. Then add evaporated milk and heat; do not boil. Serve immediately.

SERVES ▶ 6

2 tablespoons olive oil

1 onion, chopped

1 cup chopped carrots

1 cup chopped celery

2 cups diced potatoes

2 cups turkey broth

2 cups water

2 cups chopped cooked turkey

1 (15-ounce) can creamed corn

1 cup leftover mashed potatoes

1 teaspoon salt

⅛ teaspoon pepper

¼ teaspoon ground ginger

1 (15-ounce) can evaporated milk

Meatball Soup

SERVES ► 4

Extra lean ground beef is the most expensive kind. But it's necessary in this recipe, because the meatballs are cooked directly in the soup.

2 tablespoons olive oil

1 onion, chopped

3 carrots, sliced

2 stalks celery, sliced

1 teaspoon Worcestershire sauce

½ cup soft bread crumbs

1 egg, beaten

½ pound extra lean ground beef

½ teaspoon dried Italian seasoning

2 cups Beef Stock (page 80)

3 cups water

1 (14-ounce) can diced tomatoes, undrained

2 cups shredded cabbage

½ cup rice

1. In large pot, combine olive oil, onion, carrots, and celery. Cook over medium heat, stirring frequently, until onion is tender, about 6–8 minutes. Meanwhile, in medium bowl combine Worcestershire sauce, bread crumbs, and egg and mix well. Add beef and Italian seasoning and mix well.

2. Add broth and water to pot with vegetables and bring to a simmer. Form ground beef mixture into small meatballs about the size of a marble; drop into soup as you form them. Add tomatoes, cabbage, and rice and bring to a simmer. Cover and simmer for 25–35 minutes or until meatballs are cooked and rice and vegetables are tender.

Grains and Beans Soup

SERVES ► 8–10

This fabulous soup is so rich, thick, and hearty. Because legumes and grains are combined in the soup, it provides complete protein!

2 tablespoons olive oil

1 onion, chopped

4 cloves garlic, minced

1 cup dried split peas

1 cup dried green lentils

1 cup pearl barley

3 carrots, chopped

2 (10-ounce) cans condensed vegetable broth

6 cups water

1 teaspoon salt

1 teaspoon dried thyme leaves

1 (14-ounce) can diced tomatoes, undrained

½ cup bulgur

1. In large pot, heat olive oil over medium heat. Add onion and garlic; cook and stir until tender, about 5 minutes. Meanwhile, sort through peas and lentils, removing any debris; rinse and drain. Add to pot along with barley, carrots, broth, and water. Bring to a boil, cover, reduce heat, and simmer for 30 minutes.

2. Add salt, thyme, and tomatoes. Bring to a simmer again and cook for 15–25 minutes longer until barley, peas, and lentils are tender. Stir in bulgur and remove from heat. Cover and let stand for 10–15 minutes, until bulgur is tender. Stir and serve immediately.

Taco Olé Soup

COST PER SERVING $1.28

With all the vegetables and beans in this spicy and warming soup, you only need the beef for flavor and a bit of texture.

SERVES ► 6

- ½ pound extra lean ground beef
- 1 onion, chopped
- 3 cloves garlic, minced
- 1 zucchini, chopped
- 1 tablespoon chili powder
- ½ teaspoon cumin
- ½ teaspoon salt
- 3 cups water
- 1 (15-ounce) can kidney beans, drained
- 1 (14-ounce) can diced tomatoes, undrained
- 1 (8-ounce) jar salsa
- 1 (15-ounce) can corn, undrained

1. In large soup pot, combine ground beef, onion, and garlic over medium heat. Cook and stir until beef is browned; do not drain. Add zucchini, chili powder, cumin, and salt; cook and stir for 5 minutes longer.
2. Add remaining ingredients and bring to a simmer. Simmer for 10–15 minutes, stirring frequently, until soup is blended. Serve with sour cream, avocados, and tortilla chips.

Chicken Stock

COST PER CUP 42¢

Use your slow cooker to make chicken stock for a big batch with almost no work at all. Freeze in 1 cup portions or in ice cube trays.

YIELDS ► 12 CUPS

- 2 pounds chicken backs, bones, necks
- 2 onions, chopped
- 2 carrots, chopped
- 2 tablespoons olive oil
- 3 cloves garlic, minced
- 3 celery stalks, chopped
- ¼ cup chopped celery leaves
- 2 teaspoons salt
- ½ teaspoon pepper
- 10 cups water

1. Preheat oven to 400°F. Place chicken, onions, and carrots on baking sheet and drizzle with olive oil. Roast for 30–40 minutes or until chicken begins to brown.
2. Combine roasted chicken, onions, and carrots with all ingredients in a 5–6 quart slow cooker. Cover and cook on low for 8–10 hours. Strain and refrigerate overnight. The next day, remove fat from the surface of the stock and discard. Freeze stock up to 3 months.

Cheaper Chicken Stock If you buy bone-in chickens, chicken breasts, chicken thighs, or drumsticks for a recipe, save the bones in the freezer until you have a couple of pounds. Then you can make chicken stock for about 27¢ a cup. And yes, you can use the bones after they have been cooked; in that case, don't roast them first, just simmer.

Beef Stock

YIELDS ▶ 12 CUPS

3 pounds beef bones and trimmings

10 cups water

2 onions, chopped

2 carrots, chopped

3 cloves garlic, minced

2 tomatoes, chopped

2 potatoes, chopped

¼ cup chopped celery leaves

2 teaspoons salt

½ teaspoon pepper

1 bay leaf

1 teaspoon dried thyme leaves

Once again your slow cooker comes to the rescue to make a rich and flavorful beef stock.

1. Preheat oven to 400°F. Place beef bones, onions, and carrots on baking sheet. Roast for 40–50 minutes or until bones begin to brown.

2. Combine bones, onions, carrots, and trimmings with all ingredients in a 5–6 quart slow cooker. Cover and cook on low for 8–10 hours. When stock tastes rich, strain and refrigerate overnight. The next day, remove the fat from the surface of the stock and discard. Freeze stock up to 3 months.

Peanut Chicken Soup

SERVES ▶ 6–8

2 tablespoons olive oil

1 tablespoon butter

2 boneless, skinless chicken thighs

1 onion, chopped

3 cloves garlic, minced

3 stalks celery, chopped

2 tablespoons all-purpose flour

3 cups Chicken Stock (page 79)

5 cups water

1 cup peanut butter

1 (13-ounce) can evaporated milk

1 cup chopped peanuts

Peanut butter in soup? Why not—it's classic in Thai cooking, and is an inexpensive source of protein.

1. In large stockpot, heat olive oil with butter over medium heat. Cut chicken into 1" pieces and add to stockpot. Cook until browned on one side, about 4 minutes. Add onion, garlic, and celery; cook and stir for 4 minutes longer.

2. Sprinkle flour into stockpot and cook for 3 minutes. Add Chicken Stock and water and bring to a simmer. Simmer for 15 minutes or until chicken is thoroughly cooked.

3. Place peanut butter in medium bowl and gradually add evaporated milk, stirring to blend. Add ½ cup of the hot broth from the soup and mix well. Add peanut butter mixture to stockpot and heat just until steaming. Serve, garnished with peanuts.

▸ CHAPTER 6 ◂

Cheaper-Than-Takeout Sandwiches

Onion Garlic Burgers

COST PER SERVING 98¢

1 tablespoon olive oil

½ cup chopped onion

4 cloves garlic, minced

3 tablespoons dried bread crumbs

1 egg

1 tablespoon water

1 tablespoon soy sauce

½ teaspoon salt

⅛ teaspoon pepper

1 pound 80 percent lean hamburger

Adding extra ingredients to plain hamburger not only stretches the meat to serve more people, but it adds extra flavor, moisture, and nutrition too.

1. In small saucepan, heat olive oil over medium heat. Add onion and garlic; cook and stir until very tender, about 6 minutes. Remove from heat and let cool for 15 minutes. Place onion mixture in blender or food processor and add bread crumbs, egg, water, soy sauce, and salt and pepper. Blend or process until smooth and remove to large bowl.

2. Add hamburger to puréed mixture, gently mixing with hands just until combined. Cover and refrigerate for at least 4 hours.

3. Preheat grill or broiler. Form hamburger mixture into 5 patties and grill or broil until meat thermometer registers 165°F, turning carefully once. Serve on toasted buns with relish, mustard, and ketchup.

Tabbouleh Pitas

COST PER SERVING 75¢

1 cup Tabbouleh (page 102)

1 (15-ounce) can Great Northern Beans, drained

1 cup chopped tomatoes

4 Pita Breads (page 46)

This super–healthy sandwich is quick to make too. It's high in B vitamins and fiber . . . very satisfying.

In small bowl, combine tabbouleh, beans, and tomatoes and mix well. Cut pita breads in half and fill with tabbouleh mixture; serve immediately.

Gourmet Grilled Cheese Spread

COST PER SERVING
32¢

Cheese is an excellent source of protein and it's inexpensive too. Combine your favorite types to make this spread that will keep in the fridge up to 4 days.

1. In medium bowl, combine ricotta cheese with Cheddar cheese and mix well. Add remaining ingredients and mix until blended. Cover and refrigerate up to 4 days.

2. To use, spread about 3 tablespoons of the spread between two slices of bread. Butter the outsides of the bread, then grill, either on a skillet over medium heat, or on a dual contact indoor grill, until the bread is toasted and cheese melts.

> *Sharp or Mild Cheese?* Whether you buy sharp or mild cheese is really all about your tastes. If you want a lot of impact with less cheese, either for financial or health reasons, choose a sharper flavor cheese. About a cup of sharp Cheddar cheese will flavor an entire casserole or pizza.

YIELDS ▶ 2¼ CUPS
SERVING SIZE ▶ 3 TABLESPOONS

½ cup ricotta cheese

1 cup shredded sharp Cheddar cheese

1 cup shredded Swiss cheese

1 cup shredded American cheese

1 tablespoon butter or margarine

½ teaspoon dried basil leaves

Cubano Sandwiches

SERVES ▶ 4

3 tablespoons mayonnaise

¼ cup mustard

4 Potato Rolls (page 45)

4 (1-ounce) slices cooked ham

4 (1-ounce) slices cooked turkey

4 (1-ounce) slices Swiss cheese

½ cup pickle relish

2 tablespoons butter, softened

These classic sandwiches are pressed as they cook, which results in crisp bread and a melted interior.

1. In small bowl, combine mayonnaise and mustard and mix well. Cut rolls in half and spread cut sides with mayonnaise mixture.

2. Preheat dual-contact grill, panini maker, or griddle. Layer ham, turkey, and cheese on half of rolls. Spread pickle relish on other half, then put halves together to make sandwiches.

3. Spread butter on outsides of sandwiches and grill, pressing down on sandwiches if not using dual-contact grill or panini maker, until bread is crisp and golden brown and filling is hot. Serve immediately.

Packaged Meats Be sure to compare unit pricing for precooked, sliced meats that you buy in your grocer's meat department. Sometimes the least expensive package has the most expensive meat. Also consider how the meat is sliced. Shaved meat can deliver a bigger taste than plain slices, since there is more surface area available for your taste buds to sense.

Chili Quesadillas

COST PER SERVING $1.04

This hearty dish could serve 8–10 as an appetizer (cut into eighths). If you'd like, top it with sour cream and more cheese.

1. In small bowl, combine sour cream with green chiles and mix well. Place tortillas on work surface. Spread mixture onto all tortillas. Top with cheeses, then put tortillas together to make four quesadillas.

2. Melt butter on large skillet over medium heat until sizzling. Add quesadillas and cook, turning once, until tortillas are toasted and cheese is melted. While quesadillas are cooking, heat chili in microwave until hot.

3. Cut quesadillas into quarters and place on serving dish; spoon hot chili over all. Serve immediately.

SERVES ▶ 6

8 (8-inch) flour tortillas

½ cup sour cream

1 (4-ounce) can green chiles, drained

1 cup shredded Cheddar cheese

1 cup shredded Swiss cheese

2 tablespoons butter

2 cups Homemade Chili (page 32)

Grilled Tuna Apple Melts

COST PER SERVING 95¢

These melted sandwiches are open-faced, saving you both money and carbs because you only eat one slice of bread.

1. In medium bowl, combine tuna, onions, apple, celery, mustard, and mayonnaise and mix gently but thoroughly.

2. Preheat broiler. On broiler pan, place bread slices and spread with butter. Broil for 2–4 minutes or until bread is toasted. Turn bread slices over. Top each with a slice of cheese, then divide the tuna mixture and place on top. Top with another slice of cheese.

3. Broil sandwiches 6" from heat source for 3–6 minutes, watching carefully, until the cheese melts and tuna mixture is hot. Serve immediately.

SERVES ▶ 4

1 (6-ounce) can tuna, drained

2 green onions, sliced

½ cup chopped apple

¼ cup chopped celery

2 teaspoons mustard

¼ cup mayonnaise

8 slices American cheese

4 slices Artisan Whole Wheat Bread (page 39)

2 tablespoons butter or margarine

Chicken Cream Cheese Bagels

COST PER SERVING $1^{47}

SERVES ▶ 4

This simple chicken spread is colorful and flavorful too. It's delicious on bagels or any bread, and can be used as a dip with the addition of ¼ cup more milk.

2 Slow Cooker Simmered Chicken Breasts (page 145)

1 (8-ounce) package cream cheese, softened

2 tablespoons milk

¼ cup chopped green onion

½ cup dried cranberries, chopped

4 plain bagels, split

2 tablespoons butter

1. Chop chicken and set aside. In medium bowl, combine cream cheese with milk and beat until fluffy. Stir in chicken, green onions, and cranberries.

2. Split bagels and spread with butter. Toast until golden brown, then make sandwiches with the toasted bagels and the chicken spread. Serve immediately.

Chicken Sandwiches

COST PER SERVING 95¢

YIELDS ▶ 4

Using raspberry jam is an inexpensive way to get the taste of raspberries in this delicious sandwich.

2 slices bacon

2 Slow Cooker Simmered Chicken Breasts (page 145)

⅓ cup mayonnaise

6 slices Hearty White Bread (page 48)

3 tablespoons butter or margarine

3 slices butter lettuce

¼ cup raspberry jam

1. In small skillet, cook bacon until crisp; crumble and set aside. Slice chicken into ½" slices. In medium bowl, combine chicken, bacon, and mayonnaise and stir gently to coat chicken.

2. Spread bread with butter on both sides and toast in a toaster oven or under the broiler. Make sandwiches with the toasted bread, the chicken mixture, butter lettuce, and raspberry jam. Slice diagonally and serve immediately.

Substituting Meats With sandwiches, it's easy to substitute one meat for another. If you don't have chicken, use turkey or ham, or roast beef. Canadian bacon or sausage can be substituted for plain bacon. "Taste" the recipe in your mind. If you think a substitution will work, go ahead.

Crescent Ham Salsa Sandwiches

COST PER SERVING
$1⁴¹

Once you have this basic recipe down, you can vary it to make a hundred different versions. It's quick, easy, and delicious.

1. Preheat oven to 375°F. Place ham on cutting board and chop into fine pieces. Drain ¼ cup of the fruit salsa and chop finely. Combine with ham, Muenster cheese, and sour cream in small bowl.

2. Separate crescent dough into 4 rectangles, firmly pressing perforations to seal. Divide ham mixture among rectangles. Fold dough in half to make a triangular shape, sealing edges with a fork. Place on ungreased cookie sheet.

3. Bake 15–20 minutes until sandwiches are golden brown. Serve with remaining fruit salsa.

SERVES ▶ 4

3 (2-ounce) packages shaved ham

1 cup Suave Fruit Salsa (page 28), divided

½ cup shredded Muenster cheese

¼ cup sour cream

1 (8-ounce) can refrigerated crescent rolls

Avocado Smash Sandwiches

COST PER SERVING $1.01

Avocados are expensive, but with this recipe you can stretch one to feed four people.

SERVES ▶ 4–6

1 avocado

⅓ cup sour cream

¼ teaspoon salt

Pinch white pepper

1 cup grape tomatoes

1 cucumber, peeled

8 slices Artisan Whole Wheat Bread (page 39)

2 tablespoons butter, softened

4 (1-ounce) slices Swiss cheese

1. Peel avocado, remove pit, and place in small bowl. Top with sour cream, salt, and pepper, and mash, leaving some chunks. Cut grape tomatoes in half and add to avocado mixture.

2. Cut cucumber into thin slices. Toast bread until golden brown, then butter one side of each piece. Place, buttered side up, on work surface.

3. Layer cheese and cucumber on half of slices. Spread avocado mixture on other half, and put together to make sandwiches. Serve immediately.

Freezing Avocados When avocados go on sale, you can buy a bunch and freeze them. But don't freeze them whole or in slices; they will become mushy. Peel the avocado, remove the pit, and mash with 1 tablespoon lemon juice for each piece of fruit. Pack into a hard-sided container, label, and freeze for up to 3 months. They're delicious in spreads and Big Batch Guacamole (page 24).

Toasted Cheese Sandwiches

COST PER SERVING $1⁵⁴

You could use the peanut spread as a sandwich all by itself, or pair it with some sliced ham or chicken.

1. In a small bowl, combine peanuts, cream cheese, celery, and mayonnaise, mixing until combined. To make sandwiches, spread peanut spread on one side of each piece of bread. Top each with some of the cheeses, then put together. Spread butter on outsides of sandwiches.

2. Toast in a dual-contact grill or on a hot griddle, pressing down on the sandwiches as they cook. When bread is toasted and the filling is melted, cut in half and serve immediately.

> *Dual Contact Grill Substitute* You can still cook these sandwiches without a dual contact grill. Heat a regular griddle or skillet, add the sandwiches, then place a second, smaller skillet, bottom side down, on the sandwiches. Press gently on them as the sandwiches cook. Then turn and cook the second side, without the second skillet.

SERVES ► 4

½ cup chopped peanuts

1 (3-ounce) package cream cheese, softened

½ cup chopped celery

2 tablespoons mayonnaise

8 slices Artisan Whole Wheat Bread (page 39)

1 cup shredded Swiss cheese

1 cup shredded Colby cheese

2 tablespoons butter, softened

Seafood Slaw Sandwiches

COST PER SERVING $1¹¹

The dressing from the confetti slaw moistens the crab and fish fillets to make the perfect sandwich filling. Yum.

1. In medium bowl, combine crab, fish fillets, confetti slaw, and cheese and mix gently until combined.

2. Spread cut sides of buns with butter and toast under a broiler or in a toaster oven. Make sandwiches with the toasted buns and the crab filling; serve immediately.

SERVES ► 6

1 (6-ounce) can crab meat, drained

2 leftover Cornmeal Fried Fish fillets (page 173), chopped

2 cups Confetti Slaw (page 102)

1 cup shredded Swiss cheese

6 hot dog buns, sliced

2 tablespoons butter, softened

Three Bean Sandwich Spread

YIELDS ► 3 CUPS
SERVING SIZE ► ⅓ CUP

This spread is really good (and provides complete protein!) when you serve it on corn tortillas as a wrap sandwich.

2 tablespoons olive oil

5 cloves garlic, minced

1 (15-ounce) can garbanzo beans, drained

2 tablespoons lemon juice

½ teaspoon salt

⅛ teaspoon cayenne pepper

1 (15-ounce) can black beans, drained

1 (15-ounce) can kidney beans, drained

1 cup chopped celery

1 cup shredded carrots

1. In small saucepan, heat olive oil over medium heat. Add garlic; cook and stir until fragrant, about 2–3 minutes. Place in medium bowl and add garbanzo beans, lemon juice, salt, and pepper. Mash until mixture is mostly smooth.

2. Stir in black beans, kidney beans, celery, and carrot. Cover and store in refrigerator for up to 4 days. Use as a sandwich spread or as a dip for fresh vegetables and crackers.

Cooking Times for Legumes All legumes have different cooking times. You can still use them in the same recipe if you follow a couple of rules. Learn the cooking times, and add the ingredients at staggered times, working backward from the finish time. Use canned beans, which are more expensive, if you want to add all at once. And beans that are soaked overnight cook more quickly than those that have not soaked.

Tender Steak Pitas

COST PER SERVING
$1⁶⁴

Marinating round steak makes it almost as tender as filet mignon. Make this sandwich filling ahead of time to eat lunch in a flash.

SERVES ▶ 4

½ pound bottom round steak

3 tablespoons olive oil

3 tablespoons apple cider vinegar

1 tablespoon soy sauce

3 tablespoons ketchup

1 teaspoon salt

2 tablespoons water

2 Pita Breads (page 46)

1 cucumber, peeled and chopped

2 stalks celery, chopped

2 green onions, chopped

1. Place steak in heavy duty plastic zipper bag. Add olive oil, vinegar, soy sauce, ketchup, salt, and water. Close bag and squish with your hands to mix marinade. Place in large bowl and chill in refrigerator for 8 hours.

2. Preheat broiler and remove steak from marinade. Pour marinade into a small saucepan and set aside. Broil steak, 6" from heat source, turning once, for 5–9 minutes or until desired doneness. Let steak stand for 10 minutes.

3. Bring marinade to a boil over high heat; boil for 1 minute. Thinly slice steak against the grain and place in medium bowl with cucumber, celery, and green onion. Pour marinade over, cover, and place in refrigerator up to 3 days.

4. When ready to eat, slice pita breads in half and fill with drained meat mixture.

> *Marinating Meats* Marinating meats in an acidic mixture breaks down the meat structure, which results in a tender steak. Acidic ingredients include lemon juice, wine, and vinegar. But don't marinate the meat too long! Meats that have been marinated more than 24 hours can turn mushy, and the flavor could be compromised by the marinade ingredients.

Pizza Burgers

*Black beans and carrots stretch the meat and add rich
flavor and nutrition to these simple open–faced sandwiches.
You could serve the filling on toasted English muffins if you'd like too.*

SERVES ► 4–6

¾ pound 80 percent lean
ground beef

1 onion, chopped

1 tablespoon all-purpose flour

1 cup cooked black beans, chopped

1 (14-ounce) can tomato purée

½ cup grated carrots

½ teaspoon dried Italian seasoning

½ teaspoon garlic salt

¼ cup grated Parmesan cheese

1½ cups shredded sharp Cheddar
cheese, divided

4 hamburger buns, cut in half

2 tablespoons butter, softened

1. In a large saucepan, cook ground beef and onion together over medium heat, stirring occasionally, until meat is browned and cooked. Drain off excess fat and water.

2. Sprinkle flour over meat; cook and stir for 1 minute. Then add beans, tomato purée, carrots, Italian seasoning, and salt. Bring to a boil, reduce heat, and simmer for about 5–8 minutes until thickened. Stir in Parmesan cheese and ½ cup Cheddar cheese; remove from heat.

3. Preheat broiler. Spread cut sides of hamburger buns with butter and toast under broiler. Remove from oven and divide beef mixture among buns. Top with remaining Cheddar cheese. Broil 6" from heat for 4–5 minutes or until sandwiches are hot and cheese is melted and bubbly. Serve immediately.

CLTs

COST PER SERVING
$1⁵⁸

Cheese, lettuce, and tomato sandwiches are really deliciously different, especially when the tomatoes are caramelized and the cheese melted and creamy.

SERVES ▶ 4

1. Preheat toaster oven to 400°F. Drizzle small roasting pan with olive oil and add tomatoes, cut side up. Sprinkle with garlic, salt, and pepper. Roast for 20 minutes, or until tomatoes are hot and turning brown in spots.

2. Remove pan from oven and sprinkle with cheese. Cover with foil and let stand for 5 minutes.

3. Meanwhile, spread bread with butter and toast in toaster oven. Make sandwiches with toasted bread, lettuce, and tomato/cheese mixture. Serve immediately.

2 tablespoons olive oil

4 plum tomatoes, sliced

2 cloves garlic, minced

½ teaspoon salt

⅛ teaspoon pepper

1 cup shredded Mozzarella cheese

1 cup shredded sharp Cheddar cheese

4 leaves butter lettuce

8 slices Artisan Whole Wheat Bread (page 39)

2 tablespoons butter

Shredded Or Not? Usually pre-shredded cheese is more expensive than the cheese you buy in blocks and shred yourself, but not always. Be on the lookout for sales and coupons that could not only bring the price of pre-shredded cheese down, but save you some time and work as well. Be sure to seal the package of the shredded variety carefully so it doesn't dry out.

Black Bean Burgers

COST PER SERVING
$1⁴¹

SERVES ▶ 6

Wrapping these burgers in corn tortillas with cheese and guacamole adds a Tex–Mex twist.

1 tablespoon olive oil

3 cloves garlic, minced

1 jalapeño pepper, minced

¾ cup cooked black beans

1 egg, beaten

½ teaspoon salt

⅛ teaspoon pepper

1 pound 80 percent lean ground beef

6 (1-ounce) slices Pepper Jack cheese

6 (6-inch) corn tortillas

½ cup Big Batch Guacamole (page 24)

¼ cup sour cream

1. In medium microwave–safe bowl, combine olive oil, garlic, and jalapeño pepper. Microwave on high for 1 minute; remove and stir. Add black beans and mash with potato masher until smooth. Beat in egg, salt, and pepper.

2. Add beef; mix with hands just until combined. Form into 6 oval patties. Broil or sauté patties until thoroughly cooked, turning once, about 5–7 minutes. Top each with Pepper Jack cheese, cover, and let stand for 5 minutes.

3. Wrap tortillas in microwave–safe paper towels and heat on high for 45 seconds. Remove from microwave. In small bowl, combine guacamole and sour cream. Spread guacamole mixture onto tortillas and wrap each around a beef patty. Serve immediately.

CHAPTER 7

Slightly Sumptuous Salads

Sparkling Fruit Salad

COST PER SERVING 57¢

In this easy salad, the gelatin retains the bubbles from the soda, so it really sparkles!

SERVES ▶ 12

1 (15-ounce) can pineapple tidbits, drained

2 (3-ounce) packages lemon–flavored gelatin

1½ cups boiling water

2 cups sparkling white soda

1 cup fresh blueberries

1 cup green grapes, halved

1. Drain pineapple, reserving juice. Add enough water to juice to equal 1½ cups. Bring to a boil over high heat. In large bowl, combine gelatin and boiling liquid; stir until gelatin is completely dissolved.

2. Stir in sparkling soda and chill until the mixture is syrupy, about 45 minutes. Add fruits and stir gently. Pour into 9" x 13" pan and chill until set. Cut into squares to serve.

Green Bean Salad

COST PER SERVING 83¢

You can keep this green bean salad in the fridge for a couple of days; mix with lettuce just before serving.

SERVES ▶ 8

1 (16-ounce) package frozen green beans

3 tablespoons mustard

¼ cup olive oil

⅔ cup plain yogurt

⅛ teaspoon pepper

1 cup diced Swiss cheese

1 (4-ounce) jar sliced mushrooms, drained

8 cups mixed salad greens

1. Cook green beans according to package directions; rinse with cold water, drain, and set aside.

2. In medium bowl, combine mustard, olive oil, yogurt, and pepper and mix well. Add cheese, drained mushrooms, and green beans; mix well. Cover and chill for 2 hours before serving. To serve, place salad greens in bowl and top with green bean mixture. Toss and serve immediately.

Mushrooms White or button mushrooms will turn dark, even if treated with an acidic ingredient like lemon juice. Canned mushrooms are a better choice for longer-lasting salads. The darkened mushrooms still have the same amount of nutrients, but aesthetically they are less pleasing.

Pasta Cabbage Salad

COST PER SERVING
82¢

Add a can of tuna or chicken and this becomes a hearty main dish salad.

1. Bring a large pot of salted water to a boil. Meanwhile, in large bowl combine mayonnaise, yogurt, and salad dressing and mix well.

2. Wash cabbage and cut in half. Remove core and cut crosswise into ¼" thick pieces. Add to mayonnaise mixture in bowl. Add bell pepper and mushrooms.

3. Place frozen peas in a colander. Cook pasta in boiling water until al dente according to package directions. Drain over peas in colander and add to salad mixture. Toss gently to coat and serve immediately or cover and chill for 3–4 hours before serving.

SERVES ▶ 8

½ cup mayonnaise

½ cup plain yogurt

½ cup zesty Italian salad dressing

1 head purple cabbage

1 green bell pepper, chopped

1 cup sliced mushrooms

2 cups frozen peas

1 (16-ounce) package penne pasta

Wild Rice Ham Salad

COST PER SERVING
$1¹⁶

To make this salad stretch even further, serve it on top of mixed torn salad greens. For a splurge, use double the wild rice and cut the brown rice in half.

1. In small saucepan, combine wild rice with 1 cup water. Bring to a boil, reduce heat, cover, and simmer for 40–45 minutes until rice is tender. Meanwhile, in medium saucepan, combine brown rice with 2 cups water. Bring to a boil, reduce heat, cover, and simmer for 30–35 minutes until rice is tender.

2. Meanwhile, in large bowl, combine mayonnaise, mustard, olive oil, and Parmesan cheese and mix well. When rice is cooked, drain if necessary and add to mayonnaise mixture along with remaining ingredients. Stir well to coat. Serve immediately, or cover and chill before serving.

SERVES ▶ 6

½ cup wild rice

1 cup brown rice

¾ cup mayonnaise

3 tablespoons mustard

¼ cup olive oil

¼ cup grated Parmesan cheese

1 green bell pepper, chopped

1 cup diced ham

1 cup chopped celery

1 cup diced Swiss cheese

Gemelli "Crab" Salad

SERVES ▶ 6–8

1 (16-ounce) package gemelli pasta

⅔ cup mayonnaise

½ cup plain yogurt

2 teaspoons Old Bay Seasoning

2 tablespoons mustard

2 tablespoons lemon juice

¼ cup milk

2 cups frozen peas

¼ cup chopped green onions

1 cup grape tomatoes, halved

1 (8-ounce) package frozen imitation crab legs, thawed

*Imitation crab legs taste almost like the real thing,
especially when combined with lots of other ingredients.*

1. Bring a large pot of salted water to a boil. Meanwhile, in large bowl combine mayonnaise, yogurt, Old Bay Seasoning, mustard, lemon juice, and milk, and mix with wire whisk until blended.

2. Place frozen peas in a colander. Cook pasta in boiling water according to package directions until al dente. Pour over peas in colander to drain and to thaw peas. Add to mayonnaise mixture along with green onions and tomatoes and stir to coat.

3. Flake crab legs and add to salad; toss gently. Cover and chill for 2–3 hours before serving on lettuce cups.

Imitation Crab Legs Imitation crab legs, also known as surimi, are real seafood. Surimi is a fish paste made from a mild white fish like pollock that is flavored and formed to look like crab legs. The taste and texture is very similar, and the imitation crab costs about $3.50 per pound. Real lump crab costs at least $20.00 per pound.

Best Potato Salad

COST PER SERVING **96¢**

This salad has a cooked dressing and two kinds of potatoes for added interest. Serve it alongside Onion Garlic Burgers (page 82) for the perfect summer dinner.

1. In large skillet, cook bacon over medium heat until crisp. Remove bacon from pan, crumble, and refrigerate. To drippings remaining in pan, add butter, then cook onion until tender, about 5 minutes.

2. Sprinkle flour, salt, and pepper into pan; cook and stir until bubbly, about 3 minutes. Then add evaporated milk; cook and stir until thickened. Stir in vinegar and sugar and bring back to a boil. Remove from heat to small bowl, stir in mustard, cover, and chill.

3. Bring a large pot of salted water to a boil. Cook sweet potatoes until tender, about 30–40 minutes; remove to wire rack. Then add red potatoes; cook until tender, about 15–20 minutes; remove to wire rack.

4. When potatoes are cool enough to handle, take dressing out of fridge and add mayonnaise and whipped salad dressing. Peel potatoes and cut into 1" pieces, adding to the dressing as you work. Stir in green onions, radishes, and reserved bacon. Cover and chill for at least 4 hours before serving.

SERVES ▶ 8

4 slices bacon

1 tablespoon butter

½ cup finely chopped onion

3 tablespoons all-purpose flour

1 teaspoon salt

⅛ teaspoon pepper

1 (12-ounce) can evaporated milk

⅓ cup apple cider vinegar

¼ cup sugar

2 tablespoons mustard

2 large sweet potatoes

2 pounds red potatoes

½ cup mayonnaise

½ cup whipped salad dressing

½ cup chopped green onions

4 radishes, thinly sliced

Orange Almond Salad

81¢

*For a splurge, use pecans or cashews instead of the almonds
in this fabulous salad.*

SERVES ▶ 6

¼ cup slivered almonds

3 tablespoons sugar, divided

1 tablespoon brown sugar

¼ cup sliced almonds

2 (11-ounce) cans mandarin
oranges

½ cup mayonnaise

½ teaspoon dried tarragon leaves

¼ teaspoon salt

⅛ teaspoon white pepper

6 cups mixed salad greens

3 stalks celery, chopped

1. In small skillet, combine slivered almonds, 2 tablespoons sugar, and brown sugar over low heat. Cook, stirring frequently, until sugar melts. Add the sliced almonds and stir well until the melted sugar coats almonds. Remove from heat and spoon onto parchment paper; let cool and break into small pieces.

2. Meanwhile, drain mandarin oranges, reserving ½ cup liquid. In small bowl, combine mayonnaise, 1 tablespoon sugar, reserved orange juice, tarragon, salt, and pepper and mix well. Set aside.

3. When ready to serve, combine salad greens, celery, and drained oranges in large serving bowl. Drizzle half of dressing over salad and toss to coat. Sprinkle with the cooled almonds and serve remaining dressing on the side.

Melting Sugar Melting sugar isn't difficult, but it does take some patience. It can take up to 15 minutes. The melted sugar will turn liquid and also change color to a dark golden amber. Don't raise the heat because it burns easily. Be very careful with the melted sugar; its temperature is 370°F!

THE EVERYTHING MEALS ON A BUDGET COOKBOOK

Glorified Rice

COST PER SERVING
58¢

This recipe can be served as dessert. It's also a sneaky way to get more fruits into your kids!

1. Drain pineapple, reserving juice. Drain oranges, reserving juice. In large saucepan, combine rice, ½ cup reserved juice, and water. Bring to a boil, reduce heat, cover, and simmer for 20 minutes until rice is tender. Set aside to cool.

2. In saucepan, combine remaining reserved juices, with pineapple-orange juice, egg, sugar, and flour and mix well with wire whisk. Cook over medium heat, stirring, until mixture comes to a boil and thickens. Remove from heat and chill in refrigerator for ½ hour.

3. Stir rice with fork to fluff. Add egg mixture, coconut, whipped topping, pineapple, and mandarin oranges and fold together until blended. Pour into serving bowl, cover, and chill for at least 4 hours before serving.

1 (20-ounce) can crushed pineapple

1 (15-ounce) can mandarin oranges

1 cup long grain rice

1½ cups water

1 (6-ounce) can pineapple-orange juice

1 egg

½ cup sugar

3 tablespoons all-purpose flour

½ cup coconut

1 cup frozen whipped topping, thawed

Pesto Pasta Salad

COST PER SERVING
78¢

This colorful salad can be a main dish if you add chopped ham or cooked turkey. For a splurge, use a red bell pepper instead of green.

SERVES ▶ 8

1. Bring a large pot of salted water to a boil. Meanwhile, in large bowl combine pesto, mayonnaise, salad dressing, and milk and mix until blended. Cook pasta until al dente according to package directions.

2. Place peas in colander; drain pasta over peas, then add pasta and peas to pesto mixture. Stir in bell pepper, celery, and green onions. Cover and chill for 3–4 hours before serving.

½ cup Spinach Pesto (page 28)

½ cup mayonnaise

½ cup whipped salad dressing

2 tablespoons milk

1 (16-ounce) box farfalle pasta

2 cups frozen peas

1 green bell pepper, chopped

3 stalks celery, chopped

¼ cup chopped green onions

Whipped Salad Dressing Whipped salad dressing is not mayonnaise. It is found under the brand name Miracle Whip, and is used primarily as a sandwich spread. It is a cooked white dressing that is whipped until creamy and fluffy. Don't substitute mayonnaise for it, because the whipped dressing is sweeter and more tangy than mayonnaise.

Tabbouleh

COST PER SERVING
93¢

SERVES ▶ 6

*Save some Tabbouleh to make Tabbouleh Pitas (page 82)
for lunch tomorrow.*

1½ cups bulgur

3 cups boiling water

2 tablespoons lemon juice

¼ cup chopped flat leaf parsley

2 tablespoons chopped fresh mint

1 green bell pepper, chopped

1 cucumber, peeled and sliced

½ cup sliced green onions

3 tablespoons lemon juice

¼ cup olive oil

1 teaspoon salt

⅛ teaspoon pepper

1. Place bulgur in bowl and cover with boiling water; add 2 table-spoons lemon juice. Cover and let stand for 30 minutes. Drain if necessary, then add parsley and mint. Toss until steaming stops.

2. Add pepper, cucumber, and green onions. In small bowl, combine 3 tablespoons lemon juice, olive oil, salt, and pepper and mix well. Drizzle over salad and toss. Serve immediately or cover and chill for a few hours before serving.

> *Bulgur* Bulgur is cracked wheat, that is, the whole kernel of wheat cracked and packaged. Be sure to read label directions. Some bulgur has been pre-cooked or steamed and only needs to be rehydrated with cold water. Other varieties need to be cooked before use.

Confetti Slaw

COST PER SERVING
77¢

SERVES ▶ 12

*Cabbage is one of the cheapest foods available, and it is
delicious; crisp, crunchy, and slightly sweet. This salad feeds a bunch!*

½ cup mayonnaise

1 cup buttermilk

1 cup plain yogurt

⅓ cup crumbled feta cheese

1 teaspoon dried dill weed

⅛ teaspoon pepper

2 tablespoons prepared horseradish

1 head red cabbage, shredded

1 head green cabbage, shredded

6 stalks celery, sliced

1 green bell pepper, chopped

2 cups frozen peas, thawed

1. In large bowl, combine mayonnaise, buttermilk, yogurt, feta, dill, pepper, and horseradish and mix until blended.

2. Prepare cabbage and vegetables, adding them to the mayonnaise mixture as you work. When everything is added, toss gently to coat. Cover and refrigerate for at least 2 hours before serving. Store in refrigerator up to 4 days.

Corn "Cobb" Salad

COST PER SERVING
$1⁸⁰

*Because this salad is tossed rather than composed, you
can get away with using less of the expensive ingredients, like
avocado and chicken.*

1. In small saucepan, cook bacon until crisp; crumble and set
   aside. To drippings remaining in pan, add onion; cook and stir
   until crisp-tender, about 4 minutes. Remove to small bowl and
   add mayonnaise, buttermilk, dill, garlic salt, parsley, and feta
   cheese; mix well.

2. In large bowl, combine chopped chicken, corn, lettuce, tomato,
   and avocado. Drizzle with mayonnaise mixture and toss gently;
   serve immediately.

> *Dried Herbs* Compare prices carefully on dried herb jars and bot-
> tles. The smaller bottles are usually the better buy, and, since herbs last
> only 6–12 months, it's less likely that you'll throw them away. Mark the
> purchase date on the bottle or jar, and be sure to store them in a dark,
> cool, dry place.

SERVES ▶ 4

2 slices bacon

½ cup onion, finely chopped

¼ cup mayonnaise

2 tablespoons buttermilk

¼ teaspoon dried dill weed

¼ teaspoon garlic salt

1 tablespoon chopped fresh parsley

3 tablespoons feta cheese

2 Slow Cooker Simmered Chicken Breasts (page 145), chopped

1 (10-ounce) package frozen corn, thawed

4 cups lettuce

1 tomato, chopped

1 avocado, peeled and chopped

Cottage Cheese Potato Salad

COST PER SERVING **75¢**

Many people love the combination of cottage cheese and French dressing. If you're one of them, this is the salad for you!

SERVES ▶ 6

3 pounds red potatoes

½ cup French salad dressing, divided

1 cup cottage cheese

¼ cup mayonnaise

2 tablespoons milk

1 cup chopped celery

2 hard boiled eggs, chopped

1 cup frozen peas, thawed

1. Bring a large pot of salted water to a boil. Add potatoes (cut some in half if necessary so they are all about the same size), bring back to a boil, and then cook until tender, about 10–15 minutes. Drain potatoes and place on wire rack until cool enough to handle.

2. Peel warm potatoes and cut into slices. Place in large bowl with ¼ cup French salad dressing; toss to coat, and set aside.

3. In food processor or blender, combine cottage cheese, remaining ¼ cup French salad dressing, mayonnaise, and milk and blend until smooth. Pour over potatoes and add remaining ingredients. Stir gently to coat, then cover and chill for at least 4 hours before serving.

Hard Cooked Eggs To hard cook eggs, cover eggs by 1 inch with water. Bring to a boil over high heat. When water comes to a full boil, cover the pan and remove from heat. Let stand for 15 minutes for large eggs. Then place pot in the sink, uncover, and let cold water run into the pan until the eggs are cold. Crack, peel, and use.

Indian Ambrosia

COST PER SERVING
84¢

Curry powder adds a great touch of spiciness to a classic ambrosia salad. Use any canned fruits you'd like.

1. Drain pineapple tidbits, reserving 2 tablespoons juice. Drain peaches and mandarin oranges, saving the juice for another recipe. Chop peaches into pieces. Combine canned fruits in serving bowl.

2. Peel bananas and cut into slices. Add to canned fruits and mix gently.

3. In small bowl, combine sour cream, reserved pineapple juice, and curry powder and mix well. Spoon over fruits in serving bowl, do not toss. Sprinkle with toasted coconut, cover, and chill for 2–3 hours before serving.

> *Fruit Juices*   Whenever you drain a canned fruit, save the juice! You can add it to smoothies, use it as the base for a gelatin fruit salad, or even freeze the juice in ice cube trays to use in fruit drinks or as snacks for kids on a hot day. You can even mix the juice with softened ice cream and refreeze it to serve as dessert, topped with nuts or toasted coconut.

SERVES ▶ 6

1 (15-ounce) can pineapple tidbits

1 (15-ounce) can sliced peaches

1 (15-ounce) can mandarin oranges

2 bananas

½ cup sour cream

1 teaspoon curry powder

½ cup shredded coconut, toasted

Curried Waldorf
Pasta Salad

COST PER SERVING
$1.07

1 cup vanilla yogurt

¼ cup mayonnaise

1 tablespoon curry powder

¼ cup milk

2 tablespoons honey

2 Granny Smith apples, chopped

1 (16-ounce) package penne pasta

1 cup raisins

1 (12-ounce) can dark chicken meat, drained

4 stalks celery, chopped

½ cup chopped walnuts

Waldorf salad is a classic combination of apples, walnuts, celery, and raisins in a creamy dressing. This updated version adds curry, pasta, and chicken to turn it into a main dish.

1. Bring a large pot of salted water to a boil. In large bowl, combine yogurt, mayonnaise, curry powder, milk, and honey and mix well.

2. Wash apples and chop (do not peel) and add to the yogurt mixture as you work. Add pasta to boiling water and cook according to package directions until al dente.

3. Meanwhile, add raisins, chicken, celery, and walnuts to yogurt mixture and stir to coat. When pasta is done, drain and add to bowl; toss to coat. Cover and chill for 3–4 hours before serving.

Pear Cream Salad

This salad is a great choice for breakfast, and is also delicious served for brunch on the porch with Yes, Eggs Benedict (page 58).

(page 58)

SERVES ► 8

1. In large bowl, combine gelatin with ⅓ cup sugar. Drain pear slices, reserving juice. Add enough water to juice to make 3 cups total. Add 1 cup of the juice mixture to the sugar mixture. Heat remaining juice mixture just to a boil, then pour over sugar mixture along with lemon juice and stir until sugar and gelatin are completely dissolved.

2. Stir in pear slices and pour into a shallow 2-quart casserole dish. Chill until firm.

3. In small saucepan, combine remaining ⅓ cup sugar with egg, flour, and pear nectar. Cook and stir over medium heat until mixture thickens and comes to a boil. Remove from heat and chill in refrigerator until cold.

4. Fold whipped topping into egg mixture and carefully spread over gelatin mixture in pan. Chill for at least 4 hours before serving.

2 (0.25-ounce) packages unflavored gelatin

⅔ cup sugar, divided

2 (15-ounce) cans sliced pears

1 tablespoon lemon juice

1 egg

2 tablespoons all-purpose flour

1 (6-ounce) can pear nectar

1 cup frozen whipped topping, thawed

> *Unflavored Gelatin* Be sure that you are using unflavored gelatin that comes in an envelope, not the packages of flavored gelatin that are full of sugar and artificial colors. With some fruit juice and a package of unflavored gelatin, you can make many different flavors and varieties of gelatin salads that your kids will love and are nutritious too.

Frozen Banana Salad

COST PER SERVING
47¢

SERVES ► 9

*Serve this delicious frozen salad on lettuce leaves as a side
dish to ham for Easter dinner.*

3 large bananas

1 tablespoon lemon juice

1 cup sour cream

1 (6-ounce) container lemon yogurt

½ cup powdered sugar

1 (15-ounce) can crushed
pineapple, drained

½ cup dried sweetened cranberries,
chopped

1. In large bowl, mash peeled bananas with lemon juice until smooth. Stir in remaining ingredients and mix well.

2. Pour into 9" square glass dish and freeze until firm. To serve, let stand at room temperature for 15 minutes, then slice into squares.

Lettuce Salad

COST PER SERVING
38¢

SERVES ► 4

*This simple salad dressing can be served over any greens
that are on hand.*

4 cups lettuce

1 tablespoon mustard

3 tablespoons olive oil

1 tablespoon apple cider vinegar

¼ teaspoon salt

⅛ teaspoon pepper

Place lettuce in serving bowl. In small bowl, combine remaining ingredients and beat with wire whisk until blended. Pour over lettuce, toss gently, and serve immediately.

The Indispensable Leftover

8

Baked Bread Crumb Frittata

COST PER SERVING 82¢

SERVES ▶ 4

Frittatas are like heavy omelets. They can be eaten hot, warm, or cold, so they are perfect for breakfast on the run; just wrap a slice in a napkin and go!

2 tablespoons butter or margarine, divided

1 tablespoon olive oil

½ cup frozen spinach, thawed and drained

2 slices Artisan Whole Wheat Bread (page 39), toasted

6 eggs

½ cup cottage cheese

½ teaspoon salt

1 cup shredded Swiss cheese

1. Preheat oven to 375°F. Grease a 9" pie plate with 1 tablespoon butter and set aside. In medium skillet, melt 1 tablespoon butter with the olive oil over medium heat. When the butter foams, add spinach; cook and stir until liquid evaporates, about 4–5 minutes. Remove spinach from skillet and set aside.

2. Make crumbs from the toast and add to the skillet; cook and stir over medium heat until coated with butter mixture. Remove from heat.

3. In medium bowl, beat eggs with cottage cheese and salt. Add spinach, Swiss cheese, and toasted crumbs and mix well, then pour into prepared pie plate.

4. Bake for 20 minutes or until almost set. Remove from oven and sprinkle with cheese. Return to oven and bake for 10–20 minutes longer until frittata is set and top is browned. Cool for 5 minutes, then slice to serve.

Sicilian Bread Salad

COST PER SERVING **$1.02**

You need a good hearty bread for this recipe (not white bread).

1. Preheat oven to 350°F. Cut the french bread into 1" cubes, including some crust with each cube. Place on cookie sheet and drizzle with olive oil; toss to coat. Bake for 12 minutes, turning once, until golden brown and crisp. Cool on wire rack.

2. In large bowl, combine vegetables, pesto, and beans; toss until coated. Let stand for 20 minutes. Add bread and tomatoes and toss to coat. Drizzle with salad dressing and sprinkle with feta cheese. Add lettuce and toss gently; serve immediately.

Versatile Salads One of the things that makes salads such a good use for leftovers is that they are so versatile. Combine just about any cooked leftover with some spicy salad dressing and a "filler" ingredient like greens or pasta or rice and you have an easy, satisfying meal.

SERVES ▶ 4–6

6 (1-inch) slices Whole Wheat French Bread (page 47)

2 tablespoons olive oil

1 cup Roasted Vegetables (page 228)

¼ cup Spinach Pesto (page 28)

1 (15-ounce) can red beans, drained

2 tomatoes, chopped

½ cup Italian salad dressing

¼ cup crumbled feta cheese

4 cups torn lettuce leaves

Chili French Bread Pizza

COST PER SERVING **$1.11**

Any thick chili can be used in this easy and hearty recipe. You could even use a 16–ounce can of chili.

1. Preheat broiler. In large skillet, heat olive oil over medium heat. Add onion; cook and stir until crisp-tender, about 4 minutes. Add chili and undrained mushrooms and bring to a simmer. Simmer for 10 minutes, stirring frequently.

2. Meanwhile, cut bread in half lengthwise and place, cut side-up, on cookie sheet with sides. Broil 6" from the heat for 4–6 minutes or until toasted. Remove from oven; turn oven to 400°F. Top toasted bread with tomato slices. Spoon chili mixture over tomatoes, and sprinkle with cheeses.

3. Bake for 20–25 minutes or until pizzas are hot and cheese is melted and beginning to brown. Let stand for 5 minutes, then cut and serve immediately.

SERVES ▶ 6

1 tablespoon olive oil

1 onion, chopped

2 cups leftover Homemade Chili (page 132)

1 (4-ounce) can mushroom pieces, undrained

½ loaf Whole Wheat French Bread (page 47)

1 tomato, thinly sliced

1 cup shredded Cheddar cheese

1 cup shredded mozzarella cheese

⅓ cup grated Parmesan cheese

Everything Stew

SERVES ▶ 4

2 cups tomato juice

1 cup water

1 cup small pasta

1 cup cooked ground beef or chicken

2 cups cooked vegetables

½ teaspoon hot sauce

1 cup shredded Cheddar cheese

3 tablespoons potato flakes

After the stew is complete, taste it for seasoning and see if you need to add more salt or pepper.

1. In large saucepan, combine tomato juice and water and bring to a boil. Add pasta and bring back to a boil. Boil for 5 minutes, then add all remaining ingredients except cheese and potato flakes.

2. Bring back to a simmer and cook for 3–5 minutes or until pasta is tender and all ingredients are hot. Stir cheese and potato flakes into saucepan; heat and stir until cheese melts and mixture thickens. Serve immediately.

Storing Leftovers If you want to make a soup or stew from leftovers, keep a hard-sided freezer container in your freezer specifically designated for those ingredients. Add cooked meats and bits of cooked vegetables, making sure to keep track of when you started collecting the food. Use it within three months of the original preparations.

Frittata Sandwich

COST PER SERVING 80¢

Here's another way to make another meal out of the leftovers of a leftover. However, be sure that you use properly refrigerated food within 4 days of its original preparation.

1. Preheat broiler. Cut bread in half horizontally, then cut into 4 pieces each. Drizzle cut sides of bread with olive oil. Place on broiler pan; broil 6" from heat source until golden, about 3–5 minutes. Remove from oven and immediately rub cut side of each piece of bread with some of the tomato. Set aside.

2. Meanwhile, place frittata on microwave-safe plate and sprinkle with cheese. Microwave on high for 1–2 minutes or until cheese begins to melt. Let stand for 3 minutes, then cut into squares. Make sandwiches with the bread pieces and the heated frittata. Serve immediately.

SERVES ▶ 4

½ loaf Whole Wheat French Bread (page 47)

3 tablespoons olive oil

1 tomato, cut into quarters

½ Baked Bread Crumb Frittata (page 110)

1 cup shredded Swiss cheese

Meatloaf Panini

COST PER SERVING 88¢

Leftover meatloaf is not only good cold, but is truly spectacular in this hot sandwich.

1. Heat a large skillet, panini maker, or indoor dual-contact grill. Cut the bread slices on an angle. In small bowl combine sour cream and barbecue sauce. Spread on one side of each slice of bread.

2. Top half of bread slices with meatloaf, then Muenster cheese. Top with remaining bread slices, sauce side down. Spread outsides of sandwiches with softened butter.

3. Grill sandwiches until bread is toasted and cheese is melted. If grilling on a skillet, cover the skillet while the sandwiches are cooking, and press down occasionally with a spatula. Cut in half and serve immediately.

SERVES ▶ 4–6

8 slices Whole Wheat French Bread (page 47)

¼ cup sour cream

¼ cup barbecue sauce

4 slices Mom's Meatloaf (page 136)

4 slices Muenster cheese

3 tablespoons butter, softened

Pasta Toss

SERVES ▶ 4–6

1 tablespoon olive oil

½ onion, chopped

½ green bell pepper, chopped

1–2 cups leftover cooked
chopped meat

½ teaspoon salt

⅛ teaspoon pepper

1 (16-ounce) package
spaghetti pasta

2 eggs, beaten

½ cup ricotta cheese

¼ cup milk

⅓ cup grated Parmesan cheese

You can use chicken, turkey, ham, roast beef, fish fillets, or salmon as the meat in this versatile and delicious dish.

1. Bring a large pot of water to a boil. Meanwhile, in large saucepan heat olive oil over medium heat. Add onion and bell pepper; cook and stir until tender, about 5 minutes. Add meat, sprinkle with salt and pepper, cover, and turn off heat.

2. Cook pasta as directed on package until al dente. While pasta is cooking, combine eggs, ricotta cheese, milk, and Parmesan cheese in a small bowl and mix well.

3. When pasta is cooked, drain and immediately add to saucepan with meat. Place pan over medium–high heat and add egg mixture. Using tongs, toss everything together for 4–5 minutes to cook egg mixture. Serve immediately.

Leftover Vegetables When a recipe calls for cooking vegetables as a first step, if you have similar vegetables cooked and already on hand, use those instead. Just heat the cooked vegetables through on the first step; you don't want them to overcook. Be careful with seasoning. If the vegetables were seasoned the first time around, you don't want to overdo it.

Pasta Toss Omelet

COST PER SERVING 63¢

*Use the leftovers of leftovers to make another meal!
Any cooked pasta dish (or any leftovers, for that matter)
could be used in this fabulous recipe.*

1. In medium nonstick saucepan, melt butter over medium heat. In medium bowl, beat eggs with milk, salt, and pepper. Add to saucepan. Cook over medium heat, pulling edges in to let uncooked egg flow underneath, until eggs just begin to set.

2. Place pasta toss in small microwave-safe bowl; microwave on medium power for 1 minute to warm. Arrange on top of partially cooked eggs; top with peas and cheese. Cover pan and cook, shaking pan occasionally, until cheese melts, about 4–6 minutes. Fold omelet in half and slide onto serving plate; cut into wedges to serve.

SERVES ▶ 3–4

2 tablespoons butter

5 eggs

¼ cup milk

¼ teaspoon salt

⅛ teaspoon pepper

1 cup Pasta Toss (page 114)

1 cup frozen peas, thawed

1 cup shredded Cheddar cheese

Tetrazzini Soup

COST PER SERVING 81¢

*You can use this method for turning any pasta dish into
a soup. Use leftover Spaghetti and Meatballs (page 217) and
make Italian Meatball Soup.*

1. In large saucepan, combine carrots and chicken stock and bring to a simmer over medium heat. Simmer for 3–4 minutes or until carrots are crisp-tender. Add milk, cornstarch, green beans, and tetrazzini to the saucepan and bring to a simmer again.

2. Cook, stirring frequently, over low heat until mixture thickens slightly and tetrazzini blends into soup, about 3–5 minutes. Stir in cheese until melted, then serve immediately.

SERVES ▶ 4

1 cup sliced carrots

1 cup Chicken Stock (page 79)

1 cup milk

1 tablespoon cornstarch

1 cup frozen green beans, thawed

2 cups Chicken Tetrazzini (page 210), chopped

1 cup shredded Swiss cheese

Beefy Fried Rice

COST PER SERVING
87¢

SERVES ▶ 4

Any leftover rice or rice pilaf will work well in this super easy recipe. Or you could cook ¾ cup of instant rice and use it immediately.

½ cup 80 percent lean ground beef

1 onion, chopped

4 cloves garlic, minced

2 tablespoons olive oil

2 cups Vegetable Rice (page 232)

2 tablespoons soy sauce

1 cup frozen peas or green beans

3 eggs, beaten

1. In large saucepan or wok, combine ground beef with onion and garlic. Cook and stir over medium heat, stirring frequently, until beef is almost cooked. Remove from heat and drain thoroughly; wipe out saucepan or wok.

2. Return wok to heat and add olive oil. Heat over medium high heat. Then add rice; stir-fry for 1 minute. Sprinkle with soy sauce and add peas; stir-fry for 2–3 minutes longer.

3. Return ground beef mixture to saucepan. Then push food to the sides of the saucepan and pour eggs into the center. Cook eggs, stirring frequently, until set. Mix with rest of food in saucepan; stir-fry for 1–3 minutes until hot, then serve immediately.

Fried Rice Fried rice is best when the rice has been cooked and thoroughly chilled; the grains will cook separately and heat thoroughly. You can use any leftover cooked meat or vegetable in a fried rice recipe; just make sure to add the cooked ingredients at the end of the stir-fry process because they only need to be heated through.

After–Turkey Day Casserole

COST PER SERVING **73¢**

Leftovers from Thanksgiving are very valuable, and can be served in so many ways. This hearty casserole is delicious.

SERVES ► 6

1. Preheat oven to 375°F. In medium saucepan, combine 1 tablespoon butter and olive oil over medium heat. Add onion; cook and stir until crisp-tender, about 4 minutes. Add flour, salt, pepper, and basil; cook and stir until bubbly, about 3 minutes.

2. Stir in evaporated milk and milk and cook, stirring, until thickened. Add peas and turkey; bring back to a simmer. Stir in stuffing and remove from heat. Meanwhile, in medium bowl combine potatoes, sour cream, and cheese and mix until blended.

3. In small microwave-proof bowl, place remaining 2 tablespoons butter. Microwave on high for 1 minute or until melted. Stir in crumbled bread until coated.

4. Pour turkey mixture into 2-quart casserole dish. Top with spoonfuls of potato mixture, then sprinkle with the buttered bread crumbs. Bake for 40–50 minutes or until casserole is bubbly. Serve immediately.

3 tablespoons butter, divided

1 tablespoon olive oil

1 onion, chopped

2 tablespoons all-purpose flour

½ teaspoon salt

⅛ teaspoon pepper

1 teaspoon dried basil

1 (12-ounce) can evaporated milk

½ cup milk

1 cup frozen peas or leftover green beans

2 cups chopped cooked turkey

1 cup leftover turkey stuffing

2 cups leftover mashed potatoes

½ cup sour cream

1 cup shredded Cheddar cheese

2 slices leftover toasted bread, crumbled

Veggie Potato Burritos

COST PER SERVING
86¢

SERVES ▶ 6

*Once again, you can use any leftover in this basic recipe.
If you don't have leftover mashed potatoes, make some with
dried potato flakes.*

1 tablespoon olive oil

1 onion, chopped

2 cloves garlic, minced

1 (3-ounce) package cream cheese

2 tablespoons chili powder

½ teaspoon salt

⅛ teaspoon cayenne pepper

1½ cups leftover Creamy Mashed
Potatoes (page 224)

1 cup leftover cooked vegetables

1 cup shredded sharp
Cheddar cheese

8 (10-inch) flour tortillas

2 cups vegetable oil

1. In large saucepan, heat olive oil over medium heat. Add onion and garlic; cook and stir until tender, about 5 minutes. Remove from heat and add cream cheese, stirring until cheese melts and mixture combines. Stir in chili powder, salt, and pepper.

2. Add potatoes, vegetables, and Cheddar cheese and mix well. Divide mixture among the flour tortillas. Roll up tortillas, folding in ends. Fasten with toothpicks to keep closed.

3. Heat vegetable oil in large saucepan over medium-high heat. When oil reaches 375°F, add 2 burritos at a time. Deep fry, turning once, until burritos are crisp and golden brown, about 4–6 minutes. Carefully remove, drain on paper towels, and serve immediately with sour cream and salsa.

Reusing Cooking Oil You can reuse cooking oils, as long as the oil is cooled and thoroughly strained through cheesecloth or a coffee filter. But if the oil smoked during the cooking process, don't use it. It most probably developed some off-flavors, which would transfer to the next batch of fried food.

Meat and Potato Hash

COST PER SERVING
50¢

Use the meat and sauce from the Swiss Steak; combined
with Roasted Potatoes and some butter, it makes a fabulous
and quick lunch or dinner recipe.

1. Cut the steak into small pieces. Combine with the potatoes in a medium bowl. In large skillet, melt 2 tablespoons butter over medium heat. Add the onion; cook and stir for 3 minutes. Then add steak mixture; cook and stir for 5–7 minutes or until hot.

2. Meanwhile, in medium nonstick skillet, melt remaining 2 table-spoons butter. Carefully add eggs to pan and sprinkle with salt and pepper. Cook eggs for 3–4 minutes or until the whites are set. Then carefully turn eggs and cook on second side until eggs are set, about 2–3 minutes.

3. Stir the steak mixture and spread evenly in skillet. Carefully place eggs on top of steak mixture and cook for 1–2 minutes without stirring. Sprinkle with parsley and serve immediately.

Eggs Over Easy With today's problems of salmonella in eggs, you shouldn't eat raw or undercooked eggs. If, however, you just can't give up that egg sunny-side-up or over-easy, try pasteurized eggs. They can be found in the regular grocery store. They do have stringent expiration dates, though, and are more expensive.

SERVES ▶ 4

1–2 cups leftover Swiss Steak (page 129)

2 cups leftover Roasted Potatoes (page 228)

¼ cup butter, divided

1 onion, chopped

4 eggs

½ teaspoon salt

⅛ teaspoon pepper

2 tablespoons chopped parsley

"Neat" Joes

COST PER SERVING
90¢

This is a great way to remake any thick chili or casserole.
Just add more cheese and encase it in some flaky rolls. Yum!

SERVES ▶ 4

1½ cups Homemade Chili
(page 132), chilled

1 cup shredded Cheddar cheese

¼ cup grated Parmesan cheese

1 (8-ounce) can refrigerated
crescent roll dough

1. Preheat oven to 375°F. In small bowl, combine chili with Cheddar and Parmesan cheeses; mix well.

2. Unroll dough on work surface and separate into four rectangles. Press the perforations to seal. Divide chili mixture among the rectangles, keeping it on one half of the dough. Fold other half of dough over chili mixture, pressing edges to seal. Prick top with fork. Bake for 15–25 minutes or until sandwiches are deep golden brown. Let cool for 5 minutes, then serve.

Crescent Roll Dough In recent years, generic forms of crescent roll dough have appeared on the market. These products are just as good as the brand names, and they offer a significant cost savings.

Chicken BBQ Corn Bread Melts

COST PER SERVING
89¢

These rich little open–faced sandwiches use split corn bread as the bread. They're inexpensive and fabulous!

SERVES ▶ 4

2 squares Double Corn Bread
(page 41)

1½ cups chopped BBQ Chicken
(page 138)

¼ cup barbecue sauce

¼ cup mayonnaise

½ cup chopped celery

1 cup shredded sharp
Cheddar cheese

1. Preheat broiler. Carefully cut corn bread in half horizontally. Place cut side up on cooking sheet or broiler pan.

2. In small bowl, combine chopped chicken, barbecue sauce, mayonnaise, and celery. Spoon onto split corn bread. Sprinkle with cheese. Broil sandwiches 6" from heat for 2–4 minutes or until sandwiches are hot and cheese is melted and bubbling. Serve immediately.

Risotto Balls

COST PER SERVING
$1 14

*You can use any leftover cooked rice in this easy recipe;
if you do, add another egg so everything will hold together.*

1. In small saucepan, heat olive oil over medium heat. Add carrots and garlic; cook and stir until tender, about 3 minutes. Add tomato sauce and Italian seasoning and bring to a simmer. Lower heat to low and let simmer, stirring occasionally, while you make the risotto balls.

2. In medium bowl, combine risotto, egg, and ¼ cup bread crumbs; mix well. Form into 1½" balls and press a cube of cheese into the center of each ball; roll until smooth. Roll each ball into bread crumbs and set aside.

3. Heat butter in nonstick skillet over medium heat. Cook risotto balls, shaking pan and turning the balls gently, until crisp and golden brown. Serve with the tomato sauce.

> *Make Ahead* You can make these Risotto Balls ahead of time and refrigerate them up to 8 hours. You will need to cook them a bit longer, because they will be thoroughly chilled. Let them sit at room temperature for 30 minutes before you start heating the butter. Leftovers are good cold, or you can reheat them in the microwave oven.

SERVES ▶ 4

1 tablespoon olive oil

½ cup shredded carrots

3 cloves garlic, minced

1 (8-ounce) can tomato sauce

½ teaspoon dried Italian seasoning

2 cups leftover Veggie Risotto (page 182)

1 egg, beaten

¾ cup dried bread crumbs, divided

1 cup cubed mozzarella cheese

3 tablespoons butter

Curried Chicken Pot Pie

Adding curry powder to chicken pot pie elevates it to a new realm. This comforting food is delicious for a cold winter's night.

SERVES ► 6

¼ cup butter

1 onion, chopped

¼ cup all-purpose flour

½ teaspoon salt

⅛ teaspoon pepper

1 tablespoon curry powder

1 (4-ounce) can mushroom pieces

1 cup Chicken Stock (page 79)

1–2 cups leftover cooked chicken, cubed

1 cup frozen sliced carrots, thawed

1 cup frozen peas, thawed

1 cup leftover Roasted Potatoes (page 228)

1 cup cubed Swiss cheese

1 Pie Crust (page 270), unbaked

1. Preheat oven to 400°F. In large saucepan, melt butter and add onion; cook and stir until crisp-tender, about 4 minutes. Sprinkle with flour, salt, and pepper, and curry powder; cook and stir until bubbly, about 3 minutes.

2. Drain mushrooms, reserving juice. Add reserved juice and chicken stock to saucepan; cook and stir until sauce is thickened. Remove from heat and add chicken, carrots, and peas. Cut roasted potatoes into small pieces and add to sauce. Fold in cheese.

3. Pour mixture into a 10" deep dish pie plate. Top with the pie crust and cut slits in the top to let steam escape. Bake for 25–35 minutes or until chicken mixture is bubbling and crust is golden brown. Serve immediately.

> ▸ CHAPTER 9 ◂

Where's the Beef? Entrées

Corned Beef Hash — **124**

Fork Tender Pot Roast — **124**

Spinach Beef Stir-Fry — **125**

Potato Mini Burger Casserole — **126**

Beef Ragout with Polenta — **127**

Sweet and Sour Beef — **128**

Ma's Irish Stew — **128**

Swiss Steak — **129**

Pesto Rice Meatballs — **130**

Meatballs in Romesco Sauce — **131**

Beans and Meatballs — **131**

Homemade Chili — **132**

Ground Beef Stroganoff — **132**

Fake-Out Beef Wellington — **133**

Steak Stir-Fry — **134**

Sicilian Meatballs — **135**

Mom's Meatloaf — **136**

9

Corned Beef Hash

6 russet potatoes

1 tablespoon olive oil

2 tablespoons butter

1 onion, chopped

3 cloves garlic, minced

1 (12-ounce) can corned beef, diced

½ cup Beef Stock (page 80)

1 tomato, chopped

¼ cup grated Parmesan cheese

You can top each serving of this hearty dish with a fried egg if you'd like for the classic finish.

1. Scrub potatoes but do not peel. Cut potatoes into ½" pieces. In large skillet, combine olive oil and butter over medium heat. Add onion, garlic, and potatoes; cook and stir for 8–10 minutes or until potatoes are beginning to brown.

2. Add corned beef and beef stock; bring to a simmer. Cover and simmer for 10–15 minutes or until potatoes are tender. Uncover and add tomato; simmer for 3–4 minutes longer. Stir, sprinkle with cheese, and serve.

Fork Tender Pot Roast

1 (3-pound) bottom round or chuck roast

3 tablespoons all-purpose flour

1 teaspoon salt

1 teaspoon paprika

¼ teaspoon pepper

1 tablespoon olive oil

2 tablespoons butter

2 onions, chopped

4 potatoes, cubed

4 carrots, sliced

1 (10-ounce) can condensed tomato soup

2 tablespoons cornstarch

⅓ cup water

This is an entire meal in one—add a salad and bread if you'd like.

1. Trim excess fat from roast. On plate, combine flour, salt, paprika, and pepper. Dredge roast in this mixture, coating both sides. Heat olive oil and butter in large saucepan over medium heat. Add roast; brown on both sides, turning once, about 7 minutes.

2. Meanwhile, place onions, potatoes, and carrots in a 5–6 quart slow cooker. Top with the browned roast. Pour ¼ cup water and tomato soup into saucepan and bring to a boil, scraping the pan to loosen drippings. Pour over roast.

3. Cover and cook on low for 8–10 hours until meat and vegetables are very tender. If necessary, you can thicken the gravy by removing the roast and covering with foil. Then combine cornstarch and ⅓ cup water in small bowl and stir into the gravy; cover and cook on high for 20–30 minutes until thickened.

Spinach Beef Stir–Fry

COST PER SERVING
$1²³

This easy stir–fry recipe uses ingredients you probably already have around the house.

SERVES ▶ 6

1. In large skillet, crumble ground beef. Cook and stir over medium heat for 3 minutes. Add mushrooms, onion, and garlic; cook and stir until beef is browned and vegetables are crisp-tender. Drain well.

2. Drain spinach thoroughly and add to skillet along with ginger and soy sauce; cook and stir for 2 minutes until hot.

3. In small bowl, combine egg, milk, and cheese and beat well. Add to skillet; stir-fry until eggs are cooked and set. Serve immediately.

1 pound 80 percent lean ground beef

2 cups sliced mushrooms

1 onion, chopped

4 cloves garlic, minced

½ teaspoon ground ginger

2 tablespoons soy sauce

1 (10-ounce) package frozen spinach, thawed

4 eggs

¼ cup milk

⅓ cup grated Parmesan cheese

Stir–Fry Tips You don't need a wok to stir-fry; a large heavy-duty frying pan will do, preferably one without a non-stick surface. Have all the ingredients ready to cook and the sauces mixed. Heat the pan over high heat and add the ingredients in the order the recipe specifies. Keep the food moving with a sturdy spatula or wooden spoon. And be sure to serve immediately!

Potato Mini Burger Casserole

This hearty casserole is for meat and potatoes lovers. Serve it with a crisp green salad and an ice cream pie for dessert.

SERVES ▶ 6

1 tablespoon olive oil

1 onion, finely chopped

2 cloves garlic, minced

1 egg

¼ cup fine dry bread crumbs

½ teaspoon salt

⅛ teaspoon pepper

¼ cup ketchup

¾ pound 80 percent lean ground beef

4 cups frozen hash brown potatoes, thawed

1 (12-ounce) can evaporated milk

2 plum tomatoes, chopped

½ cup shredded sharp Cheddar cheese

¼ cup grated Parmesan cheese

1. In large skillet, heat olive oil over medium heat. Add onion and garlic; cook and stir until tender, about 5 minutes. Remove from heat. Remove ¼ cup of onion mixture to medium bowl and add egg, bread crumbs, salt, pepper, and ketchup; mix well. Add ground beef; mix until combined. Form into 8 small hamburgers.

2. Remove remaining onion mixture from skillet and place in 2-quart casserole dish; do not wipe skillet. Place hamburgers in skillet; cook, turning once, over medium heat until hamburgers are almost fully cooked, about 6–8 minutes. Remove hamburgers to paper towel to drain. Drain fat from skillet.

3. Add potatoes, milk, and plum tomatoes to skillet; bring to a simmer. Pour into casserole dish and mix with onion mixture. Add cooked hamburger patties, stirring gently. Sprinkle with cheeses. Bake for 30–40 minutes or until casserole is bubbling and cheese is melted.

Beef Ragout with Polenta

COST PER SERVING 1^{88}

Perfect for a cold winter's night, a ragout is made from beef simmered with vegetables and tomatoes. The crisp polenta is the perfect finishing touch.

SERVES ► 6

1. Cut beef into 1" pieces and place in medium bowl. Sprinkle with vinegar, olive oil, and salt, mix well, and set aside for 30 minutes.

2. Drain beef, reserving marinade. Toss beef with flour, then melt butter in large saucepan over medium heat. Add beef to saucepan; cook and stir until browned, about 4–6 minutes. Remove beef from pan. Add onions and garlic to pan; cook and stir for 3 minutes. Drain mushrooms, adding liquid to reserved beef marinade. Then add mushrooms to saucepan; cook and stir for 2 minutes longer.

3. Add tomatoes, tomato paste, beef stock, oregano, pepper, and reserved marinade; bring to a simmer. Cook for 10 minutes, then return beef to pan. Cover, reduce heat to low, and simmer for 20–30 minutes or until beef is tender.

4. Prepare polenta and fry as directed in that recipe. Serve ragout in individual bowls topped with polenta.

¾ pound beef sirloin tip

2 tablespoons red wine vinegar

2 tablespoons olive oil

½ teaspoon salt

2 tablespoons all-purpose flour

2 tablespoons butter

2 onions, chopped

4 cloves garlic, minced

1 (4-ounce) jar mushroom pieces

1 (14-ounce) can diced tomatoes, undrained

2 tablespoons tomato paste

½ cup Beef Stock (page 80)

½ teaspoon dried oregano leaves

⅛ teaspoon pepper

12 squares Polenta (page 228), fried until crisp

Stretching Beef   When you're purchasing steak or ground beef, you can get an extra meal's worth of beef "free" by simply trimming off several ounces, up to ¼ pound, and freezing it. When you have another ½ to ¾ pound of beef, you can use it in another recipe. Be sure to label the bag or container you use to store the beef clearly, and use it all within 6 months.

Sweet and Sour Beef

The acidic ingredients make the beef meltingly tender.
For a splurge, double the amount of meat.

SERVES ▶ 4

1 pound sirloin tip, cubed

3 tablespoons all-purpose flour

½ teaspoon salt

⅛ teaspoon pepper

2 onions, chopped

1 (20-ounce) can pineapple tidbits

¼ cup apple cider vinegar

3 tablespoons sugar

2 tablespoons soy sauce

2 cups sliced carrots

1 cup frozen green beans

1½ cups Beef Stock (page 80)

2 tablespoons cornstarch

1. Toss cubed meat with flour, salt, and pepper. Combine in 3–4 quart slow cooker with onions. Drain pineapple, reserving liquid. Add pineapple to slow cooker along with vinegar, sugar, and soy sauce; stir until blended.

2. Add carrots, green beans, and stock. Cover and cook on low for 8–10 hours until beef is very tender.

3. In bowl, combine cornstarch with ½ cup reserved pineapple liquid. Add to slow cooker, stir, cover, and cook on high for 30 minutes or until sauce is thickened. Serve over hot cooked rice.

Ma's Irish Stew

This thick and rich stew is a classic.

SERVES ▶ 6

1 pound beef stew meat

¼ cup all-purpose flour

1 teaspoon salt

⅛ teaspoon pepper

3 slices bacon

1 onion, chopped

3 cloves garlic, minced

5 carrots, sliced

3 potatoes, cubed

1 parsnip, peeled and cubed

1 cup water

3 cups Beef Stock (page 80)

1 (8-ounce) can tomato sauce

1 bay leaf

1. Cut stew meat into 1" pieces. On plate, combine flour, salt, and pepper and mix well. Coat meat in flour mixture and set aside. In large saucepan, cook bacon until crisp; remove bacon, crumble, and set aside. Sauté meat in bacon drippings in saucepan, stirring frequently, until browned, about 3–4 minutes.

2. In 5–6 quart slow cooker, place onion, garlic, carrots, potatoes, and parsnips. Top with beef and bacon. To drippings remaining in saucepan, add 1 cup water and bring to a boil, scraping the bottom. Pour into slow cooker.

3. Pour beef stock and tomato sauce into slow cooker and add bay leaf. Cover and cook on low for 8–10 hours until vegetables are tender. Remove bay leaf and serve.

Swiss Steak

COST PER SERVING $1.90

This traditional and comforting recipe is just plain delicious. Serve it with Creamy Mashed Potatoes (page 224) and Sautéed Peas and Radishes (page 223).

1. Cut cube steak into 6 portions if necessary. On shallow platter combine flour, salt, and pepper and mix well. Dredge steaks in this mixture on both sides.

2. Heat olive oil in large skillet over medium heat. Add steaks; brown on both sides, turning once, about 3–5 minutes. Remove steaks from heat. Add onion to drippings in skillet; cook and stir until crisp-tender, about 4 minutes.

3. Add tomatoes, carrots, mushrooms, Worcestershire sauce, and marjoram to skillet and bring to a simmer. Return steaks to skillet, covering with the sauce. Reduce heat to low, cover, and simmer for 60–80 minutes or until meat is very tender. Serve immediately.

Cube Steaks Cube steaks from the supermarket have been run through a tenderizing machine. You can make your own cube steaks by buying thin cuts of bottom round and cutting into individual portions. Cover the meat with plastic wrap, and pound vigorously with a meat mallet or rolling pin. This breaks down the meat fibers, tenderizing the steak.

SERVES ▶ 6

1½ pounds cube steak

¼ cup all-purpose flour

1 teaspoon salt

⅛ teaspoon pepper

3 tablespoons olive oil

1 onion, diced

2 (14-ounce) cans diced tomatoes, undrained

1 cup grated carrot

1 (4-ounce) can mushroom pieces, undrained

1 tablespoon Worcestershire sauce

½ teaspoon dried marjoram leaves

Pesto Rice Meatballs

COST PER SERVING
$1.27

SERVES ▶ 5

Partially cooking the rice adds moisture to the meatballs and ensures that the rice becomes nice and tender, even on the inside of each meatball.

⅓ cup long grain rice

¾ cup water

1 egg

⅓ cup Spinach Pesto (page 28)

2 tablespoons milk

¼ cup grated Parmesan cheese

1 pound 80 percent lean ground beef

2 tablespoons olive oil

1 (10-ounce) can condensed tomato soup

1 cup water

1. In small saucepan, combine rice and water. Bring to a boil, then reduce heat, cover, and simmer for 10 minutes to cook rice partially. Drain rice if necessary.

2. In large bowl, combine rice, egg, pesto, milk, and cheese and mix well. Add beef; mix gently but thoroughly until combined. Form into 1" meatballs.

3. Heat olive oil in large skillet over medium heat. Cook meatballs, turning frequently, until lightly browned, about 5 minutes. Drain pan, then add soup, water, and bring to a simmer. Stir gently, then cover and simmer for 30–40 minutes or until meatballs are thoroughly cooked. Serve immediately.

Leftover Meatballs If you have leftover meatballs, they make fabulous sandwiches. Heat the meatballs with the sauce, or if you need more sauce, add some pasta or tomato sauce. Then split a couple of hoagie buns, toast them, top with the meatballs, sauce, and some cheese. Broil until the cheese melts and bubbles, then serve.

Meatballs in Romesco Sauce

COST PER SERVING **$1**⁹²

Serve this wonderful entrée over cooked pasta or rice.

1. Preheat toaster oven or regular oven to 400°F. Place almonds on a small baking sheet and toast for 4–7 minutes until light golden brown, watching carefully so they don't burn. Cool completely, then grind in food processor; set aside.

2. In large saucepan, heat olive oil and butter over medium heat. Add onion; cook and stir for 3 minutes. Add undrained tomatoes, chopped plum tomatoes, salt, pepper, paprika, beef stock, and ground almonds and bring to a simmer.

3. Crumble bread into fine pieces and add to sauce along with vinegar and sugar. Bring back to a simmer. Add meatballs and simmer, stirring frequently, for 7–9 minutes or until meatballs are hot and sauce has thickened. Serve immediately.

SERVES ► 4

½ cup slivered almonds

1 tablespoon olive oil

1 tablespoon butter

½ onion, chopped

1 (14-ounce) can diced tomatoes, undrained

2 plum tomatoes, chopped

½ teaspoon salt

⅛ teaspoon cayenne pepper

½ teaspoon paprika

1 cup Beef Stock (page 80)

1 slice Oatmeal Bread (page 53)

1 tablespoon red wine vinegar

1 teaspoon sugar

12 Sicilian Meatballs (page 135)

Beans and Meatballs

COST PER SERVING **$1**⁴¹

You can use any kind of canned beans you'd like in this easy recipe. Chili beans, chick peas, cannelloni beans, and black beans all work well. You do need one can of pork and beans, though.

1. Preheat oven to 350°F. In large saucepan, warm olive oil over medium heat. Add onion and garlic; cook and stir until tender, about 5 minutes. Add ketchup, brown sugar, and mustard and bring to a simmer.

2. Drain kidney beans and add with pork and beans to saucepan; mix well and remove from heat.

3. Cut meatballs in half and add to bean mixture. Pour into 2-quart casserole. Bake for 50–60 minutes or until casserole is bubbling.

SERVES ► 6

1 tablespoon olive oil

1 onion, chopped

2 cloves garlic, minced

½ cup ketchup

2 tablespoons brown sugar

2 tablespoons mustard

1 (15-ounce) can kidney beans

1 (15-ounce) can pork and beans

8 Sicilian Meatballs (page 135), cooked

Homemade Chili

COST PER SERVING $1.39

This chili cooks all day in the slow cooker, so you can do other things. It's thick, hearty, and filling; all the things chili should be!

SERVES ▶ 6

1 pound 80 percent lean ground beef
1 onion, chopped
3 cloves garlic, minced
2 (15-ounce) cans kidney beans, drained
2 (14-ounce) cans diced tomatoes, undrained
1 (6-ounce) can tomato paste
1 tablespoon chili powder
1 teaspoon cumin
1½ cups water
½ teaspoon salt
2 tablespoons cornstarch
¼ cup water

1. In large skillet, cook ground beef, onion, and garlic until beef is browned and vegetables are tender, stirring occasionally. Drain well. Combine with all remaining ingredients except cornstarch and ¼ cup water in 4–5 quart slow cooker.

2. Cover and cook on low for 8–10 hours. In small bowl, combine cornstarch with ¼ cup water and mix well. Stir into chili, then turn heat to high and cook for 15–20 minutes or until chili is thickened. Serve immediately.

Canned Beans Canned beans often go on sale; when they do, stock up! Mark the purchase date on each can with an indelible marker or grease pencil and store the cans in your pantry. Be sure to rotate the cans and use the oldest first. Discard any cans that are dented, bulging, or leaking.

Ground Beef Stroganoff

COST PER SERVING $1.25

For a splurge, use 1–2 pounds of sirloin tip, cut into cubes. This rich stroganoff is delicious and hearty.

SERVES ▶ 6–8

1 pound ground beef
2 onions, chopped
4 cloves garlic, sliced
3 cups Beef Stock (page 80)
2 cups sliced carrots
2 (4-ounce) cans mushroom pieces, undrained
1 cup sour cream
3 tablespoons all-purpose flour
1 (3-ounce) package cream cheese
1 (12-ounce) package egg noodles

1. In large saucepan, cook ground beef until browned. Drain and place in 3–4 quart slow cooker with onions, garlic, stock, carrots, and mushrooms with their liquid. Cover and cook on low for 7–9 hours.

2. Bring a large pot of salted water to a boil. Meanwhile, in small bowl combine sour cream and flour with wire whisk. Add ½ cup of the liquid from slow cooker and blend well. Stir into slow cooker. Cube cream cheese and stir into slow cooker. Cover and cook on high for 20–30 minutes.

3. When stroganoff has thickened and sauce is smooth, add egg noodles to water. Cook according to package directions until al dente. Drain well and stir into slow cooker. Serve immediately.

Fake-Out Beef Wellington

COST PER SERVING
$2³⁴

Marinated round steak is almost as tender as filet mignon, and the mushroom mixture (called duxelles) adds a rich meaty flavor. Save this recipe for a special occasion.

SERVES ▶ 4

1. The day before, cut round steak into 4 portions and trim off excess fat. Pierce steaks with fork. Place in 9" glass baking dish and drizzle with olive oil, lemon juice, and pepper. Turn steaks to coat. Cover and refrigerate for 24 hours.

2. In food processor, combine mushrooms, garlic, and onion and process until finely chopped. In medium saucepan, melt butter over low heat and add mushroom mixture. Cook for 15–20 minutes, stirring frequently, until mixture is deep golden brown and all the liquid evaporates.

3. Sprinkle mixture with salt and add cream and thyme leaves; bring to a simmer. Remove from heat and cool; cover and refrigerate.

4. The next day, warm a large nonstick skillet over medium heat. Drain steaks and pat dry; discard marinade. Sauté steaks for 3 minutes on one side, then turn and cook for 1–2 minutes on other side. Remove to platter and let stand for 20 minutes to cool.

5. Preheat oven to 400°F. On lightly floured surface, roll puff pastry to a 14" square. Cut into four 7-inch squares. Divide mushroom mixture in the center of each sheet the size of each piece of steak. Place steak on top. Bring corners to center to completely cover meat and seal edges. Place seam-side-down on baking sheet; cut decorative swirls into the top.

6. Bake for 20–30 minutes or until deep golden brown. Serve immediately.

1 pound round steak
2 tablespoons olive oil
3 tablespoons lemon juice
⅛ teaspoon pepper
1 (4-ounce) can mushroom pieces, drained
4 cloves garlic, minced
½ onion, chopped
1 tablespoon butter
½ teaspoon salt
2 tablespoons heavy cream
½ teaspoon dried thyme leaves
1 (8-ounce) sheet frozen puff pastry, thawed

Duxelles If you like the flavor of duxelles, make a large batch and freeze it in ½ cup portions. It adds wonderful richness to almost any main dish recipe. Stir it into stew, add it to a beef casserole or stir-fries, or spread it on top of grilled or sautéed steaks to stretch the meat and add a meatier flavor.

Steak Stir-Fry

SERVES ▶ 4

Stir–fries are easy and fun to make. You can use any vegetable you'd like, as long as all of the vegetables cook at about the same rate.

1 cup long grain rice

2 cups water

¾ pound round steak

2 tablespoons red wine vinegar

2 tablespoons olive oil, divided

1 onion, chopped

2 cups frozen broccoli florets, thawed

1 (4-ounce) can mushroom pieces, drained

1 cup Beef Stock (page 80)

2 tablespoons cornstarch

1 tablespoon soy sauce

⅛ teaspoon pepper

1. In medium saucepan, combine rice and water and bring to a boil. Cover, reduce heat to low, and simmer for 20–25 minutes or until rice is tender. Meanwhile, trim steak and cut across the grain into thin strips. Place in medium bowl and sprinkle with vinegar and 1 tablespoon olive oil. Toss and let stand while you prepare the vegetables.

2. In a large saucepan or wok, heat 1 tablespoon olive oil over medium-high heat. Drain meat, reserving marinade. Add meat to skillet; stir-fry for 4 minutes until browned. Remove steak from saucepan.

3. Add onion to skillet; stir-fry until crisp-tender, about 5–6 minutes. Return beef to pan along with drained broccoli and mushroom pieces. Stir-fry for 2 minutes.

4. Add stock, cornstarch, soy sauce, and pepper to reserved marinade and stir well. Add to saucepan and bring to a boil. Cook for 1–2 minutes until sauce is thickened and beef and vegetables are tender. Serve over rice.

Sicilian Meatballs

COST PER MEATBALL
36¢

These meatballs are baked because it's less work and generates less waste. When meatballs are fried, you'll always lose a little bit that sticks to the pan.

1. Preheat oven to 350°F. In small saucepan, heat olive oil over medium heat. Add onion; cook and stir until onion is tender, about 4 minutes. Stir in tomato paste, lower heat to low, and cook, stirring occasionally, until the tomato paste begins to brown in spots (this adds a rich flavor to the meatballs).

2. When the tomato paste has begun to brown, add water to the saucepan; stir to loosen brown bits from the pan. Then remove the mixture to a large bowl. Add the bread crumbs, cheese, Italian seasoning, nutmeg, and egg and mix well. Then add the ground beef, working gently with hands to combine.

3. Form into 15 meatballs and place them on a broiler pan. Bake for 20–30 minutes or until meatballs are thoroughly cooked (165°F). Use immediately in a recipe or cool and chill for 1 day before using. Freeze for up to 3 months.

> *Meatballs* Meatballs can be used in so many ways. Combine a batch with some grape jelly and chili sauce in a slow cooker for a delicious appetizer. Add them to a sub sandwich for a meatball sub. You can also use them in Spaghetti and Meatballs (page 217) or Meatballs with Romesco Sauce (page 131).

YIELDS ► 15 MEATBALLS
SERVING SIZE ► 3

1 tablespoon olive oil

½ cup finely chopped onion

2 tablespoons tomato paste

2 tablespoons water

¾ cup dried bread crumbs

¼ cup grated Parmesan cheese

1 teaspoon dried Italian seasoning

⅛ teaspoon nutmeg

1 egg

1 pound ground beef

Mom's Meatloaf

COST PER SERVING
$1 16

This meatloaf is pure comfort food. Leftovers are great crumbled into spaghetti sauce, or used for the classic meatloaf sandwich.

SERVES ▶ 8

1 tablespoon olive oil

1 tablespoon butter

1 onion, chopped

1 cup mushrooms, chopped

½ cup sour cream

2 slices Oatmeal Bread (page 53)

1 teaspoon salt

⅛ teaspoon pepper

1 pound ground beef

½ pound ground pork

⅓ cup ketchup

3 tablespoons mustard

2 tablespoons brown sugar

1. In small saucepan, heat olive oil and butter over medium heat. Add onion and mushrooms; cook and stir until vegetables are tender and mushrooms have given up their liquid. Continue cooking until the liquid evaporates. Remove to large bowl and let stand for 10 minutes.

2. Preheat oven to 350°F. Crumble the oatmeal bread into bread crumbs and add sour cream, bread crumbs, salt, and pepper to mushroom mixture and mix well. Then add ground meats, mixing with your hands until combined. Form into two loaves and place on a broiler pan.

3. In small bowl, combine ketchup, mustard, and brown sugar and spoon over loaves. Bake for 60–70 minutes or until meat thermometer registers 165°F. Tent meatloaves with foil and let stand for 10 minutes before serving.

Meatloaf Tips For the best meatloaf, be sure to combine all of the ingredients before you add the meat. Work the mixture as little as possible and don't compact it. Let it stand for 10 minutes, covered, after it's cooked. Be sure to refrigerate leftovers promptly. Leftover meatloaf can be used in place of meatballs in many recipes, and it makes a great sandwich.

Chicken Cheap Cheep!

10

BBQ Chicken

COST PER SERVING
70¢

Making your own barbecue sauce lets you use your imagination. You could add bell peppers, celery, more herbs and spices, or even chili sauce.

2 tablespoons olive oil

1 onion, chopped

3 cloves garlic, minced

¼ cup apple cider vinegar

¼ cup brown sugar

1 tablespoon mustard

1 teaspoon chili powder

1 teaspoon salt

2 tablespoons Worcestershire sauce

1 cup ketchup

2 tablespoons lemon juice

1 teaspoon Tabasco sauce

3 pounds cut-up chicken

1 teaspoon salt

¼ teaspoon white pepper

1. In large saucepan, heat olive oil over medium heat. Add onion and garlic; cook and stir until tender, about 5 minutes. Add vinegar, brown sugar, mustard, chili powder, salt, Worcestershire sauce, and ketchup and bring to a simmer. Reduce heat to low and simmer for 30 minutes. Stir lemon juice and Tabasco sauce into sauce and set aside.

2. Preheat oven to 375°F. Sprinkle chicken with 1 teaspoon salt and white pepper and arrange in large roasting pan. Bake for 45 minutes. Pour sauce over chicken and bake for 30–40 minutes longer until chicken is thoroughly cooked. Serve chicken with sauce.

Barbecue Sauce Barbecue sauces are almost always tomato-based, with spices and seasonings added. Ketchup is a standard ingredient, as is Tabasco sauce, vinegar, and some type of sugar. You can make your own barbecue sauce by adding more of any of these ingredients, or by adding mustard and spices such as chili powder, cumin, or garlic powder.

Chicken Wings in Honey–Garlic Sauce

COST PER SERVING 1^{37}

Serve these wings with Creamy Mashed Potatoes (page 224) topped with melted butter and some cooked peas for a finger–licking dinner.

1. The day before, in a saucepan, combine honey, brown sugar, soy sauce, garlic, orange juice, and vinegar and bring to a boil. Meanwhile, arrange chicken wings in a 9" x 13" glass baking dish. Pour marinade over chicken wings and turn to coat. Cover tightly and refrigerate for at least 24 hours before baking.

2. When ready to eat, preheat oven to 350°F. Bake the wings, uncovered, for 30 minutes. Turn wings with tongs and bake for 30 minutes longer. Baste with marinade in bottom of pan and sprinkle with red pepper flakes. Bake for another 20–30 minutes or until chicken wings are dark golden brown and thoroughly cooked. Serve immediately.

SERVES ▶ 4

⅓ cup honey

2 tablespoons brown sugar

¼ cup soy sauce

8 cloves garlic, sliced

¼ cup orange juice

1 tablespoon balsamic vinegar

2 pounds chicken wings

½ teaspoon red pepper flakes

Hot and Sweet Meatloaf

COST PER SERVING 1^{21}

Ground turkey makes a nice change from beef in this flavorful meatloaf. Leftovers make fabulous meatloaf sandwiches.

1. Preheat oven to 375°F. In small skillet, melt butter over medium heat. Add onion and jalapeño pepper; cook and stir until tender, about 5 minutes. Remove to large bowl; let cool for 10 minutes.

2. Add ½ cup chili sauce, Worcestershire sauce, bread crumbs, egg, salt, and pepper and mix well. Add turkey and cheese; work gently but thoroughly with hands until combined.

3. Form into a loaf on a cookie sheet with a rim. In small bowl, combine remaining ¼ cup chili sauce with brown sugar. Spread over loaf. Bake for 55–65 minutes or until internal temperature registers 165°F. Cover with foil and let stand for 5 minutes, then slice and serve.

SERVES ▶ 4

1 tablespoon butter

1 onion, finely chopped

1 jalapeño pepper, minced

¾ cup chili sauce, divided

1 tablespoon Worcestershire sauce

½ cup dried bread crumbs

1 egg

½ teaspoon salt

⅛ teaspoon cayenne pepper

1 pound ground turkey or ground chicken

1 cup shredded mozzarella cheese

2 tablespoons brown sugar

Fruited Chicken Drumsticks

COST PER SERVING $1³⁹

Serve this recipe with rice to soak up the wonderful sauce.

SERVES ► 5

8 drumsticks, skinned
1 (15-ounce) can fruit cocktail
½ cup chili sauce
1 onion, chopped
3 cloves garlic, minced
2 tablespoons cornstarch

1. Drain fruit cocktail, reserving juice. Place fruit in blender or food processor with chili sauce, onion, and garlic. Blend until smooth.

2. Place drumsticks in 4–5 quart slow cooker and add fruit mixture. Cover and cook on low for 7–9 hours until internal temperature reaches 170°F.

3. In small bowl combine ½ cup reserved fruit juice with cornstarch and mix well. Stir into slow cooker, cover, and cook on high for 30 minutes until juice is thickened. Serve immediately.

Skinning Chicken Most chicken skin is already loose on one side of each piece. Just grasp the skin firmly, using a paper towel to help tighten your grip, and gently pull away the skin. You might need to use a knife to help start the process, especially on drumsticks. Just discard the skin.

Chicken Succotash

COST PER SERVING $1⁷²

Succotash usually includes okra, but this version doesn't. You can add it.

SERVES ► 4

½ cup chopped chorizo sausage
2 boneless, skinless chicken breasts
2 tablespoons all-purpose flour
½ teaspoon ground ginger
½ teaspoon salt
⅛ teaspoon cayenne pepper
1 tablespoon olive oil
1 onion, chopped
2 cloves garlic, minced
1 (10–ounce) package frozen lima beans, thawed
1 (10–ounce) package frozen corn, thawed
1 cup Chicken Stock (page 79)
1 tomato, chopped

1. In large saucepan, place chorizo sausage over medium heat. Cook, stirring frequently, until crisp, about 7–9 minutes. Meanwhile, cut chicken into 1" pieces and toss with flour, ginger, salt, and pepper.

2. Remove chorizo from saucepan. Add olive oil to drippings and add onion and garlic. Cook, stirring frequently, until crisp-tender, about 4 minutes.

3. Add chicken to saucepan with onions; cook and stir for 4 minutes. Then add chorizo, lima beans, corn, and chicken stock. Bring to a simmer, reduce heat, and simmer for 5 minutes, stirring occasionally, until sauce thickens.

4. Stir in tomato and simmer for 2 minutes, then stir again and serve immediately over hot cooked rice.

Spinach Stuffed Chicken Breasts

COST PER SERVING
$1⁸⁹

You could use any semi–soft cheese you'd like to flavor this recipe. Cheddar, Havarti, and Swiss are all great choices.

SERVES ▶ 4

1. Carefully cut the meat away from the bone, leaving the skin attached. Save the bone for Chicken Stock (page 79). Using your fingers, loosen the skin from the flesh, leaving the skin attached at one side. Set aside.

2. In large saucepan, heat olive oil over medium heat. Add garlic; cook and stir for about 1 minute until fragrant. Then add the spinach; cook and stir until liquid evaporates, about 4 minutes. Remove from heat and place spinach in a small bowl; add bread crumbs, thyme, basil, half of the salt, the pepper, and the Muenster cheese and mix well.

3. Stuff this mixture between the chicken and the skin, spreading evenly and smoothing the skin back over the flesh.

4. Preheat oven to 450°F. Melt the butter in same saucepan. Sprinkle the remaining salt over the chicken, and place, skin side down, in the hot butter. Cook for 3 minutes without moving the chicken. Then shake the pan to loosen chicken and cook for 2–4 minutes longer until skin is brown and crisp.

5. Carefully turn chicken, then move pan to preheated oven and cook for 10–14 minutes longer until the chicken registers 170°F. Let stand for 5 minutes, then serve.

4 bone-in, skin-on chicken breasts

2 tablespoons olive oil

3 cloves garlic, minced

1 cup frozen chopped spinach, thawed

3 tablespoons dried bread crumbs

½ teaspoon dried thyme leaves

½ teaspoon dried basil leaves

½ teaspoon salt, divided

⅛ teaspoon pepper

½ cup shredded Muenster cheese

2 tablespoons butter

Making It Safe You can make any stuffing for poultry ahead of time and refrigerate or freeze it. What you shouldn't do is stuff the poultry ahead of time. For safety reasons, you can heat the stuffing in the microwave before you stuff the chicken or turkey. This helps quickly bring the stuffing up to a safe temperature.

Chicken Sausage Patties

COST PER SERVING 45¢

*Making your own sausage patties means you can control
what goes into them. You can reduce or omit the salt if you'd like.*

SERVES ► 8

1 Granny Smith apple, peeled

½ cup finely chopped onion

2 cloves garlic, minced

3 tablespoons butter, divided

1 teaspoon salt

½ teaspoon dried thyme leaves

⅛ teaspoon cayenne pepper

1½ pounds chicken pieces

1. Finely chop the apple, and combine with the onion, garlic, and 2 tablespoons butter in a small saucepan. Cook over medium heat, stirring frequently, until onion is tender. Remove from heat, pour into large bowl, and let cool, about 20 minutes.

2. Add salt, thyme, and cayenne pepper to onion mixture and blend well. Remove skin and bones from chicken (reserve for Chicken Stock, page 79). In food processor, grind chicken with the pulse feature until mixture is even. Add to onion mixture and mix well with hands just until blended.

3. Form mixture into eight patties. In large nonstick skillet, melt 1 tablespoon butter. Cook chicken patties, turning once, for 8–12 minutes or until patties are deep golden brown and chicken is thoroughly cooked, 165°F. Serve immediately, or freeze for longer storage.

Ground Chicken Once chicken or other poultry is ground it should be used within 24 hours. Mix dark and light meat together for best taste and lower cost. Save the skin and bones for Chicken Stock (page 79). Place them in the freezer in a large bag or hard-sided container marked for the stock recipe.

Chicken Filo Cigars

COST PER SERVING $1.15

This fabulous recipe disguises canned chicken in a delicious and crisp roll that's fun to make and eat.

SERVES ► 6–8

1. Preheat oven to 400°F. In large saucepan, heat olive oil over medium heat. Add onion and garlic; cook and stir until crisp-tender, about 4 minutes.

2. Thoroughly drain spinach and add to saucepan; cook and stir until water evaporates. Sprinkle with flour; cook and stir for 2 minutes. Add ricotta, lemon zest, and chicken; remove from heat. Let mixture cool for 20 minutes, then stir in feta cheese.

3. Unroll filo sheets and cover with a damp cloth. Place one rectangle on work surface, brush with melted butter and sprinkle with a teaspoon of Romano cheese. Cover with another rectangle. Place ¼ cup of the chicken mixture on the short side of the rectangle, leaving a 1" border at sides. Roll up, folding in sides, to make a fat cylinder. Brush with more butter and place on parchment paper-covered cookie sheets.

4. Repeat with remaining filo, butter, Romano cheese, and chicken filling. When all cigars are assembled, bake for 15–25 minutes or until they are crisp and golden brown. Let cool for 5 minutes, then serve.

1 tablespoon olive oil

1 onion, finely chopped

3 cloves garlic, minced

1 (10-ounce) package frozen chopped spinach, thawed

1 tablespoon all-purpose flour

½ cup ricotta cheese

1 teaspoon lemon zest

1 (12-ounce) can light and dark chicken meat, drained

½ cup crumbled feta cheese

32 (14" x 9") filo pastry sheets, thawed (recently filo sheets are being made smaller)

⅓ cup butter, melted

⅓ cup grated Romano cheese

Filo Dough Each box of filo (or phyllo) dough contains about 40 sheets. You must thaw the entire box according to the package directions, even if you're only using half of the dough. Luckily, it can be refrozen again and again. Make sure that you keep the dough that's waiting well covered, and reseal the package carefully.

Chicken and Sausage

COST PER SERVING $1.04

This hearty dish can be served by itself or over hot cooked rice or pasta. Choose hot Italian sausages for a spicier dish.

SERVES ► 8

1 tablespoon olive oil

1 tablespoon butter

1 pound boneless, skinless chicken breasts

½ teaspoon salt

⅛ teaspoon pepper

2 tablespoons all-purpose flour

½ teaspoon paprika

8 ounces bulk Italian sausage

1 green bell pepper, chopped

1 cup sliced mushrooms

1 (14-ounce) can diced tomatoes, undrained

3 tablespoons tomato paste

½ cup water

½ teaspoon dried basil leaves

1. In heavy saucepan, combine oil and butter over medium heat. Meanwhile, cut chicken into 1" pieces. On shallow plate, combine salt, pepper, flour and paprika; toss chicken in flour mixture to coat. Add chicken to saucepan; cook for 4 minutes, then add sausage and continue cooking for 8–10 minutes longer until almost cooked. Remove to plate; pour off drippings.

2. Add bell pepper and mushrooms to drippings remaining in saucepan; cook and stir for 3 minutes. Add tomatoes, tomato paste, water, and basil leaves and bring to a boil. Lower heat and simmer for 10 minutes.

3. Return sausage and chicken to saucepan; simmer for 5 minutes or until thoroughly cooked.

Cheesy Chicken Quiche

COST PER SERVING 89¢

You can fill this basic quiche recipe with chopped ham or cheese.

SERVES ► 8

2 tablespoons butter

1 onion, chopped

2 tablespoons all-purpose flour

½ teaspoon salt

⅛ teaspoon pepper

½ cup milk

½ cup sour cream

1 tablespoon mustard

4 eggs

1 Slow-Cooker Simmered Chicken Breast (page 145)

1 Pie Crust (page 270), unbaked

⅓ cup sliced black olives

1½ cups shredded Swiss cheese

3 tablespoons grated Parmesan cheese

1. Preheat oven to 350°F. In medium saucepan, melt butter over medium heat. Add onion; cook and stir until tender, about 5 minutes. Add flour, salt, and pepper; cook and stir until bubbly, about 3 minutes longer.

2. Stir in milk and cook until thick, about 3 minutes. Remove from heat and add sour cream and mustard. Beat in eggs one at a time, beating well after each addition.

3. Remove meat from chicken breast and dice meat; discard bones or save for stock. Sprinkle in bottom of pie crust along with olives and Swiss cheese. Pour egg mixture over all. Sprinkle with Parmesan cheese and bake for 40–50 minutes or until quiche is puffed and set.

Slow Cooker Simmered Chicken Breasts

COST PER SERVING
83¢

This chicken is perfect for Chicken with Linguine (page 146). Use it to make your own chicken salad too.

SERVES ▶ 6–8

6 bone-in, skin-on chicken breasts
1 teaspoon salt
⅛ teaspoon white pepper
½ cup water

1. Sprinkle chicken with salt and pepper and arrange in 4–6 quart slow cooker. Pour water into slow cooker, cover, and cook on low, rearranging once during cooking, for 7–9 hours or until chicken is fully cooked.

2. Remove chicken to a baking dish and pour any juices remaining in slow cooker over. Cover and chill for 2–3 hours or until chicken is cold. Remove meat from chicken in large pieces and refrigerate up to 2 days, or freeze up to 3 months. Freeze skin and bones for making Chicken Stock (page 79).

3. You can cook chicken thighs or drumsticks using this method too; just increase the cooking time to 8–10 hours.

> *Chicken in the Slow Cooker* Newer slow cookers cook at hotter temperatures than those manufactured 10 years ago. Because of this change, chicken breasts can overcook. Check boneless, skinless chicken breasts after 5 hours on low. Bone-in breasts should be checked for an internal temperature of 170°F after 7 hours. Dark meat, because it has more fat, isn't in as much danger of overcooking.

Chicken Newburg

SERVES ▶ 6

Newburg is usually made with seafood. Chicken is a less expensive alternative and it's just as delicious.

3 boneless, skinless chicken breasts

½ teaspoon salt

⅛ teaspoon pepper

1 red bell pepper, sliced

1 green bell pepper, sliced

2 tablespoons butter

2 tablespoons olive oil

1 onion, chopped

1 (12-ounce) can evaporated milk

1 (8-ounce) package cream cheese

1 egg yolk

1 tablespoon cornstarch

2 tablespoons lemon juice

1 teaspoon dried thyme leaves

1½ cups shredded Colby cheese

1. Sprinkle chicken breasts with salt and pepper and cut into 1" pieces. In large skillet, combine butter and olive oil over medium heat. Add chicken; stir until cooked, about 6–8 minutes; remove from pan. Add bell peppers; cook and stir for 3–4 minutes until crisp-tender; remove from pan.

2. Add onion to skillet; cook and stir until tender, about 5 minutes. Reduce heat to low and add milk, cream cheese, egg yolk, cornstarch, lemon juice, and thyme. Cook, stirring constantly with wire whisk, until mixture is smooth and hot.

3. Add chicken and bell peppers to sauce; cook and stir over low heat for 2–3 minutes. Stir in cheese; cook and stir until melted, about 2–3 minutes. Serve over hot cooked rice or pasta.

Chicken with Linguine

SERVES ▶ 6

Serve this elegant dish immediately so there is still contrast between the creamy chicken and crunchy croutons.

4 slices bacon

2 tablespoons olive oil

1 onion, chopped

3 Slow Cooker Simmered Chicken Breasts (page 145), sliced

½ teaspoon dried basil leaves

½ cup half-and-half cream

1 pound linguine pasta

2 tablespoons butter or margarine

1 cup shredded Swiss cheese

½ cup garlic croutons, crushed

2 tablespoons grated Parmesan cheese

1. Bring a large pot of salted water to a boil. Meanwhile, in a large skillet, cook bacon over medium heat until crisp. Remove bacon, crumble, and set aside. Drain drippings from skillet and discard; do not wipe out skillet.

2. Add olive oil and onion to skillet and cook over medium heat until tender, about 5 minutes. Add pasta to boiling water and cook according to package directions until al dente.

3. When onion is tender, add chicken, basil, and half-and-half to skillet and bring to a simmer. Drain pasta and add to skillet along with Swiss cheese, crushed croutons, and Parmesan cheese; toss gently and serve immediately.

Chicken Marengo

Chicken Marengo is a classic French dish that uses lobster.
This version, with canned crab, is just as elegant but less expensive.

1. Cut chicken into 2" pieces and toss with flour, salt, and pepper. In large skillet, heat olive oil and butter over medium heat. When butter melts, add chicken; cook and stir until browned, about 4 minutes.

2. Add onion and mushrooms; cook and stir until crisp-tender, about 4 minutes longer. Add stock, tomato paste, and thyme and bring to a simmer. Reduce heat to low, cover, and simmer for 10 minutes until chicken is tender and thoroughly cooked.

3. Drain crab meat and pick through to remove any cartilage. Stir in crab and lemon juice and serve immediately over hot cooked rice.

SERVES ► 6

2 tablespoons olive oil

2 tablespoons butter

6 boneless, skinless chicken breasts

3 tablespoons all-purpose flour

½ teaspoon salt

⅛ teaspoon pepper

1 onion, chopped

2 cups sliced fresh mushrooms

2 cups Chicken Stock (page 79)

½ cup tomato paste

½ teaspoon dried thyme leaves

1 (6-ounce) can crab, drained

2 tablespoons lemon juice

4 cups hot cooked rice

Chicken Potato Casserole

This comforting, hearty casserole uses just enough wild rice to add
flavor and texture, but not enough to significantly increase the cost.

1. In 4–5 quart slow cooker, layer onions, wild rice, potatoes, and carrots. Place chicken on top. In small bowl, combine soup, water, pepper, and tarragon and mix well. Pour over chicken.

2. Cover and cook on low for 7–9 hours or until chicken is tender and thoroughly cooked, wild rice is tender, and potatoes are cooked.

3. Remove chicken from slow cooker and cut into 2" pieces. Return to slow cooker, stir, and serve.

SERVES ► 6

2 onions, chopped

½ cup wild rice

5 potatoes, cubed

3 carrots, sliced

4 boneless, skinless chicken thighs

1 (10-ounce) can cream of chicken soup

1 cup water

⅛ teaspoon pepper

½ teaspoon dried tarragon leaves

Rice in a Slow Cooker Most rice doesn't cook well in a slow cooker. Brown rice and wild rice are the exceptions, as is instant rice stirred in at the very end of the cooking time. Make sure that the brown or wild rice is at the bottom of the slow cooker, completely covered by the liquid used in the recipe. Stir well before serving.

Chicken Chops

COST PER SERVING $1 50

This hearty stovetop recipe is the perfect meal for a cold winter night. You can eat the skin or not—it's your choice!

SERVES ▶ 5

½ pound hot Italian sausages
1 onion, chopped
3 cloves garlic, minced
1 cup chopped mushrooms
½ cup ricotta cheese
5 boneless, skin-on chicken thighs
¼ cup all-purpose flour
½ teaspoon salt
⅛ teaspoon cayenne pepper
1 (14-ounce) can diced tomatoes with garlic, undrained
½ cup red wine or Chicken Stock (page 79)

1. In large skillet, cook sausage, onion, garlic, and mushrooms together over medium heat until the sausage is browned, stirring frequently. Remove mixture from skillet with slotted spoon and place in medium bowl. Remove skillet from burner.

2. Add ricotta cheese to sausage mixture. Loosen skin from the chicken pieces, leaving it attached at one end. Stuff sausage mixture between skin and flesh, then smooth skin back over meat. On plate, combine flour, salt, and pepper. Dredge chicken in this mixture.

3. Return skillet to burner and heat until hot. To drippings remaining in skillet, add chicken, skin side down. Cook for 4–6 minutes without moving, then turn chicken and add tomatoes and red wine or stock.

4. Bring to a boil, reduce heat, cover, and simmer for 30–40 minutes or until chicken is thoroughly cooked and sauce is reduced. Serve over spaghetti or hot cooked rice.

Chicken Chops Chicken chops are usually made from the bone-in chicken thigh. Sometimes a "chop" is made from the leg and thigh combination, or chicken quarter that is boneless. It's really just a piece of tender dark meat chicken, browned and simmered until tender. Cooking it with the skin on keeps it moist and doesn't add many calories to a dish if you don't eat it.

Pork by the Pound

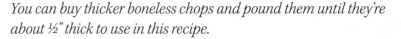
Spicy Pork with Tomato Sauce

You can buy thicker boneless chops and pound them until they're about ½" thick to use in this recipe.

SERVES ▶ 4

1 teaspoon cumin seeds

¼ teaspoon ground ginger

⅛ teaspoon cayenne pepper

½ teaspoon salt

2 garlic cloves

2 tablespoons olive oil, divided

4 thin boneless (4-ounce) pork chops

1 tablespoon butter

1 cup chopped plum tomatoes

1 cup Chicken Stock (page 79)

2 tablespoons chopped flat-leaf parsley

1. In small bowl, combine cumin seeds with ginger, cayenne pepper, salt, and garlic cloves. Work with back of spoon to mash garlic and grind seeds. Then stir in 1 tablespoon olive oil and blend until smooth.

2. Rub this mixture on both sides of pork chops, coating thoroughly. Let stand for 10 minutes.

3. Heat butter and remaining 1 tablespoon olive oil in large skillet over medium heat. Add the chops and cook without moving for 3–4 minutes, until the chops can be moved without sticking. Turn the chops and cook for 2–4 minutes on second side or until pork is just slightly pink in center, then remove from pan.

4. To drippings remaining in pan, add tomatoes, stock, and 1 tablespoon parsley. Bring to a boil and boil until reduced, about 4 minutes; pour over chops, sprinkle with remaining parsley, and serve over hot cooked rice.

Pork Chops Pork chops freeze like a dream, and they can be cooked frozen. You no longer need to cook pork to well-done; a nice light pink color is what you're shooting for. Pork is much leaner than it was 20 years ago, and healthier too. The mild flavor accepts many seasonings; change any recipe by changing the herbs and spices you use.

Hot German Potato Salad

By leaving the skins on these potatoes, you're getting the most fiber, nutrition, and yield. Plus, because they've been roasted, they're crisp and delicious!

1. Preheat oven to 400°F. Scrub potatoes and cut into 1" pieces, including some skin with each piece. Place in large roasting pan along with onion and garlic. Drizzle olive oil over all and toss. Roast for 30 minutes, turn vegetables with a spatula, return to oven, and roast for 30–45 minutes longer until potatoes are tender and skins are crisp.

2. When potatoes are done, cook bacon slices in large saucepan over medium heat until crisp. Remove bacon from pan, crumble, and set aside. Heat Polish sausage in drippings until hot; remove and add to plate with bacon.

3. Add butter to drippings in pan and melt over medium heat. Add flour, celery salt, and pepper; cook and stir until bubbly, about 3 minutes. Add water, vinegar, and honey and bring to a boil. Stir in yogurt.

4. Add potato mixture, sausage, and bacon to pan and mix gently until combined. Serve immediately.

> *Hot Salads* Hot salads may sound unusual to you, but they can be very delicious. These inexpensive dishes are so easy to make and they are very hearty and filling. Be sure to refrigerate the Hot German Potato Salad leftovers promptly; the next day, leftovers heat up in the microwave oven.

SERVES ▶ 8

7 russet potatoes

1 onion, chopped

3 cloves garlic, minced

3 tablespoons olive oil

4 slices bacon

1 pound fully cooked Polish sausages, sliced

1 tablespoon butter

3 tablespoons all-purpose flour

1 teaspoon celery salt

⅛ teaspoon pepper

1 cup water

½ cup apple cider vinegar

¼ cup honey

½ cup plain yogurt

Bean and Sausage Chowder

COST PER SERVING **91¢**

This hearty soup is perfect for cold winter evenings. It stretches one pound of Italian sausage to serve eight people! To splurge, add some cooked link sausage.

SERVES ► 8

1 pound Great Northern beans

1 pound sweet Italian sausage

8 cups water

1 onion, chopped

4 cloves garlic, minced

3 potatoes, peeled and chopped

2 zucchinis, chopped

2 (14-ounce) cans diced tomatoes, undrained

1 (8-ounce) can tomato sauce

1 teaspoon salt

⅛ teaspoon pepper

1. Sort beans and rinse thoroughly. Drain and place in pot; cover with water. Bring to a boil and boil for 2 minutes. Then cover pot, remove from heat, and let stand for 1 hour. Meanwhile, cook sausage in large skillet until browned; drain off all but 1 tablespoon drippings. Cook onion and garlic in drippings over medium heat until crisp-tender, about 4 minutes.

2. Drain and rinse beans. Cut sausage into 1" pieces. Combine in 4–5 quart slow cooker with water, onion, garlic, and potatoes. Cover and cook on low for 8 hours. Stir in zucchini, tomatoes, tomato sauce, salt, and pepper; cover and cook on low for 1–2 hours longer, until beans and potatoes are tender. Mash some of the beans and potatoes, leaving others whole, for a thicker chowder.

Slow Cooker Curried Pork Casserole

COST PER SERVING **$1⁷⁴**

Instant rice cooks well in the slow cooker. And instant brown rice may cost a little bit more, but it is more nutritious and has better texture.

SERVES ► 6

1 pound pork chops

2 onions, chopped

4 cloves garlic, minced

4 stalks celery, chopped

2 cups sliced carrots

1 (4-ounce) can mushroom pieces, undrained

2 (14-ounce) cans diced tomatoes

1 tablespoon curry powder

½ teaspoon salt

½ teaspoon paprika

½ cup raisins

1 cup instant brown rice

1. Cut pork chops into 2" pieces and combine in 4–5 quart slow cooker with onions, garlic, celery, carrots, and mushrooms.

2. Empty half of one can of tomatoes into the slow cooker. Add curry powder, salt, and paprika to remaining tomatoes in can and stir. Add with second can of tomatoes to slow cooker. Add raisins. Cover and cook on low for 7–9 hours or until pork is tender.

3. Stir in the brown rice; cover, and cook on high for 15–20 minutes or until rice is tender. Stir and serve immediately.

Pulled Pork Sandwiches

COST PER SERVING $1⁴⁷

Pork shoulder becomes velvety tender shredded meat when cooked in the slow cooker.

1. In 4–5 quart slow cooker, place onion and top with pork roast. Rub roast with pepper and paprika. In bowl combine vinegar, brown sugar, and Worcestershire sauce and mix well. Pour over pork. Cover and cook on low for 8–10 hours until very tender.

2. Remove meat from slow cooker and shred. Return to slow cooker, add chili sauce, and cook for another hour.

3. Make sandwiches with the pork mixture, slaw, and hamburger buns. Serve immediately.

> *Shredded Pork* Shredded pork can be made into tacos or burritos too. Combine the pork mixture with enchilada or taco sauce and canned beans. Roll up inside flour or corn tortillas or place into taco shells with some shredded cheese, and bake or microwave until the burritos are hot.

SERVES ▶ 6

1 onion, chopped

1½ pounds shoulder pork roast

⅛ teaspoon cayenne pepper

½ teaspoon paprika

¼ cup apple cider vinegar

3 tablespoons brown sugar

2 tablespoons Worcestershire sauce

½ cup chili sauce

2 cups Confetti Slaw (page 102)

6–8 hamburger buns

Choucroute

COST PER SERVING $1⁸⁰

This classic and hearty French dish is perfect comfort food. Cooking it in the slow cooker means the dish will be delicious with little effort.

1. In 5–6 quart slow cooker, layer cabbage, carrots, onion, garlic, and potatoes. Cut pork chops into 2" pieces and add to slow cooker. Slice sausage into 1" pieces and add to slow cooker.

2. Drain sauerkraut, rinse, and drain again. In medium bowl, combine sauerkraut with brown sugar, caraway, vinegar, and water and mix well. Pour into slow cooker.

3. Cover and cook on low for 7–9 hours or until pork is cooked and potatoes are tender. Serve in soup bowls.

SERVES ▶ 6

3 cups shredded cabbage

4 carrots, sliced

1 onion, chopped

3 cloves garlic, sliced

1 sweet potato, peeled and chopped

1 russet potato, chopped

4 (4-ounce) pork chops

½ pound Polish sausage

1 (14-ounce) can sauerkraut

2 tablespoons brown sugar

1 teaspoon caraway seeds

¼ cup apple cider vinegar

½ cup water

Mexican Rice

COST PER SERVING $1⁰⁹

COST PER SERVING $1⁰⁹

You could add some sliced olives or corn to this recipe, or serve warmed corn tortillas and shredded cheese so your guests can make burritos.

SERVES ► 6

¾ pound ground pork sausage
1 onion, chopped
1 tablespoon olive oil
1 tablespoon butter
1½ cups long grain rice
1½ cups water
1 (14-ounce) can diced tomatoes, undrained
1 (4-ounce) can green chiles, undrained
½ cup chili sauce
1 tablespoon chili powder
½ teaspoon salt
⅛ teaspoon cayenne pepper

1. In large saucepan, cook sausage and onion over medium heat, stirring frequently, until sausage is almost cooked. Drain. Add olive oil and butter to saucepan and stir in rice. Cook and stir for 2–4 minutes until rice turns opaque.

2. Add water, tomatoes, and remaining ingredients and bring to a boil. Cover, reduce heat, and simmer for 20–25 minutes or until rice is tender and liquid is absorbed. Let stand for 5 minutes, then stir and serve immediately.

> *Brown Rice* If you want to use brown rice the cooking time will be longer. Read the directions to find out the exact cooking time for the brand of rice you choose. Usually, brown rice takes twice as long to cook, but some varieties, including brown Basmati rice, have shorter cook times.

Slow Cooker Pork and Beans

COST PER SERVING $1²⁸

This recipes stretches a pound of pork chops to serve eight people. The beans are rich and filling; each serving is about 300 calories.

SERVES ► 8

4 (4-ounce) boneless pork chops
2 onions, chopped
3 cloves garlic, minced
2 (28-ounce) cans pork and beans, undrained
½ cup ketchup
3 tablespoons mustard

Cut pork chops into 1" pieces and combine with remaining ingredients in a 4-quart slow cooker. Cover and cook on low for 7–9 hours or until pork is tender and mixture is blended.

Sausage and Greens with Pasta

COST PER SERVING
96¢

Kale is an inexpensive and very hearty green that is full of vitamins, minerals, and fiber.

1. Bring a large pot of salted water to a boil. In large saucepan, cook sausage with onion and garlic, stirring to break up pork, until browned. Drain off all but 1 tablespoon drippings.

2. Add kale to skillet and sprinkle with salt. Let kale cook down for about 4–5 minutes, then add chicken stock and sugar. Cover pan and simmer for 10–15 minutes, until kale is tender.

3. Add pasta to boiling water; cook according to package directions until al dente. Drain and add with hot sauce to pan with kale mixture; cook and stir for 2 minutes. Sprinkle with cheese and serve.

> *Cooking Dark Greens* Dark leafy greens include kale, collard greens, spinach, and mustard greens. They cook down dramatically in volume; 4 cups cooks down to about 1–2 cups. The longer the cooking time, the less bitter the greens will be. Clean them thoroughly by submerging in water in order to remove all the grit or sand.

SERVES ▶ 6

½ pound pork sausage

1 onion, chopped

4 cloves garlic, chopped

1 pound chopped kale

½ teaspoon salt

1½ cups Chicken Stock (page 79)

1 tablespoon sugar

1 (16-ounce) package linguine pasta

½ teaspoon hot sauce

⅓ cup grated Parmesan cheese

Cranberry Stuffed Ham

This festive dish is perfect for the holidays. Serve it with scalloped potatoes and some roasted green beans.

SERVES ▶ 6

1 tablespoon butter

1 onion, chopped

1 cup rice

2 cups water

½ teaspoon salt

⅛ teaspoon pepper

1 apple, peeled and chopped

1 (15-ounce) can whole berry cranberry sauce

1 pound thin ham slices (about 14)

½ cup Chicken Stock (page 79)

1. In large saucepan, melt butter over medium heat. Add onion; cook and stir until crisp-tender, about 4 minutes. Add rice; cook and stir for 2 minutes longer. Add water, salt, and pepper and bring to a boil. Cover, reduce heat, and simmer for 10 minutes.

2. Stir in apple and simmer for 10–15 minutes longer until rice is tender. Remove from heat and let cool for 30 minutes. Stir in half of cranberry sauce.

3. Preheat oven to 375°F. Place ham slices on work surface and divide rice mixture among them. Roll up ham to enclose filling. Add chicken stock to remaining cranberry sauce in can and mix well. Spread a thin layer in the bottom of a 13" × 9" glass baking pan.

4. Arrange filled ham rolls in pan, seam side down. Spoon remaining cranberry sauce mixture over rolls. Cover with foil and bake for 20–30 minutes until ham rolls are hot. Serve immediately.

Thinly Sliced Ham There are several types of thinly sliced ham. The type used for stuffing is sliced about ⅛" thick. Do not use shaved ham, or the type packaged in 2-ounce containers because it will not hold the filling. If the ham slices are too thick, though, they will be difficult to roll. You can ask a deli person to slice the ham to the correct thickness.

Tex–Mex Turnovers

COST PER SERVING 1^{15}

These turnovers are perfect for a party. You can make them about half this size by cutting the filo into two 14" × 4½" rectangles and serve as appetizers.

1. In large saucepan, combine sausage and onion over medium heat. Cook and stir until sausage is browned. Drain well, then add chili powder, cumin, refried beans, and water and mix well. Simmer for 5 minutes. Let cool for 20 minutes.

2. Unwrap filo sheets and cover with damp towel. Place one rectangle on work surface, brush with melted butter, and top with another rectangle. Place about ¼ cup sausage mixture at short end of rectangle, leaving about a ½" border. Top with a spoonful of salsa and 2 tablespoons cheese.

3. Starting at short end, roll the filo over the filling. Fold sides in, then continue rolling to the end. Seal edge with melted butter. Brush with butter and place on cookie sheet.

4. Repeat with remaining filo, filling, salsa, and cheese. Preheat oven to 375°F. Bake turnovers for 20–30 minutes or until pastries are golden brown. Serve with salsa and sour cream, if desired.

SERVES ▶ 8

½ pound ground pork sausage

1 onion, chopped

1 tablespoon chili powder

1 teaspoon cumin

1 (15-ounce) can refried beans

2 tablespoons water

32 (14" × 9") filo pastry sheets, thawed

⅓ cup butter, melted

1 cup Quick and Easy Salsa (page 20)

2 cups shredded Cheddar cheese

Corny Ham Dumpling Stew

COST PER SERVING 88¢

Corn muffin mix not only makes the dumplings in this easy stew, but it thickens the stew as well.

SERVES ▶ 8

2 cups milk

4 cups Chicken Stock (page 79), divided

1 (6-ounce) package corn muffin mix, divided

2 tablespoons olive oil

1 onion, chopped

3 potatoes, peeled and diced

4 cups water

2 cups chopped ham

¼ teaspoon pepper

1 teaspoon dried oregano leaves

1 egg, beaten

1 tablespoon milk

1 cup frozen sliced carrots

2 cups frozen corn

1 cup frozen cut green beans

1. In medium bowl, combine milk, ½ cup chicken stock, and ¾ cup of the muffin mix; mix well and set aside.

2. In large pot, heat olive oil over medium heat. Add onion; cook and stir until translucent. Add potatoes, remaining chicken stock, water, ham, pepper, and oregano, and bring to a simmer. Cover and cook until potatoes are tender, about 10–15 minutes.

3. For dumplings, while soup is simmering, in small bowl combine remaining corn muffin mix, beaten egg, and 1 tablespoon milk and mix just until combined.

4. Add carrots, corn, green beans, and chicken stock/muffin mix mixture to soup and stir well; bring to a simmer. Drop dumplings onto soup by one tablespoon amounts. Cover pot and simmer for 12–14 minutes or until dumplings are no longer doughy in center and soup has thickened and blended. Serve immediately.

Sausage Quiche

COST PER SERVING $1¹⁸

A quiche is always an elegant lunch or dinner, and it's easy to make too.

1. Preheat oven to 400°F. In large saucepan, cook sausage and onion over medium heat, stirring to break up sausage, until pork is browned, about 5–7 minutes. Drain fat. Add bell pepper to saucepan; cook and stir for 1 minute longer.

2. Sprinkle with flour, salt, and pepper; cook and stir for 3 minutes. Add milk; cook and stir until thickened.

3. In large bowl, beat eggs until foamy. Stir sausage mixture into eggs. Sprinkle cheeses into pie crust and pour sausage mixture over. Bake for 25–35 minutes or until quiche is puffed, set, and top is beginning to brown.

SERVES ▶ 6

½ pound pork sausage

1 onion, chopped

1 green bell pepper, chopped

2 tablespoons all-purpose flour

½ teaspoon salt

⅛ teaspoon pepper

1 (12-ounce) can evaporated milk

3 eggs

1 cup shredded Cheddar cheese

½ cup shredded Swiss cheese

1 Pie Crust (page 270), unbaked

Pita Scramblers Sandwiches

COST PER SERVING $1⁰⁷

Other vegetables, like chopped red bell pepper, chopped mushrooms, or summer squash could be substituted for the tomatoes. These sandwiches are great for lunch or breakfast.

1. Cut pita breads in half and set aside. In large skillet, cook sausage until brown; drain off fat. In medium bowl, combine eggs, sour cream, salt, and pepper and beat well. Add to skillet with sausage; cook and stir until eggs are set but still moist.

2. Sprinkle with cheese, remove from heat, and cover. Let stand for 4 minutes. In small bowl, combine tomato and green onion.

3. Spoon egg mixture into pita breads and top with tomato mixture. Serve immediately.

SERVES ▶ 4

2 Pita Breads (page 46)

¼ pound pork sausage

6 eggs

¼ cup sour cream

½ teaspoon salt

⅛ teaspoon pepper

1 cup shredded Cheddar cheese

1 tomato, chopped

2 green onions, chopped

Corn Dogs

SERVES ▶ 8

If you purchase premade corn dogs, they cost about $1.00 apiece. These are less than half the cost, and they taste much better.

½ cup all-purpose flour

¼ cup cornmeal

1 tablespoon sugar

½ teaspoon baking powder

¼ teaspoon baking soda

¼ teaspoon dry mustard

½ teaspoon salt

¼ teaspoon pepper

3 tablespoons butter

1 egg

½ cup buttermilk

8 hot dogs

3 cups vegetable oil

1. In medium bowl, combine flour, cornmeal, sugar, baking powder, baking soda, mustard, salt, and pepper and mix well. Cut in butter until particles are fine. In small bowl, combine egg and buttermilk and beat well. Stir into flour mixture. Let stand for 10 minutes.

2. In large, deep saucepan heat vegetable oil to 350°F. Push wooden sticks into the end of the hot dogs and pat hot dogs dry.

3. Dip hot dogs into the batter and let excess drip off. Carefully lower into the hot oil, two at a time, and fry until deep golden brown. Let drain on paper towels, then serve.

The Best Corn Dogs Make sure that the hot dogs are completely dry so the batter will stick to them. You may want to dust the hot dogs with a bit of cornstarch or all-purpose flour before dipping them into the batter. Make sure the oil is around 350°F for best results. Use a thermometer, and don't fry more than two dogs at once to keep the temperature constant.

Ham Sweet Potato Stir-Fry

COST PER SERVING $1¹⁴

The dense sweetness of sweet potatoes is a nice contrast to the chewy, salty ham in this easy dish.

SERVES ▶ 4

1. Peel sweet potato and cut in quarters lengthwise, then cut into ¼" thick slices; set aside. In small bowl, combine soy sauce, ketchup, sugar, vinegar, chicken stock, and cornstarch.

2. In large skillet or wok, heat olive oil over medium-high heat. Add onion and sweet potato; stir-fry for 4 minutes. Add carrot, then add water, cover, and simmer for 5–9 minutes or until sweet potato is tender.

3. Uncover skillet and add broccoli and ham; stir-fry for 2 minutes. Then stir cornstarch mixture and add to skillet. Bring to a simmer and stir-fry until sauce thickens. Serve immediately over hot cooked rice.

1 sweet potato

3 tablespoons soy sauce

3 tablespoons ketchup

2 tablespoons brown sugar

2 tablespoons apple cider vinegar

1 cup Chicken Stock (page 79)

2 tablespoons cornstarch

1 tablespoon olive oil

1 onion, chopped

1 cup sliced carrot

¼ cup water

1 cup frozen chopped broccoli, thawed and drained

1½ cups cubed ham

Freezing Ham Ham freezes well, but its texture will change and will become softer. You can freeze it up to 2 months. Use the thawed ham in recipes such as stir-fries and soups, not sandwiches. Ham will keep more of its quality if you freeze it in a liquid; pineapple juice is a good choice.

BBQ Spareribs

These are fingerlickin' good! Serve with Best Potato Salad (page 99) for the perfect summer meal.

SERVES ▶ 6

2 pounds country-style pork spareribs

1 teaspoon salt

¼ teaspoon pepper

2 onions, chopped

1 teaspoon chili powder

¼ cup lemon juice

2 tablespoons Worcestershire sauce

¼ teaspoon cayenne pepper

½ cup chili sauce

½ cup ketchup

¼ cup brown sugar

3 tablespoons mustard

3 tablespoons cornstarch

¼ cup water

1. Sprinkle ribs with salt and pepper. Heat a skillet over medium-high heat. Brown ribs on all sides, turning frequently, for 5–7 minutes. Place ribs in a 5–6 quart slow cooker; drain fat from skillet and add onions. Cook and stir for 2–3 minutes, scraping pan to remove drippings. Add to slow cooker.

2. In small bowl, combine remaining ingredients, except cornstarch and water, and mix well. Pour over ribs in slow cooker. Cover and cook on low for 8–9 hours or until ribs are very tender.

3. If the sauce needs to be thickened, combine cornstarch and water in small bowl and mix well. Add to slow cooker; cover and cook on high for 20–30 minutes.

Yes, You Can Afford Seafood

12

Fish 'n Chips Dinner

SERVES ▶ 6

This is a complete meal, for under $2.00 per serving. The fresh coleslaw is a great contrast to the hot and crisp potatoes and fish.

2 cups shredded red cabbage

3 cups shredded cabbage

1 cup shredded carrots

¾ cup mayonnaise

⅓ cup buttermilk

½ teaspoon dried dill weed

4 cups frozen french-fried potatoes

1 tablespoon chili powder

1 (21-ounce) package breaded fish fillets

1. In large bowl, combine red cabbage, cabbage, and carrots. In small bowl combine mayonnaise, buttermilk, and dill weed and blend well. Pour over cabbage mixture and stir to coat; cover and refrigerate.

2. Preheat oven to 425°F. Place french fries on a cookie sheet and sprinkle with the chili powder. Toss to coat. Spread in an even layer, and arrange the fish fillets on the same pan.

3. Bake for 25–35 minutes or until the fish and potatoes are golden brown and crisp. Serve with the coleslaw.

Salmon Linguine

SERVES ▶ 6

Bacon and salmon is one of the most perfect combinations of flavors and textures. Keep these ingredients on hand for a fabulous dinner.

4 slices bacon

3 cloves garlic, minced

½ cup heavy cream

1 (3-ounce) package cream cheese, softened

1 (12-ounce) package linguine

½ cup Spinach Pesto (page 28)

½ (14-ounce) can salmon, drained

½ cup coarsely chopped walnuts

1. Bring a large pot of salted water to a boil. Meanwhile, in large saucepan cook bacon until crisp. Remove bacon, crumble, and set aside. Drain bacon drippings from pan but do not wipe pan. Add garlic; cook and stir until fragrant, about 2 minutes. Add cream and cream cheese; remove from heat.

2. Cook pasta according to package directions until al dente. Drain, reserving ⅓ cup pasta cooking water, and add pasta to saucepan with cream mixture.

3. Return saucepan to medium heat and add pesto and salmon. Toss with tongs until sauce is blended, adding some reserved pasta water as necessary to make a smooth sauce. Sprinkle with walnuts and serve.

Poor Fisherman's Chowder

COST PER SERVING $1¹⁷

This rich and thick chowder is accented with just enough seafood. If you want to splurge, increase the amount of seafood; more crabmeat would be a fabulous addition.

1. In large saucepan, bring water to a boil over high heat. Add potatoes and carrots. Cover and bring back to a boil; reduce heat and simmer for 8 minutes. Stir in celery and fish fillets; simmer for 3 minutes. Stir in shrimp; simmer for 2–4 minutes until shrimp turn pink and the fish flakes. Cover and set aside off the heat.

2. In medium saucepan, combine olive oil and onion over medium heat; cook and stir until tender, about 5–6 minutes. Stir in flour, salt, and pepper; cook and stir until bubbly. Add milk; cook and stir until mixture begins to thicken. Add cheese; cook and stir until melted.

3. Stir cheese sauce into fish mixture. Cook and stir over medium heat until mixture blends and soup starts to steam; do not boil. Serve immediately.

Seafood on Sale Grocery stores often have seafood on sale. When that happens, buy a couple of packages and freeze them. Most seafood freezes very well. If the fish or shrimp isn't in freezer bags, repackage them into freezer-safe bags or containers, label with the purchase date, and freeze. Use within three months.

SERVES ► 8

5 cups water

3 potatoes, peeled and diced

2 carrots, sliced

2 stalks celery, sliced

½ pound fish fillets

1 cup small raw shrimp

3 tablespoons olive oil

1 onion, chopped

¼ cup all-purpose flour

1 teaspoon salt

⅛ teaspoon white pepper

2 cups milk

2 cups shredded Cheddar cheese

Sweet and Sour Fish

COST PER SERVING
$1⁶⁴

The trick to stir-frying is to have all the ingredients prepared and ready to go before you start heating anything. Then dinner is ready in about 20 minutes!

6 frozen crunchy fish fillets

1½ cups long grain rice

3 cups water

2 tablespoons olive oil

1 onion, chopped

2 cloves garlic, minced

2 green bell peppers, chopped

1 cup sliced carrot

1 (8-ounce) can pineapple tidbits

⅓ cup ketchup

2 tablespoons sugar

2 tablespoons apple cider vinegar

2 tablespoons cornstarch

2 tablespoons soy sauce

½ teaspoon ground ginger

⅛ teaspoon cayenne pepper

1. In large saucepan, combine rice and water and bring to a boil. Reduce heat, cover, and simmer for 20–25 minutes or until rice is tender and liquid is absorbed. Preheat oven to 350°F. Prepare fish as directed on package.

2. Meanwhile, in large saucepan heat olive oil over medium heat. Add onion and garlic; stir-fry for 3 minutes. Add bell pepper and carrot; stir-fry for 3–5 minutes longer.

3. Drain pineapple, reserving juice. Add pineapple to saucepan and stir. In small bowl, combine reserved pineapple juice, ketchup, sugar, vinegar, cornstarch, soy sauce, ginger, and pepper and mix well. Add to saucepan, bring to a simmer, and cook until thickened, about 3–5 minutes.

4. When rice is done, place on serving plate and top with vegetable mixture. Cut fish fillets in half and place on top of vegetables. Serve immediately.

Salmon Patties

COST PER SERVING
80¢

Serve these old-fashioned patties with Creamy Mashed Potatoes (page 224) and a green salad for a retro meal. Save the rest of the salmon to make Salmon Linguine (page 164).

1. In small saucepan, combine rice and water. Bring to a boil, reduce heat, cover, and simmer for 30–40 minutes or until rice is tender and liquid is absorbed.

2. In large saucepan, heat olive oil over medium heat. Add onion and carrot; cook and stir for 4 minutes. Remove from heat and combine with almonds, flour, sour cream, salt, pepper, and egg in a medium bowl. Stir in cooked rice, then add salmon and stir gently. Add cheese and mix.

3. Form mixture into four patties. Wipe out large saucepan and melt butter over medium heat. Add patties and cook for 3–5 minutes on each side, turning once, until patties are crisp and brown. Serve immediately.

> *Freezing Fish* Leftover canned fish, like salmon and tuna, freezes very well. If you don't use a whole can, remove the rest from the can and place it in a freezer bag or container, seal, label, and freeze for up to 3 months. To thaw, place in refrigerator overnight. Never store fish in the can, even in the refrigerator or freezer.

SERVES ▶ 4

⅓ cup brown rice

⅔ cup water

1 tablespoon olive oil

¼ cup finely chopped onion

⅓ cup shredded carrot

¼ cup ground almonds

2 tablespoons flour

1 tablespoon sour cream

½ teaspoon salt

⅛ teaspoon pepper

1 egg

½ (14-ounce) can salmon, drained

¼ cup grated Parmesan cheese

2 tablespoons butter

Uptown Tuna Casserole

SERVES ▶ 8

By making the white sauce instead of relying on canned condensed soup, this casserole has a more sophisticated flavor than most tuna casseroles.

5 tablespoons butter, divided

1 onion, finely chopped

3 tablespoons all-purpose flour

½ teaspoon salt

1 tablespoon curry powder

1½ cups milk

3 stalks celery, chopped

1 cup shredded Swiss cheese

1 (12-ounce) package gemelli pasta

1 (12-ounce) can tuna, drained

1½ cups red grapes

1 slice Oatmeal Bread (page 53), toasted

2 tablespoons Romano cheese

1. Preheat oven to 375°F. Spray a 2-quart casserole with nonstick cooking spray and set aside. Bring a large pot of salted water to a boil.

2. Meanwhile, in large saucepan, melt 3 tablespoons butter over medium heat. Add onion; cook and stir until tender, about 4 minutes. Add flour, salt, and curry powder; cook and stir until bubbly, about 3 minutes.

3. Stir in milk, whisking until smooth. Then add celery. Cook, stirring frequently, until sauce thickens. Stir in Swiss cheese and remove from heat.

4. Cook pasta according to package directions until al dente. Drain and add along with tuna and grapes to milk mixture. Pour into prepared casserole.

5. Melt remaining 2 tablespoons butter. Crumble the toasted bread and combine with the butter and Romano cheese. Sprinkle on top of casserole. Bake for 20–30 minutes or until casserole is bubbly and topping is browned and crisp.

What Kind of Tuna? Canned tuna varies in cost depending on the type and form. Solid pack tuna is the most expensive. Albacore, or white tuna, is the most expensive packed tuna because the fish is larger and costs more to catch. "Light" tuna is the other type most commonly sold in the U.S. It is darker and less expensive, and actually contains *less mercury* than the larger albacore.

Crisp Polenta with Salmon Cream

COST PER SERVING $1⁴⁸

The combination of flavors and textures in this simple recipe is sublime. For a splurge, use more salmon.

1. In medium bowl, combine sour cream, onions, and cheese; mix well and set aside. Sprinkle salmon fillets with salt and pepper.

2. Combine olive oil and butter in large skillet over medium heat. Add salmon fillets; cook for 4 minutes, then carefully turn salmon and cook for 2–4 minutes longer or until just cooked. Remove to plate and cover with foil to keep warm.

3. Add polenta squares to pan; cook until brown and crisp, about 4 minutes, then turn and cook on second side until brown and crisp, about 3 minutes.

4. Flake salmon and add to sour cream mixture. Spoon over hot polenta and top with salsa. Serve immediately.

Canned, Fresh, or Frozen? When it comes to seafood, canned is going to be the least expensive. You can substitute canned for fresh or frozen when the recipe calls for flaking the fish after it is cooked. Unless you live on the coast, fresh seafood in your grocer's case has been frozen; usually it's frozen on the boat or the same day it's caught.

SERVES ▶ 4

⅔ cup sour cream

3 green onions, chopped

¼ cup grated Parmesan cheese

2 (4-ounce) salmon fillets

¼ teaspoon salt

⅛ teaspoon pepper

2 tablespoons butter

1 tablespoon olive oil

4 (3" × 3") squares Polenta (page 228)

1 cup Quick and Easy Salsa (page 20)

Seafood Stuffed Shells

SERVES ▶ 6

Now this is one elegant dish! You will be proud to serve it to guests, even the director of the board.

1 tablespoon butter

1 onion, finely chopped

1 green bell pepper, chopped

1 (8-ounce) package cream cheese

½ cup milk

½ teaspoon salt

⅛ teaspoon pepper

½ teaspoon dried thyme leaves

1 (6-ounce) can crab meat

4 ounces frozen cooked
small shrimp, thawed

⅓ cup grated Parmesan cheese

1 cup Quick and Easy Salsa
(page 20)

1 (12-ounce) package jumbo
macaroni shells

1 cup shredded Swiss cheese

1. Preheat oven to 400°F. Bring a large pot of salted water to a boil. In medium saucepan, melt butter over medium heat. Add onion and bell pepper; cook and stir until crisp-tender, about 4 minutes.

2. Cut cream cheese into cubes and add to saucepan along with milk, salt, pepper, and thyme. Bring to a simmer and cook, stirring, until sauce blends. Reserve ½ cup sauce.

3. Drain crab and pick over meat, discarding any shell or cartilage. Add to mixture in saucepan along with shrimp and Parmesan cheese. Stir in half of salsa and set aside.

4. Cook shells in water until almost al dente according to package directions. Drain, rinse shells in cold water and drain again. Stuff shells with seafood mixture.

5. Combine remaining salsa with the reserved sauce and place in a 1½ quart baking dish. Top with the stuffed shells; sprinkle shells with Swiss cheese. Bake for 20–25 minutes or until dish is hot and cheese melts and begins to brown.

About Seafood You can substitute most seafood for other types in most recipes. Crab is a good substitute for shrimp, which is a good substitute for clams or mussels. Seafood should always smell sweet or slightly briny, never "fishy." If you buy it fresh, use it within 1–2 days or freeze it immediately in freezer-proof bags or wraps.

Spicy Fish Tacos

These crisp and creamy tacos are full of flavor and color. For a splurge, add some halved cherry tomatoes and fresh chopped avocado.

1. Preheat oven to 400°F. In medium bowl, combine sour cream, lemon juice, green onion, and corn; mix well. Add salsa; stir and set aside.

2. Place fish fingers on cookie sheet. In small bowl combine chili powder, cayenne pepper, and paprika; mix well. Sprinkle this mixture over the fish fingers and toss to coat. Bake fish according to package directions.

3. Heat taco shells in oven according to package directions as soon as fish is done; for about 4–5 minutes or until hot.

4. Assemble tacos by starting with the sour cream mixture, adding fish fingers, then topping with lettuce, cheese, and guacamole. You can let diners assemble their own tacos. Serve immediately.

SERVES ▶ 4–6

½ cup sour cream

1 tablespoon lemon juice

3 green onions, chopped

1 cup frozen corn, thawed and drained

½ cup Quick and Easy Salsa (page 20)

24 frozen fish fingers

1 tablespoon chili powder

¼ teaspoon cayenne pepper

½ teaspoon paprika

8 taco shells

1½ cups shredded lettuce

1½ cups shredded Cheddar cheese

1 cup Big Batch Guacamole (page 24)

Seafood Quiche

Most cooked frozen shrimp comes with the tails attached. Thaw the shrimp according to directions and gently pull off and discard the tail.

1. Preheat oven to 350°F. In medium bowl, combine eggs, milk, mayonnaise, mustard, flour, and dill weed and beat to combine.

2. Arrange mushrooms, shrimp, crab, and Swiss in layers in pie crust. Pour egg mixture over. Sprinkle with Parmesan cheese.

3. Bake for 40–50 minutes or until quiche is puffed and golden brown. Serve immediately.

About Crabmeat Whether you use canned or frozen crabmeat, it always has to be picked over before use. In processing, small bits of shell or pieces of cartilage get into the meat. Drain the crab, then spread it on a kitchen towel or paper towel and run your fingers through it. Pick out and discard anything that feels hard or sharp.

SERVES ▶ 6

3 eggs

½ cup milk

⅓ cup mayonnaise

1 tablespoon mustard

1 tablespoon all-purpose flour

½ teaspoon dried dill weed

1 (4-ounce) can mushroom pieces, drained

4 ounces small frozen cooked shrimp, thawed

1 (6-ounce) can crabmeat, drained

1 cup shredded Swiss cheese

1 Pie Crust (page 270), unbaked

¼ cup grated Parmesan cheese

Fish with Veggie Slaw

Simply seasoned and baked fish is served on cold and crisp coleslaw for a delicious lunch or dinner.

SERVES ▶ 4

1 tablespoon olive oil

1½ pounds frozen pollock fillets, thawed

½ teaspoon salt

⅛ teaspoon pepper

½ teaspoon paprika

1 lemon, very thinly sliced

4 cups Confetti Slaw (page 102)

1. Preheat oven to 400°F. Pat fish dry and cut into serving size portions. Tear four sheets of foil about 18" long. Place foil, shiny side down, on work surface. Grease a part of the foil that is the size of the fillets with olive oil.

2. Place fish on greased area of foil. Sprinkle with salt, pepper, and paprika. Place thin slices of lemon on top. Fold foil around the fish to enclose, leaving some room for heat expansion.

3. Place foil packets on a cookie sheet. Bake for 15–20 minutes or until fish flakes when tested with fork.

4. Divide slaw among plates and top with fish. Serve immediately.

> **Preparing Fish** Fish is such a delicate meat it must be prepared in a way that preserves the moisture. Baking in foil, or *en papillote*, is an easy way to keep the fish moist. You can also poach fish by placing it in simmering water or fish stock and cooking for 10 minutes per inch of thickness. Fish is also tasty broiled for about 8–10 minutes per inch of thickness.

Crabby Corn Pie

COST PER SERVING $1¹⁴

Surimi is imitation crabmeat that looks and tastes just like the real thing.

1. Preheat oven to 350°F. In medium bowl, combine cracker crumbs with melted butter. Mix well, then press into bottom and up sides of a 9" pie pan. Set aside.

2. In large skillet, heat olive oil over medium heat. Add onion; cook and stir until tender, about 4 minutes. Add flour, salt, and basil; cook and stir for 3 minutes. Add milk; cook and stir until thickened. Add corn and eggs; stir well. Cook for 1 minute.

3. Chop surimi into bite-sized pieces and arrange with cheese in pie crust. Carefully pour in corn mixture. Bake for 30–40 minutes or until the pie is set, puffed, and golden brown. Let stand for 5 minutes, then serve.

SERVES ▶ 6

1½ cups crushed soda crackers

⅓ cup butter or margarine, melted

2 tablespoons olive oil

1 onion, chopped

2 tablespoons all-purpose flour

½ teaspoon salt

½ teaspoon dried basil leaves

1 cup milk

2 cups frozen corn, thawed and drained

2 eggs, beaten

1 (8-ounce) package frozen surimi, thawed and drained

1 cup shredded Swiss cheese

Cornmeal Fried Fish

COST PER SERVING $1²⁷

If you have a fisherman in your family, the cost per serving will drop to about 30 cents!

1. In small bowl, combine flour, cornmeal, salt, and pepper and mix well. Cut butter into small pieces and add to flour mixture; cut in with two knives until mixture is finely blended. In shallow bowl, combine egg and milk and beat well.

2. Pat fish dry. Dip into egg mixture, then into cornmeal mixture, coating both sides. Let stand on a wire rack for 10 minutes.

3. Heat oil in large skillet until it reaches 375°F. Fry fish over medium heat, turning once, until golden brown, about 8–12 minutes. Drain on paper towels and serve immediately.

SERVES ▶ 6

⅓ cup all-purpose flour

⅓ cup cornmeal

1 teaspoon salt

⅛ teaspoon pepper

3 tablespoons butter

1 egg

¼ cup milk

2 pounds fish fillets

1 cup vegetable oil

Tex-Mex Fish Burritos

COST PER SERVING $1.29

SERVES ▶ 8–10

Burritos can be baked or deep fried, or covered with sauce. The method used in this recipe, baking, has the fewest calories, and is delicious for lunch.

1 tablespoon olive oil

1 onion, chopped

1 (15-ounce) can refried beans

1 (4-ounce) can green chiles, drained

48 frozen fish fingers

1 tablespoon chili powder

1 teaspoon cumin

1 green bell pepper, thinly sliced

1 cup Quick and Easy Salsa (page 20)

1½ cups shredded Monterey Jack cheese

8 (12-inch) flour tortillas

1. Preheat oven to 400°F. In large saucepan, heat olive oil over medium heat. Add onion; cook and stir until crisp-tender, about 4 minutes. Then stir in refried beans. Drain chiles and chop; add to bean mixture and bring to a simmer. Lower heat and let cook while you prepare the fish.

2. Place fish fingers on cookie sheet and sprinkle with chili powder and cumin. Arrange in single layer. Bake according to package directions.

3. Prepare bell pepper and cheese. When fish is done, remove from oven. Make wraps by spreading bean mixture on tortillas, then topping each with six fish fingers, green pepper slices, salsa, and cheese. Wrap up, folding in ends, and place, seam side down, on cookie sheet. Bake for 15–25 minutes or until tortillas start to brown and cheese is melted. Cut each in half and serve immediately.

> *Fish Fingers* Fish fingers are usually sold in very large packages, about 3–5 pounds. Store the package in the coldest part of your freezer, and be sure to reseal the package carefully after you remove some food. And be sure to abide carefully by the use-by dates on the package. Shop around for the best deal; these products often go on sale.

Shrimp with Grits

COST PER SERVING $2.39

Grits, that Southern staple, is a wonderful complement to tender and sweet shrimp served in a spicy tomato sauce. This is a dish to serve when you entertain!

1. In large saucepan, combine water with milk and bring to a boil over high heat. Stir in the grits and salt. Reduce heat to medium and cook for 5–6 minutes until grits are thick. Add cheese, butter, and hot sauce, stir, cover, and remove from heat.

2. In large saucepan, cook bacon until crisp. Remove bacon, crumble, and set aside. To drippings in skillet, add onion and garlic and cook until crisp-tender, about 4 minutes. Add bell pepper; cook and stir for 3 minutes longer. Drain tomatoes and mushrooms, reserving liquid.

3. Add drained tomatoes and mushrooms to saucepan and bring to a simmer. Add shrimp and stir. In small bowl, combine reserved tomato liquid and mushroom liquid with cornstarch and mix well. Stir into saucepan and bring to a simmer; simmer until thickened.

4. Spoon grits into a serving dish and top with shrimp mixture. Sprinkle with reserved bacon and serve immediately.

SERVES ▶ 6

3 cups water

2 cups milk

1¼ cups quick-cooking grits

½ teaspoon salt

1 cup grated sharp Cheddar cheese

2 tablespoons butter

½ teaspoon hot sauce

5 slices bacon

2 onions, chopped

4 cloves garlic, minced

1 green bell pepper, chopped

1 (14-ounce) can diced tomatoes

1 (8-ounce) jar mushroom pieces

12 ounces frozen cooked small shrimp, thawed

2 tablespoons cornstarch

Tangy Fish Fillets

COST PER SERVING $1⁴³

Dressing up breaded fish fillets is a delicious way to add flavor and fun to your meals. And it's so inexpensive!

SERVES ▶ 6

1 lemon

1 (21-ounce) package breaded fish fillets

¼ cup mayonnaise

2 tablespoons mustard

2 tablespoons lemon juice

½ teaspoon ground ginger

½ cup grated Parmesan cheese

1. Preheat oven to 400°F, or as package directs. Place fish fillets in a 15" × 10" jelly roll pan. Bake for 20 minutes.

2. Meanwhile, in small bowl, combine remaining ingredients except cheese and mix well.

3. Remove fish from oven and spread each with some of the mayonnaise mixture. Sprinkle with Parmesan cheese. Return to oven and bake for 5–10 minutes longer or until fish is thoroughly cooked and topping is bubbling.

Baked Tuna Mac and Cheese

COST PER SERVING 84¢

This super easy casserole can be made without the onion, or add other cooked leftover vegetables to the tuna mixture.

SERVES ▶ 4

1 tablespoon olive oil

1 onion, chopped

1 (5-ounce) package macaroni and cheese mix

¼ cup milk

1 egg, beaten

1 cup Quick and Easy Salsa (page 20)

1 (6-ounce) can tuna, drained

¼ cup grated Parmesan cheese

1. Preheat oven to 350°F. Spray a 9" baking dish with nonstick cooking spray and set aside. Bring a saucepan of water to a boil. Meanwhile, in small saucepan combine olive oil and onion over medium heat; cook and stir until onion is tender, about 5 minutes.

2. Add macaroni from mix to boiling water and cook until tender, according to package directions. Drain and return macaroni to saucepan. Add powdered cheese from mix, milk, egg, and onion mixture to macaroni and stir over low heat until combined.

3. Pour macaroni mixture into prepared dish. In small bowl, combine salsa with drained tuna and mix well. Spoon over macaroni mixture and sprinkle with cheese. Bake for 15–25 minutes or until casserole is bubbling. Serve immediately.

Thrifty Meatless Entrées

Cheesy Fruit Omelet

COST PER SERVING $1.12

Omelets are easy, as long as you pay attention and keep moving the egg mixture. You could use any fruits or veggies you'd like in the filling.

SERVES ▶ 3

1 apple, peeled and chopped
½ cup finely chopped onion
2 tablespoons butter or margarine, divided
6 eggs
2 tablespoons water
½ teaspoon salt
1 cup shredded Colby cheese

1. In large nonstick skillet, melt 1 tablespoon butter over medium heat. Add apples and onion; cook and stir until tender, about 5 minutes. Remove from skillet and set aside.

2. In medium bowl, combine eggs with water and salt; beat until fluffy. Return skillet to heat, add remaining tablespoon butter to skillet and pour in egg mixture. Cook without stirring over medium heat for 2 minutes. Then, using a rubber spatula, gently run it under the edges of the omelet, lifting to let the uncooked egg flow underneath. Shake pan occasionally to prevent sticking.

3. When eggs are almost cooked but still moist on top, add apple filling to half of the omelet and sprinkle with cheese. Cover and cook for 2–3 minutes longer, then fold over and slide onto serving plate. Serve immediately.

Omelet Tricks To make the best omelet, be sure to beat the egg mixture well, and cook the omelet quickly. To speed up the cooking, gently lift the edges of the egg as they start to set, letting the uncooked egg flow underneath. Make sure that the diners are ready for the omelet because they should be eaten immediately. And don't overcook them; cook just until the egg is set.

Meatless Chili

Chili is so good for you; it's full of fiber and vitamins A and C. In addition, the leftovers can be used in so many ways, including Chili French Bread Pizza (page 111) and "Neat" Joes (page 120).

1. Combine beans, 1 can of the tomatoes, onions, and garlic in 4–5 quart slow cooker. Add half of remaining can of tomatoes to the slow cooker, then mix the tomato paste into the can of tomatoes to help dissolve tomato paste. Add salt, chili powder, and oregano to the can of tomatoes and stir well; add to slow cooker.

2. Cover and cook on low for 7–9 hours or until chili is bubbling. If necessary, you can thicken chili by combining cornstarch with water in a small bowl. Stir this mixture into the chili and cook on high for 30 minutes, until thickened.

SERVES ▶ 6

1 (15-ounce) can black beans

2 (15-ounce) cans kidney beans

1 (15-ounce) can cannelloni beans

2 (14-ounce) cans diced tomatoes, undrained

2 onions, chopped

4 cloves garlic, minced

1 (6-ounce) can tomato paste

½ teaspoon salt

1 tablespoon chili powder

½ teaspoon dried oregano leaves

2 tablespoons cornstarch

¼ cup water

Tomato and Bean Pasta

The bit of butter in the sauce helps mellow the tomatoes and adds just a bit of richness.

1. Bring a large pot of salted water to a boil. Meanwhile, in large saucepan, combine butter and olive oil over medium heat. Add onion; cook and stir until onion is tender, about 5 minutes.

2. Cook pasta according to package directions until al dente. Meanwhile, drain cannelloni beans but do not rinse. Add to saucepan along with tomatoes and bring to a simmer, stirring occasionally. Add Italian seasoning and stir.

3. Drain pasta, reserving ⅓ cup pasta cooking water. Add pasta to saucepan and toss using tongs. Add reserved pasta water as necessary to make a sauce. Sprinkle with cheese and serve immediately.

SERVES ▶ 4

1 tablespoon butter

1 tablespoon olive oil

1 onion, chopped

1 (16-ounce) package spaghetti pasta

1 (15-ounce) can cannelloni beans

1 (14-ounce) can diced tomatoes, undrained

½ teaspoon dried Italian seasoning

⅓ cup grated Parmesan cheese

Slow Cooker Black Beans and Rice

COST PER SERVING
62¢

This recipe must be stirred, unlike most slow cooker recipes, so the beans cook evenly.

SERVES ▶ 6

2 cups dried black beans

1 tablespoon olive oil

1 cup brown rice

1 onion, chopped

3 garlic cloves, minced

1 (10.75-ounce) can condensed vegetable broth

3 cups water

1 (14-ounce) can diced tomatoes

1 teaspoon cumin

½ teaspoon salt

⅛ teaspoon cayenne pepper

1. The night before you want to serve this dish, sort beans and rinse well. Cover with cold water and soak overnight. In the morning, drain beans and rinse.

2. Heat olive oil in medium saucepan. Add rice; cook and stir for 3–5 minutes or until rice is fragrant. Combine in 4–5 quart slow cooker along with beans, onion, garlic, vegetable broth, and water. Cover and cook on low for 6 hours, stirring every two hours.

3. Then add tomatoes, cumin, salt, and pepper, stirring well. Cover and cook on low for 2–3 hours longer until rice and beans are tender.

> **About Tomatoes and Beans** Always cook beans and legumes in a low-acid and low-salt solution. Tomatoes and salt, along with salty ingredients such as bacon or ham, and ingredients high in calcium such as cheese and milk, will slow the softening process. Add these ingredients toward the end of cooking time, especially when you're cooking with a slow cooker.

Sicilian Stuffed Cabbage

COST PER SERVING $1¹⁶

*Using a small amount of wild rice is a nice splurge that
adds great texture and flavor to this comfort food recipe.*

SERVES ▶ 6

1 head cabbage

½ cup brown rice

½ cup wild rice

2 cups water

1 teaspoon salt

¼ cup mustard

2 eggs

1 cup shredded Swiss cheese

2 tablespoons olive oil

1 onion, chopped

3 cloves garlic, minced

1 cup chopped celery

1 (14-ounce) can diced tomatoes, undrained

1 (10.75-ounce) can tomato soup

1. Remove the outer layers of the cabbage and discard. Cut out the core and gently remove the outside eight leaves. Place in a large bowl and cover with hot water; set aside. Chop remaining cabbage.

2. In large saucepan, combine brown rice and wild rice and add water. Bring to a boil, then cover, reduce heat, and simmer for 30–40 minutes or until rice is almost tender. Drain if necessary, and add salt, mustard, eggs, and cheese and mix well. Add chopped cabbage.

3. In large skillet, heat olive oil over medium heat. Add onion and garlic; cook and stir until crisp-tender, about 4 minutes. Add celery; cook and stir for 1 minute longer. Add tomatoes and tomato soup and bring to a simmer.

4. Drain cabbage leaves and place on work surface. Divide rice filling among leaves, using about ½ cup for each, and roll up. Place, seam side down, in 13" x 9" glass baking dish. Pour tomato mixture over everything. If there is leftover rice mixture, arrange around stuffed leaves.

5. Place in oven and turn heat to 350°F. Bake for 60–70 minutes or until casserole is bubbly. Serve immediately.

Veggie Risotto

COST PER SERVING
$1 03

SERVES ▶ 6

Here's a shocker: you can make risotto with regular long grain rice. You don't need to buy that expensive Arborio rice. Just keep stirring!

2 tablespoons olive oil

3 tablespoons butter, divided

4 cups Chicken Stock (page 79)

1 onion, finely chopped

3 cloves garlic, minced

½ cup chopped mushrooms

1 cup frozen chopped spinach, thawed

½ teaspoon salt

2 cups long grain rice

½ cup grated Parmesan cheese

½ cup grated Muenster cheese

1. In large saucepan, combine olive oil and 1 tablespoon butter. In a medium saucepan, bring the stock to a very slow simmer.

2. When the butter melts, add the onion, garlic, and mushrooms. Cook, stirring frequently, until tender, about 5 minutes. Then add the drained spinach and salt; cook and stir for 3–4 minutes longer. Add the rice; cook and stir for 3 minutes.

3. Add stock, ½ cup at a time, stirring frequently and cooking until the rice absorbs the broth. Continue adding stock, stirring, until the rice is tender. Add the cheese and remaining 2 tablespoons butter; cover and remove from heat. Let stand for 4 minutes, then stir and serve.

> **Cooking Risotto** When rice is cooked slowly and manipulated by stirring, the starch cells break open and thicken the liquid. Arborio rice is usually used because it's very high in starch. But regular rice works just as well. You do have to keep an eye on the rice, and stir very frequently, both to help release the starch and to prevent the risotto from burning.

Potato Tacos

COST PER SERVING $1<u>03</u>

Tacos are delicious, inexpensive, and easy on the cook.
Let diners assemble their own tacos.

SERVES ▶ 4–6

1. Preheat oven to 400°F. Scrub potatoes and cut into 1" pieces, including some of the skin on each piece. Combine in roasting pan with onion and garlic. Drizzle with olive oil and sprinkle with salt and pepper and toss to coat. Roast for 30 minutes, then turn vegetables with a spatula and roast for 15–20 minutes longer until potatoes are tender and browned.

2. When potatoes are done, combine evaporated milk and undrained chiles in a saucepan. Bring to a boil over high heat, then reduce heat to low and simmer for 5 minutes or until mixture begins to reduce.

3. Stir in potato mixture until coated. Heat taco shells in the oven until crisp, about 3–4 minutes. Make tacos with potato mixture, cheese, guacamole, and chopped tomatoes.

3 russet potatoes

1 onion, chopped

3 cloves garlic, minced

2 tablespoons olive oil

½ teaspoon salt

⅛ teaspoon pepper

1 (12-ounce) can evaporated milk

1 (4-ounce) can chopped green chiles, undrained

6 taco shells

1 cup shredded Pepper Jack cheese

½ cup Big Batch Guacamole (page 24)

½ cup chopped tomato

Red Beans and Rice

COST PER SERVING $1<u>08</u>

Onion, green pepper, and celery is known as the "holy trinity"
in Cajun cooking. It adds flavor to this simple and hearty main dish.

SERVES ▶ 6

1. In saucepan, combine rice, water and salt. Bring to a boil, reduce heat, cover, and simmer for 20 minutes or until rice is tender.

2. Meanwhile, heat olive oil and 1 tablespoon butter in a large saucepan. Add onion and cook for 3 minutes. Add bell pepper and celery; cook and stir for 3–4 minutes longer. Then add drained but not rinsed beans, green chiles, chili sauce, and pepper. Bring to a simmer.

3. When rice is cooked, add 2 tablespoons butter, remove from heat and let stand, covered, for 5 minutes. Then fluff with fork and place on serving plate. Pour bean mixture over and serve immediately.

1½ cups long grain rice

3 cups water

½ teaspoon salt

1 tablespoon olive oil

3 tablespoons butter, divided

1 onion, chopped

1 green bell pepper, chopped

3 stalks celery, chopped

2 (15-ounce) cans red kidney beans, drained

1 (4-ounce) can green chiles, undrained

½ cup chili sauce

⅛ teaspoon cayenne pepper

Double Egg Quiche

Using sliced hard-cooked eggs along with an egg custard in this quiche makes it extra–rich.

SERVES ▶ 6

4 hard-cooked eggs

1 cup shredded Swiss cheese

1 Pie Crust (page 270), unbaked

4 eggs

1 cup light cream

¼ cup milk

1 tablespoon mustard

2 tablespoons all-purpose flour

½ teaspoon salt

⅛ teaspoon pepper

1 cup frozen peas, thawed

¼ cup grated Parmesan cheese

1. Preheat oven to 350°F. Peel and slice hard-cooked eggs. Layer with Swiss cheese in the bottom of pie crust; set aside.

2. In medium bowl, combine eggs, cream, milk, mustard, flour, salt, and pepper and mix well with wire whisk until blended.

3. Sprinkle peas over ingredients in Pie Crust and pour egg mixture over. Sprinkle with Parmesan cheese. Bake for 45–55 minutes or until quiche is puffed and golden brown. Serve immediately.

Thawing Frozen Vegetables Thaw frozen vegetables gently. One of the fastest ways that preserves the color and texture of the vegetables is to empty the package into a colander. Run cold water over the vegetables until they thaw. Be sure to drain the vegetables well before adding them to the recipe so you don't add too much water.

Veggie Tofu Stir-Fry

Firm tofu is sold in blocks in the dairy or vegetarian section of the supermarket. To stir-fry, it must be well-drained to remove excess water.

SERVES ▶ 4

1 (14-ounce) package firm tofu

1 tablespoon chili powder

½ teaspoon salt

⅛ teaspoon pepper

⅔ cup water

2 tablespoons soy sauce

1 tablespoon brown sugar

1 tablespoon cornstarch

½ teaspoon ground ginger

2 tablespoons olive oil

1 onion, chopped

1 (16-ounce) package frozen mixed vegetables, thawed

1. Place tofu between several layers of paper towel and press gently to thoroughly drain. Remove paper towels and repeat this process. Cut the tofu into 1" cubes and sprinkle with chili powder, salt, and pepper; set aside.

2. In small bowl, combine water, soy sauce, brown sugar, cornstarch, and ginger and mix well; set aside.

3. In skillet or wok, heat olive oil over medium-high heat. Add onion; stir-fry until crisp-tender, about 4 minutes. Drain mixed vegetables and add to skillet; stir-fry for 3 minutes or until hot.

4. Stir cornstarch mixture and add to skillet along with tofu cubes. Bring to a simmer, then stir-fry for 5 minutes or until sauce thickens and food is heated. Serve over hot cooked rice.

Tex-Mex Rice Timbales

COST PER SERVING **93¢**

Timbales are an old-fashioned recipe using leftover rice and anything else you have on hand. These molded rice cups are fun to eat.

1. Preheat oven to 350°F. Grease 6 (10-ounce) custard cups and set on a cookie sheet; set aside. In large saucepan, heat olive oil over medium heat. Add onion, garlic, and jalapeño; cook and stir until crisp-tender, about 4 minutes. Add rice; stir gently to break up rice. Then add kidney beans and remove from heat.

2. In small bowl, combine cream, milk, salt, pepper, and egg and mix well. Stir into rice mixture and mix to combine. Add cheeses and mix well. Spoon mixture into custard cups and pack down with back of spoon. Cover timbales with foil and bake for 20–25 minutes or until rice mixture is set.

3. Run a knife around the timbales to loosen, then invert onto serving plate. Top each with some of the salsa and serve.

> *Cooked Rice* If you don't have cooked rice leftover but still want to make timbales, you can stop at an Asian take-out restaurant and buy a container of hot cooked rice. This is very inexpensive and it saves you work and time. When you're cooking rice for any dish, make some extra and freeze it in 1-cup amounts for up to 3 months.

SERVES ▶ 6

2 tablespoons olive oil

1 onion, finely chopped

3 cloves garlic

1 jalapeño pepper, minced

3 cups Vegetable Rice (page 232) or leftover cooked rice

1 (15-ounce) can kidney beans, drained

3 tablespoons heavy cream

½ cup milk

½ teaspoon salt

⅛ teaspoon cayenne pepper

2 eggs, beaten

1 cup shredded Pepper Jack cheese

¼ cup grated Parmesan cheese

1½ cups Quick and Easy Salsa (page 20)

Couscous Salad

SERVES ▶ 6

1 cup water
½ cup Chicken Stock (page 79)
1¼ cups couscous
1 tablespoon mustard
3 tablespoons olive oil
2 tablespoons apple cider vinegar
½ teaspoon salt
⅛ teaspoon pepper
1 (15-ounce) can black or red beans, drained
1 cup chopped celery
½ cup chopped parsley
1 cup cubed Swiss or other cheese

Always have a box of couscous on hand to make this easy salad. Just toss in whatever fresh, frozen, or canned veggies you have.

1. In medium saucepan, combine water and stock and bring to a boil. Stir in couscous, cover, remove from heat, and let stand for 10 minutes.

2. In large bowl, combine mustard, oil, vinegar, salt, and pepper and stir well. Fluff couscous with fork and add to bowl along with remaining ingredients. Toss gently and serve immediately, or cover and refrigerate for 4 hours.

> *Cheap Salads* Growing vegetables in a garden or pots on a porch is the best way to add fresh foods inexpensively to your diet. You could also offer to buy some of your neighbor's produce if they have a garden. Many gardeners try to get rid of produce in the late summer and fall!

Lentils, Rice, and Chickpeas

SERVES ▶ 6

1 tablespoon olive oil
1 onion, chopped
3 cloves garlic, minced
1 tablespoon curry powder
1 cup lentils, rinsed
1 cup long-grain brown rice
1 (10.75-ounce) can condensed vegetable broth
2½ cups water
½ teaspoon salt
⅛ teaspoon pepper
1 (15-ounce) can chickpeas, drained
1 (14-ounce) can diced tomatoes, undrained

Combining lentils, legumes, and rice makes a complete protein in this hearty vegetarian main dish recipe.

1. In large saucepan, heat olive oil over medium heat. Add onion, garlic, and curry powder; cook and stir for 4 minutes. Then add lentils and brown rice and stir for 1 minute longer.

2. Add vegetable broth and water and bring to a boil. Cover, reduce heat to low, and simmer 30–35 minutes or until lentils and rice are tender.

3. Stir in salt, pepper, chickpeas, and tomatoes and bring back to a simmer. Simmer for 5 minutes until mixture is combined. Serve immediately.

Egg and Cheese Burritos

COST PER SERVING **81¢**

These can be served for breakfast, or for a late-night dinner or snack. Serve them with sour cream and Big Batch Guacamole (page 24) for a real treat.

SERVES ▶ 6

1. In large saucepan, melt butter over medium heat. Add jalapeño and garlic; cook and stir until fragrant, about 3 minutes. Meanwhile, in medium bowl combine eggs, water, milk, salt, and pepper and mix well.

2. Add egg mixture to saucepan; cook eggs, stirring occasionally, until set but still moist, about 4 minutes. Remove from heat.

3. Arrange tortillas on work surface. Place about 2 tablespoons salsa on each tortilla and divide egg mixture and cheese among them. Roll up, tucking in sides to enclose filling.

4. Place in single layer on microwave-safe baking dish and cover with microwave-safe paper towel. Microwave on high for 1–2 minutes or until hot. Let stand for 4 minutes, then serve.

2 tablespoons butter

1 jalapeño pepper, minced

3 cloves garlic, minced

8 eggs

2 tablespoons water

4 tablespoons milk

½ teaspoon salt

⅛ teaspoon pepper

1 cup shredded Cheddar cheese

1 cup Quick and Easy Salsa (page 20)

6 (10-inch) flour tortillas

Freezing Burritos All burritos freeze really well. Start by placing filled burritos on a cookie sheet and freeze until solid. Then wrap in freezer wrap and pack into a freezer bag. Label, seal, and freeze up to 3 months. To thaw and reheat, unwrap each burrito and microwave, one at a time, on high power for 1–2 minutes until hot. Let stand for 3 minutes and eat.

Bean Tacos

COST PER SERVING
$1 25

SERVES ► 8

1 cup dried chickpeas

1 cup dried black beans

1 cup dried red kidney beans

7 cups water

1 large onion, chopped

5 cloves garlic, minced

2 jalapeño peppers, minced

1 cup sour cream

2 tomatoes, chopped

½ teaspoon salt

⅛ teaspoon pepper

8 taco shells

1 cup Big Batch Guacamole (page 24)

2 cups shredded Pepper Jack cheese

2 cups shredded lettuce

This bean filling cooks all day in your slow cooker, so when you come home all you do is add a few ingredients and make tacos.

1. Sort chickpeas and beans and rinse; place in large bowl and cover with cold water. Let soak overnight.

2. In the morning, drain peas and beans, rinse, then combine with 7 cups water, onion, garlic, and jalapeño pepper in a 4–5 quart slow cooker. Cover and cook on low for 8–10 hours or until beans are tender.

3. Preheat oven to 400°F. Drain beans and place in large bowl with sour cream, tomatoes, salt and pepper; mix well. Place taco shells on a cookie sheet and bake for 8–10 minutes or until hot.

4. Make tacos using bean mixture, guacamole, cheese, and lettuce. Serve immediately.

Dried Beans Dried beans are very inexpensive and so good for you. They're high in fiber and B vitamins, and also high in protein when combined with grains. They must be sorted before use, because in the harvesting process some dirt or twigs can be included. For the least "gassy effect" soak the beans overnight, then drain off the water and cook in fresh water.

Tex-Mex Pizza

COST PER SERVING
$1⁵⁶

Read the label carefully on the refried beans. Most companies make a vegetarian version that uses vegetable oil instead of lard.

SERVES ► 8

1. In large bowl, combine 1 cup flour, ½ cup whole wheat flour, and ½ cup cornmeal with yeast and salt. Mix well. Add vegetable oil and warm water and beat well. Add remaining whole wheat flour and cornmeal (minus 2 tablespoons of the cornmeal), then enough remaining all-purpose flour to form a firm dough. Cover and let rise for 1 hour.

2. Punch down dough and let stand for 10 minutes. Grease two cookie sheets with shortening and sprinkle with 2 tablespoons cornmeal. Divide dough into two parts and roll out directly onto cookie sheets. Set aside while you prepare the topping. Preheat oven to 400°F.

3. In large saucepan, heat olive oil over medium heat. Add onions; cook and stir until tender, about 5 minutes. Remove from heat and stir in refried beans, taco sauce, and green chiles.

4. Bake the crusts for 10 minutes, then remove from oven. Divide bean mixture between the crusts, spreading evenly. Sprinkle with the three cheeses. Bake for 10 minutes longer, then reverse and rotate the pizzas and continue baking for 10–15 minutes or until crust is crisp and cheese is melted and browned. Serve immediately.

2 cups all-purpose flour
1 cup whole wheat flour
1 cup cornmeal
1 (0.25-ounce) package instant blend yeast
½ teaspoon salt
¼ cup vegetable oil
1½ cups warm water
2 tablespoons olive oil
2 onions, chopped
1 (15-ounce) can vegetarian refried beans
1 (20-ounce) can taco sauce
1 (4-ounce) can green chiles, undrained
2 cups shredded Cheddar cheese
2 cups shredded mozzarella cheese
½ cup grated Cotija cheese

> **Cotija Cheese** Cotija cheese is made in Mexico. It's a hard grating cheese very similar to Parmesan and Romano. The flavor is also similar to Parmesan cheese but is more intense. It can be found in the regular grocery store, but you may have to visit a Mexican grocer or ethnic foods store to find it. It's worth the trip!

Polenta Pesto Benedict

COST PER SERVING
$1²⁵

This version of eggs Benedict features a nice smear of pesto on crisp polenta cakes, topped with some scrambled eggs, veggies, and cheese. Yum.

SERVES ▶ 4

4 eggs

3 tablespoons sour cream

½ teaspoon salt

⅛ teaspoon pepper

2 tablespoons butter

1 onion, chopped

½ cup chopped mushrooms

½ cup chopped yellow summer squash

4 (4-inch) squares Polenta (page 228)

¼ cup Spinach Pesto (page 28)

1 cup shredded Swiss cheese

1. In small bowl, combine eggs with sour cream, salt, and pepper and beat well. In medium skillet, melt butter over medium heat. Add onion, mushrooms, and squash; cook and stir for 5 minutes. Add egg mixture. Cook over medium heat, stirring occasionally, until eggs are set but still moist.

2. Meanwhile, preheat broiler. Place polenta squares on greased broiler pan and broil 6" from heat for 2–4 minutes until brown. Turn polenta and broil for 1 minute longer. Spread each with 1 tablespoon pesto and top with egg mixture.

3. Sprinkle with cheese and broil for 2–5 minutes longer until food is hot and cheese melts and begins to bubble and brown. Serve immediately.

> *Benedict* The term *Benedict* involves a type of cooked egg on top of a starch, topped with cheese, and broiled until hot. Use your imagination when thinking about this dish. Polenta is one excellent base; also consider using waffles, hash brown cakes, or even refried beans spread on tortillas. Top with a cooked egg and cheese and eat.

Make a Meal from (Almost) Nothing

14

Spanish Rice

You can make this with leftover rice too; just sauté the onion, add the rice, then add remaining ingredients and bake the dish.

SERVES ▶ 6

1 tablespoon olive oil

1 onion, chopped

2 cups rice

4 cups water

½ cup sliced green olives

2 (8-ounce) cans tomato sauce

1 egg, beaten

1 teaspoon salt

⅛ teaspoon cayenne pepper

1 cup diced Cheddar cheese

1. In large saucepan, heat olive oil over medium heat. Add onion; cook and stir until crisp-tender, about 4 minutes. Add rice, then add water and bring to a boil. Cover, reduce heat, to medium low, and simmer for 15 minutes or until rice is almost tender.

2. Remove from heat and stir in olives, tomato sauce, egg, salt, pepper, and cheese. Pour into 1½ quart casserole and bake for 20–25 minutes or until bubbly.

Thick Potato Chowder

If you have potatoes on hand, you have a meal! This thick chowder will feed a crowd and won't cost you an arm and a leg.

SERVES ▶ 6–8

6 large russet potatoes

2 onions, chopped

3 cups Chicken Stock (page 79) or water

3 cups water

1 teaspoon salt

⅛ teaspoon pepper

1 (13-ounce) can evaporated milk

¼ cup potato flakes

1 cup grated Swiss cheese

½ teaspoon dried thyme leaves

1. Peel potatoes and cut into cubes. Place in 4–5 quart slow cooker along with onions, stock, water, salt, and pepper. Cover and cook on low for 6–8 hours until potatoes are tender.

2. Using a potato masher, mash some of the potatoes directly in the slow cooker. Stir in evaporated milk, potato flakes, cheese, and thyme. Cover and cook for 20–30 minutes longer until soup is thick and cheese has melted. Serve immediately.

28-Cent Split Pea Potage

COST PER SERVING
28¢

*When you or a relative has ham for the holidays, ask for the
ham bone! It's full of flavor and adds a real richness to this soup.*

SERVES ▶ 6

1. Rinse split peas and sort to remove any debris. Combine all ingredients in 4-quart slow cooker. Cover and cook on low for 6–8 hours or until split peas are tender.

2. Remove ham bone from slow cooker and cut off any meat remaining on the bone; discard bone. Using a potato masher or immersion blender, blend some of the soup to help thicken it. Turn heat to high and cook for 20–30 minutes, then serve.

1 (1-pound) package split peas
6 cups water
2 carrots, sliced
1 onion, chopped
3 cloves garlic, chopped
1 ham bone, if desired
1 teaspoon salt
⅛ teaspoon pepper
½ teaspoon dried thyme leaves

Complete Proteins This soup can be made without the ham bone; just add another half pound of split peas. Foods like split peas and other legumes are "incomplete proteins;" your body can't use them unless missing amino acids are added. For a complete protein add grains such as Freezer Whole Wheat Rolls (page 37) or Double Corn Bread (page 41).

Anything Quiche

COST PER SERVING
54¢

*Any leftover or bits and pieces of cooked food can be used in
a quiche. Add you need is eggs, milk, and cheese.*

SERVES ▶ 6

1. Preheat oven to 375°F. In pie crust, arrange meat, vegetables, and cheese; set aside.

2. In medium bowl, combine eggs, milk, flour, salt, and pepper and beat well with wire whisk or eggbeater until smooth. Pour into pie crust and sprinkle with Parmesan cheese.

3. Bake for 25–35 minutes or until quiche is puffed and set, and top is beginning to brown. Let stand for 5 minutes. Slice to serve.

1 Pie Crust (page 270), unbaked
½ to 1 cup cooked meat
½ to 1 cup cooked vegetables
1 cup shredded cheese
4 eggs
1 cup milk
2 tablespoons all-purpose flour
½ teaspoon salt
⅛ teaspoon pepper
¼ cup grated Parmesan cheese

Freezing Quiche Quiches freeze beautifully. To freeze, cut quiches into individual serving sizes and place in a hard-sided freezer container. Freeze until firm, then store up to 3 months. To thaw, heat in the microwave on high for 1–2 minutes.

Classic Cheese Soufflé

SERVES ▶ 4

Believe it or not, soufflés are one of the cheapest entrées you can make. They're made of eggs, butter, cheese, flour, and milk; that's it!

¼ cup butter

¼ cup finely chopped onion

3 tablespoons all-purpose flour

½ teaspoon salt

⅛ teaspoon pepper

1 tablespoon mustard

1 cup milk

4 eggs, separated

1 cup shredded Cheddar cheese

¼ cup grated Parmesan cheese

1. Preheat oven to 350°F. Grease the bottom of a 1-quart soufflé or casserole dish. Tear off a strip of aluminum foil 3" longer than the circumference of the dish. Fold in thirds so you have a long thin strip and butter one side. Wrap the foil around the top of the dish, buttered-side in, so 2" extends above the top of the dish.

2. In small saucepan, combine butter and onion. Cook and stir over medium heat until onion is very tender, about 5 minutes. Add flour, salt, and pepper; cook and stir for 3 minutes. Then add mustard and milk; cook and stir until thick and bubbly. Remove from heat and stir in egg yolks, one at a time. Then stir in cheeses. Set aside.

3. In medium bowl, beat egg whites until stiff peaks form. Stir a dollop of the whites into the cheese mixture. Then carefully fold in remaining egg whites. Pour into prepared pan. Bake for 50–55 minutes or until soufflé is puffed and deep golden brown. Serve immediately.

> **Soufflé Tips** For the best soufflés, here are a few rules. Be sure that the flour is thoroughly cooked in the butter before you add the milk. Stir sauce with a wire whisk to avoid lumps. Beat the egg whites last; don't make them first and let them sit. You can vigorously stir the first dollop of egg whites in the cheese sauce, but carefully fold the rest in.

Rich Baked Beans

COST PER SERVING **37¢**

On the coldest day of winter, have these beans simmering in the oven to fill your home with warmth and fabulous aroma. Serve with warm, tender Brown Bread (page 54).

Serve with warm, tender Brown Bread (page 54).

1. Sort the beans and rinse well; drain. Cover with cold water and soak overnight. The next day, drain the beans well and rinse again. Place beans in a large soup pot and cover with more cold water; bring to a boil over medium heat.

2. Simmer, uncovered, for 1½ hours. Drain beans, reserving liquid.

3. Pour beans into a 3-quart casserole dish and add onion, salt, mustard, brown sugar, ketchup, tomato paste, molasses, and pepper and mix thoroughly until well combined.

4. Add reserved bean liquid to just cover the beans. Cover the dish tightly with aluminum foil and place in oven. Bake at 325°F for 4 hours, checking once during cooking time and adding reserved bean liquid as necessary, until mixture is thick and beans are tender. Serve immediately.

SERVES ▶ 8

1 pound navy beans

1 onion, finely chopped

1 teaspoon salt

3 tablespoons mustard

½ cup brown sugar

½ cup ketchup

3 tablespoons tomato paste

½ cup molasses

¼ teaspoon pepper

Dressed-Up Macaroni and Cheese

This dinner can be whipped up in a few minutes, and it feeds three people generously for very little cost.

SERVES ► 3

2 tablespoons butter or margarine

½ cup chopped onion

1 (5.5-ounce) box macaroni and cheese mix

⅓ cup milk

2 tablespoons mustard

1 cup frozen peas, thawed

1. In medium saucepan, melt butter over medium heat. Add onion; cook and stir until tender, about 5 minutes.

2. Meanwhile, bring a large pot of water to boil. Add macaroni from package and cook according to package directions until al dente. Drain macaroni and return to pot.

3. Stir in powdered mix from package, cooked onions with butter, milk, mustard, and peas and stir until sauce is creamy and mixture is hot. Serve immediately.

Boxed Dinner Mixes There are several choices for boxed dinner mixes on the market. Often they are good buys, especially when stores have them on sale for three boxes for a dollar. They can be "dressed up" with many ingredients and are a bargain when you can add foods from your garden, like chopped tomatoes, bell peppers, zucchini, or herbs.

Scrambled Egg Crepes

COST PER SERVING
70¢

This recipe is great for brunch when you have company or as a late-night dinner. It elevates scrambled eggs to a gourmet dish; for pennies!

SERVES ▶ 6

1 cup all-purpose flour

1 cup milk

8 eggs, divided

1 tablespoon oil

½ teaspoon salt, divided

¼ cup sour cream

2 tablespoons butter

1 cup shredded Swiss cheese

1 cup shredded Cheddar cheese

1. In a blender or food processor, combine flour, milk, two eggs, oil, and ¼ teaspoon salt and blend or process until smooth. Let stand for 15 minutes.

2. Then heat an 8" nonstick skillet over medium heat and brush with ½ tablespoon butter. Pour ¼ cup batter into skillet and turn and twist skillet to spread batter evenly. Cook until the crepe can be moved, about 2 minutes, then carefully flip and cook 30 seconds on other side. Flip out onto kitchen towel. Repeat, making 8 crepes in all; do not stack hot crepes.

3. Preheat oven to 350°F. In medium bowl, beat remaining 6 eggs with sour cream and ¼ teaspoon salt. Melt remaining 1½ table-spoons butter in the nonstick skillet and pour in eggs. Cook, stirring frequently, until eggs are set but still moist.

4. Place crepes, light side up, on work surface. Divide eggs among the crepes and sprinkle with half of each of the cheeses. Roll up crepes and place, seam side down, in 9" glass baking dish. Sprinkle with remaining cheeses. Bake for 10–15 minutes or until cheeses melt. Serve immediately.

Crepes Crepes are quite easy to make, and they help you turn left-overs into a fancy dish. For the best crepes, make sure the batter is very smooth. Let it stand for a few minutes before cooking. Also, quickly turn and twist the skillet as soon as the batter hits the hot surface so the crepes are thin and even.

Spicy Thai Peanut Noodles

COST PER SERVING **53¢**

SERVES ▶ 6

1 tablespoon olive oil

1 onion, chopped

5 cloves garlic, minced

1 (16-ounce) package spaghetti pasta

½ cup Chicken Stock (page 79) or water

½ cup peanut butter

½ teaspoon ground ginger

2 tablespoons brown sugar

3 tablespoons soy sauce

⅛ teaspoon cayenne pepper

1 cup chopped peanuts

To make this even spicier, you could add a minced jalapeño pepper, or some crushed red pepper flakes if you have some on hand.

1. Bring a large pot of salted water to a boil. In large saucepan, heat olive oil over medium heat. Add onion and garlic; cook and stir until tender, about 5 minutes.

2. When water comes to a boil, add the spaghetti and cook according to package directions until al dente. Meanwhile, add stock, peanut butter, ginger, brown sugar, soy sauce, and cayenne pepper to onions. Bring to a simmer and cook, stirring, for 3 minutes.

3. When pasta is done, drain, reserving ½ cup pasta cooking water. Add pasta to saucepan; cook and stir until pasta is coated, about 1–2 minutes. Add reserving cooking water as needed to make a smooth sauce. Sprinkle with peanuts and serve immediately.

Broccoli Quiche

COST PER SERVING **69¢**

SERVES ▶ 6

1 tablespoon butter

1 onion, chopped

1 cup frozen broccoli pieces, thawed

1 (10.75-ounce) can cream of broccoli soup

3 eggs

½ cup milk

1 cup shredded mozzarella cheese

1 Pie Crust (page 270), unbaked

3 tablespoons grated Parmesan cheese

You can use this method with any flavor of soup. Use chopped cooked ham with cream of potato soup, or cooked ground beef with condensed cheese soup.

1. Preheat oven to 350°F. In medium saucepan, melt butter over medium heat. Add onion; cook and stir until tender, about 4 minutes. Add drained broccoli; cook and stir until water evaporates, about 3 minutes. Remove from heat.

2. Stir in undiluted soup, eggs, and milk and beat well until combined. Stir in mozzarella cheese, then pour mixture into pie crust. Sprinkle with Parmesan cheese. Bake for 40–50 minutes or until quiche is puffed and set. Serve immediately.

Double Cheese Quesadillas

COST PER SERVING **45¢**

Quesadillas are so easy to make and you can vary the recipe in countless ways. For example, you can use colored or corn tortillas or vary the cheese. To splurge, add ingredients like cooked ground beef, chicken, or bacon.

SERVES ▶ 4

1 cup grated Cheddar cheese

1 cup grated Swiss cheese

½ teaspoon dried Italian seasoning

8 (8-inch) flour tortillas

2 tablespoons butter, softened

1. In small bowl, combine cheeses and Italian seasoning; toss well. Place four tortillas on work surface; divide cheese mixture among them. Top with remaining tortillas.

2. Heat a large skillet over medium heat. Spread butter on both sides of each quesadilla and place in skillet. Cook, pressing down with a spatula, until first side is golden brown, about 3–5 minutes. Carefully turn each quesadilla and cook, pressing down with a spatula, until cheese is melted and second side is golden brown, about 2–5 minutes. Remove to serving plate, cut into quarters, and serve, with salsa for dipping, if you like.

Tortillas Tortillas freeze beautifully and they thaw in minutes. Make sure that you put them into a freezer bag; don't freeze them in the original wrapper. You might want to separate each one with some waxed paper so you can remove them individually. To thaw, microwave on 30 percent power for about 30 seconds.

Cheese Pizza

SERVES ▶ 6

You don't need yeast to make this pizza crust. It's flaky and light and is made in a flash. For a splurge, add pepperoni or cooked sausage or ground beef.

1 tablespoon cornmeal

2 cups all-purpose flour

1 teaspoon baking powder

½ teaspoon salt

⅓ cup solid shortening

⅓ cup water

⅓ cup milk

1 (8-ounce) can tomato sauce

3 tablespoons mustard

2 cups shredded mozzarella cheese

1. Preheat oven to 425°F. Grease a 12" pizza pan with solid short-ening and sprinkle with cornmeal. In large bowl combine flour, baking powder, and salt and mix well. Cut in shortening until particles are fine. Add water and milk and stir until a dough forms. Press into prepared pizza pan and bake for 10 minutes.

2. While crust is baking, in small bowl combine tomato sauce and mustard. Remove crust from oven and spread sauce over dough. Sprinkle with cheese. Bake for 15–25 minutes or until crust is deep golden brown and cheese is melted and beginning to brown. Serve immediately.

Pizza Toppings Almost any leftover makes a great pizza topping. Chili, of course, is a no brainer. Any cooked meat or vegetable is delicious, as is any leftover cheese. In fact, save up the bits and ends of cheeses as you use them and combine them all for a special pizza blend.

Lentil Soup

COST PER SERVING
54¢

*Add any vegetables you have around to this easy soup.
Chopped carrots or celery would be a nice addition.*

1. In soup pot, heat olive oil over medium heat. Add onions and garlic; cook and stir until tender, about 5 minutes. Meanwhile, sort over lentils and rinse.

2. Add lentils to the pot along with water, drained (but not rinsed) beans, and tomatoes. Bring to a boil, then reduce heat, cover, and simmer for 1–2 hours or until lentils are soft. Season with salt and pepper and serve.

SERVES ▶ 6

2 tablespoons olive oil

2 onions, chopped

5 cloves garlic, minced

1½ cups lentils

6 cups water

1 (15-ounce) can beans, kidney or black

1 (14-ounce) can diced tomatoes, undrained

1 teaspoon salt

⅛ teaspoon pepper

Simple Spaghetti

COST PER SERVING
41¢

Garlicky toasted bread crumbs are the cheese substitute in this amazing dish that is made out of almost nothing at all. You can even omit the tomato topping if you don't have any.

1. Bring a large pot of salted water to a boil. In small bowl, combine tomatoes, basil, salt, and pepper and mix well; set aside. Make crumbs out of the bread and set aside.

2. Cook pasta according to package directions until al dente. Meanwhile, in large saucepan heat olive oil and butter over medium heat. Add garlic; cook and stir for 2 minutes. Add bread crumbs; cook and stir for 5–6 minutes or until bread is golden brown and toasted.

3. As soon as pasta is done, drain and add to pan with bread crumbs. Toss with tongs and place in serving bowl. Top with tomato mixture and serve immediately.

SERVES ▶ 6

1 tomato, chopped

½ teaspoon dried basil leaves

1 teaspoon salt

⅛ teaspoon pepper

4 slices Oatmeal Bread (page 53)

1 (16-ounce) package spaghetti

2 tablespoons olive oil

2 tablespoons butter

5 cloves garlic, minced

Easiest Cheese Soufflé

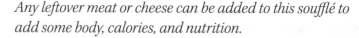
COST PER SERVING
55¢

SERVES ▶ 4

5 eggs, separated

1 (11-ounce) can condensed cheese soup

½ cup grated Cheddar cheese

1 cup leftover vegetables, if desired

1 cup leftover cooked meat, if desired

Any leftover meat or cheese can be added to this soufflé to add some body, calories, and nutrition.

1. Preheat oven to 325°F. Grease the bottom of a 1½-quart soufflé dish or casserole dish and set aside. In large bowl, beat egg yolks until light and lemon colored. Add soup and cheese, beating well.

2. In small bowl, beat egg whites until very stiff. Stir a dollop of the egg whites into the egg yolk mixture. Then carefully fold remaining egg whites into the egg yolk mixture.

3. Place vegetables and meat, if using, in the bottom of the prepared soufflé dish. Pour egg mixture carefully over the vegetables. Bake for 45–55 minutes or until soufflé is puffed and deep golden brown. Serve immediately.

Egg Whites Egg are easiest to separate when they're cold, straight from the fridge, and beat to the highest volume when they are warmer. Let egg whites sit at room temperature for about 30 minutes before beating them. A bit of acid will help stabilize the foam; add a pinch of cream of tartar or about a teaspoon of lemon juice before you start beating.

Hash Brown Pizza

COST PER SERVING
81¢

Shred potatoes directly into a bowl of ice water to keep them from turning brown, then drain well before tossing with the onion. For a splurge, add pepperoni!

SERVES ▶ 6

1. Preheat broiler. Brush a 12" ovenproof skillet with olive oil. Drain potatoes well in a kitchen towel. In large bowl, toss potatoes with half of onion, salt, and pepper. Heat skillet over medium-high heat until very hot. Carefully add potatoes; arrange in an even layer and press down with a spatula.

2. Cook for 5 minutes, occasionally shaking the pan so the potatoes don't stick, until potatoes are golden brown on the bottom. Transfer to the broiler; broil for 3–6 minutes or until top is golden brown. Set aside. Turn oven to bake at 425°F.

3. In small bowl, combine tomato sauce, tomato paste, and Italian seasoning; mix well. Spread over potatoes and sprinkle with cheeses. Bake pizza for 15–20 minutes or until hot and cheese is melted and bubbling.

2 tablespoons olive oil

3 potatoes, shredded

1 onion, finely chopped and divided

½ teaspoon salt

⅛ teaspoon pepper

1 (8-ounce) can tomato sauce

2 tablespoons tomato paste

1 teaspoon dried Italian seasoning

1 cup shredded Cheddar cheese

1 cup shredded mozzarella cheese

⅓ cup grated Parmesan cheese

Pasta Primavera

Use any fresh vegetable that is in your crisper. Or, you could use any canned vegetable you have on hand; just drain it and add at the very end of cooking.

SERVES ▶ 4

1 tablespoon olive oil

1 onion, chopped

1 cup chopped yellow summer squash or zucchini

2 cloves garlic, minced

1 (12-ounce) package spaghetti pasta

½ cup milk

⅓ cup sour cream

1 tablespoon cornstarch

¼ teaspoon salt

2 tablespoons mustard

⅓ cup grated Parmesan cheese

1. Bring a large pot of salted water to a boil. Meanwhile, in large saucepan combine olive oil and onion. Cook and stir until crisp-tender, about 4 minutes. Add squash and garlic; cook for 3 minutes longer.

2. When water boils, add pasta; cook until al dente according to package directions. In small bowl, combine milk, sour cream, cornstarch, salt, and mustard and mix well. Add to saucepan with vegetables; heat until simmering.

3. Drain pasta and add to saucepan; toss with tongs until coated. Sprinkle with cheese and serve.

Whole Wheat Pasta Whole wheat pastas are fairly new on the supermarket scene. Generally they are about twice as expensive as plain white pastas. But if you are concerned about your fiber intake or the consumption of "empty" carbs, you may want to consider using them. They're still much cheaper than any type of meat, and they are delicious too.

Pasta for Pennies

Creamy Fettuccine

COST PER SERVING
65¢

SERVES ▶ 6

½ cup heavy cream

¼ cup milk

4 eggs

¼ cup grated Parmesan cheese

½ teaspoon salt

⅛ teaspoon pepper

2 cups frozen peas

1 (16-ounce) package spaghetti

⅓ cup shredded Parmesan cheese

This super simple recipe is perfect for the days when all you have is pasta, cheese, eggs, and milk on hand.

1. Bring a large pot of salted water to a boil. Meanwhile, in medium bowl combine cream, milk, eggs, cheese, salt, and pepper and mix with wire whisk; set aside.

2. Place peas in colander and place in sink. Cook spaghetti until al dente according to package directions. Drain over peas in colander and return to pot.

3. Stir egg mixture again and add to pot. Toss together with pasta and peas over medium heat for 2–3 minutes or until sauce forms and mixture is hot. Sprinkle with shredded Parmesan cheese and serve immediately.

Linguine with Mushroom Sauce

COST PER SERVING
69¢

SERVES ▶ 6

1 tablespoon olive oil

1 tablespoon butter

1 onion, chopped

3 cloves garlic, minced

1 (4-ounce) can mushroom pieces, drained

1 (10.75-ounce) can condensed cream of mushroom soup

1¼ cups milk

⅛ teaspoon nutmeg

1 (16-ounce) package linguine

⅓ cup grated Parmesan cheese

When condensed soups go on sale, stock up! They are an excellent addition to many recipes and can be used as sauce for chicken or beef.

1. Bring a large pot of salted water to a boil. Meanwhile, in large saucepan, combine olive oil and butter over medium heat. Add onion and garlic; cook and stir until tender, about 5 minutes.

2. Add mushrooms; cook and stir for about 3 minutes. Add soup, milk, and nutmeg; stir and bring to a simmer.

3. Cook linguine until al dente according to package directions. Drain and add to saucepan with mushroom mixture. Sprinkle with half of cheese and toss to coat. Serve immediately, topped with remaining cheese.

Pasta e Fagioli

COST PER SERVING
$1 10

This dish is usually served as a soup, but this version is a very thick stew studded with beans, onions, and garlic.

SERVES ▶ 10

1. Sort beans and rinse; drain, then cover with cold water. Let soak overnight. In the morning, drain beans and set aside.

2. In large soup pot, cook onion, garlic, and celery in olive oil until crisp-tender, about 4 minutes. Add the beans, ham bone, water, and pepper, and bring to a boil. Reduce heat, then cover and simmer for 3 hours, stirring occasionally.

3. Remove ham bone and cut meat off bone. Return meat to pot and discard bone.

4. Using a potato masher, mash some of the beans. Add Italian seasoning, tomatoes, pasta, and red pepper flakes to pot. Bring to a boil and cook until pasta is tender, about 6–8 minutes or according to package directions. Serve with pesto and Parmesan cheese.

1 pound dried navy beans

2 tablespoons olive oil

2 onions, chopped

5 cloves garlic, minced

3 stalks celery, chopped

1 ham bone

8 cups water

⅛ teaspoon pepper

1 teaspoon dried Italian seasoning

1 (14-ounce) can diced tomatoes, undrained

1 (12-ounce) package ditalini or small shell pasta

¼ teaspoon red pepper flakes

½ cup Spinach Pesto (page 28)

½ cup shredded Parmesan cheese

> **Pasta in Soup** When pasta is cooked directly in soup or stews, it takes a few minutes longer to reach al dente. But it will be more flavorful, because it absorbs herbs and spices from the broth or liquid while it is cooking. Just be sure to stir occasionally and taste the pasta until it reaches the perfect texture.

Amatriciana

COST PER SERVING
92¢

SERVES ▶ 6

This classic Italian dish is usually prepared with pancetta instead of bacon and without onions. For a splurge, you can make it that way too.

4 slices bacon

4 links pork sausage

2 tablespoons olive oil

2 onions, chopped

1 jalapeño pepper

4 cloves garlic, minced

1 (14-ounce) can diced tomatoes

1 (6-ounce) can tomato paste

¼ teaspoon red pepper flakes

1 (16-ounce) package linguine

½ cup grated Romano cheese

1. Bring a large pot of salted water to a boil. Meanwhile, cook bacon in a large skillet until crisp. Remove bacon from pan, crumble, and set aside. Cook sausage in drippings remaining in skillet, turning frequently, until browned. Remove to paper towel and cut into ½" pieces.

2. Drain fat from skillet but do not clean. Add olive oil and heat over medium heat. Add onions, jalapeño, and garlic and cook for 5 minutes. Add undrained tomatoes, tomato paste, and red pepper flakes and cook, stirring frequently, until blended; add reserved bacon and sausage.

3. When water comes to a boil, cook pasta until al dente according to package directions. Drain pasta, reserving ½ cup cooking water. Add cooking water to saucepan to help thin the sauce. Add pasta and toss over medium heat for 2–3 minutes. Sprinkle with cheese and serve immediately.

Pork Lo Mein

COST PER SERVING $1.52

Hoisin sauce, made from garlic, vinegar, and fermented soybeans, adds great flavor to this or any stir-fry, and it lasts forever when stored in the fridge.

1. Bring a large pot of salted water to a boil. In small bowl, combine chicken stock, soy sauce, hoisin sauce, cornstarch, sugar, and vinegar and set aside.

2. Cook pasta as directed on package until almost al dente, then drain and rinse with cold water; set aside.

3. In large skillet or wok, heat olive oil over medium high heat. Add pork chops; stir-fry until almost cooked, about 3–4 minutes. Remove pork from skillet. Add onion and garlic; stir-fry for 3 minutes. Then add bell pepper and squash; stir-fry for 2 minutes longer.

4. Stir cornstarch mixture and add to skillet along with reserved pork; bring to a simmer. Add pasta; stir-fry for 3–4 minutes or until pasta is tender. Add bean sprouts, stir-fry for 1 minute. Serve immediately.

> *Lo Mein* Lo Mein is like a combination of Asian and Italian foods; stir-fry using spaghetti instead of rice. Cook the pasta until almost al dente; it will continue cooking in the last few minutes with the rest of the ingredients, and will soak up the flavors of the sauce. Leftovers from these recipes are excellent in frittatas.

SERVES ▶ 6

1 cup Chicken Stock (page 79)

¼ cup soy sauce

3 tablespoons hoisin sauce

2 tablespoons cornstarch

1 tablespoon sugar

2 tablespoons apple cider vinegar

1 (12-ounce) package thin spaghetti

2 tablespoons olive oil

4 (4-ounce) pork chops, thinly sliced

1 onion, chopped

4 cloves garlic, minced

1 green bell pepper, chopped

1 yellow summer squash, sliced

1 cup bean sprouts

Chicken Tetrazzini

COST PER SERVING $1.03

SERVES ▶ 8

This classic recipe looks complicated, but it goes together quickly. In addition, it makes a fabulous casserole to serve a crowd with only three chicken breasts!

2 tablespoons olive oil

2 tablespoons butter

1 onion, chopped

4 cloves garlic, minced

3 Slow Cooker Simmered Chicken Breasts (page 145)

2 (4-ounce) cans mushroom pieces

¼ cup all-purpose flour

½ teaspoon salt

⅛ teaspoon pepper

½ teaspoon thyme leaves

1 (16-ounce) package spaghetti pasta

1 cup Chicken Stock (page 79)

1 cup light cream or whole milk

1 tablespoon mustard

½ cup sour cream

1 cup shredded Muenster cheese

⅓ cup grated Parmesan cheese

1. Preheat oven to 350°F. Grease a 2-quart casserole dish and set aside. Bring a large pot of salted water to a boil. In large saucepan, combine olive oil and butter over medium heat. When butter melts, add onion and garlic; cook and stir until crisp-tender, about 4 minutes.

2. Remove meat from chicken; chop and set aside. Drain mushrooms, reserving juice. Add mushrooms to saucepan and cook for 1 minute. Sprinkle with flour, salt, pepper, and thyme leaves; cook and stir until bubbly, about 3 minutes.

3. Cook pasta until almost al dente according to package directions. Add stock, light cream, and reserved mushroom liquid to flour mixture in saucepan and bring to a simmer. Cook until thickened, about 5 minutes.

4. Drain pasta and add to sauce along with chicken. Stir in mustard, sour cream, and Muenster cheese and pour into prepared casserole. Sprinkle with Parmesan cheese and bake for 30–40 minutes or until casserole bubbles and begins to brown on top. Serve immediately.

Chicken Puttanesca

COST PER SERVING $1$35

Chicken thighs add a rich flavor to this easy and delicious pasta recipe.

SERVES ▶ 4

1. Bring a large pot of salted water to a boil over high heat. Meanwhile, in large skillet heat olive oil over medium heat. Sprinkle chicken with flour, salt, and pepper. Add chicken to skillet and cook for 5 minutes without moving. Turn chicken and cook for 3 minutes on the second side; remove to a platter.

2. To drippings remaining in skillet, add garlic and anchovy paste; cook and stir to melt anchovy paste for 2–3 minutes. Add tomatoes and tomato paste and bring to a simmer. Shred chicken and return to sauce. Simmer sauce for 10 minutes.

3. Cook pasta as directed on package until al dente. Stir olives into sauce and continue simmering. Drain pasta and add to skillet with sauce. Toss over low heat for 2 minutes, then serve.

3 tablespoons olive oil

2 boneless, skinless chicken thighs

2 tablespoons all-purpose flour

½ teaspoon salt

⅛ teaspoon cayenne pepper

4 cloves garlic, minced

1 tablespoon anchovy paste

1 (14-ounce) can diced tomatoes, undrained

¼ cup tomato paste

½ cup chopped green olives

1 (12-ounce) package spaghetti

Puttanesca Puttanesca literally means "pasta of the ladies of the evening." Where did the name originate? History is blurry on this subject. It may be because the dish is hot and spicy, or because it's an inexpensive dish that can be made quickly. The dish always includes anchovies, garlic, and some hot spice, either cayenne pepper, Tabasco sauce, or red pepper flakes.

Linguine with Clam Sauce

COST PER SERVING
$1³⁵

If you love garlic, add more! This creamy clam sauce is delicious served blended with perfectly cooked pasta. Just add some garlic bread and eat.

SERVES ► 6

3 tablespoons butter

2 tablespoons olive oil

1 onion, chopped

5 cloves garlic, minced

1 (16-ounce) package linguine

2 (6.5-ounce) cans minced clams, undrained

1 (4-ounce) can mushroom pieces, undrained

½ teaspoon dried basil leaves

3 tablespoons lemon juice

¼ cup sour cream

1 tablespoon cornstarch

¼ cup minced parsley

1. Bring a large pot of salted water to a boil. Meanwhile, in large saucepan, combine butter and olive oil over medium heat. When butter melts, add onion and garlic; cook and stir until tender, about 5 minutes.

2. Add pasta to boiling water and cook until almost al dente according to package directions. Meanwhile, add undrained clams, mushrooms, basil, and lemon juice to saucepan and bring to a simmer.

3. When pasta is done, drain and add to saucepan with sauce. In small bowl, combine sour cream and cornstarch and blend with wire whisk. Add to saucepan; cook and stir until mixture bubbles, about 4–6 minutes. Sprinkle with parsley and serve.

Homemade Pasta

COST PER SERVING 6¢

You can vary the amount of whole wheat flour you use in this recipe, but don't exceed a ratio of 2 parts all-purpose flour to 1 part whole wheat.

SERVES ► 4

1 cup all-purpose flour

½ cup whole wheat flour or all-purpose flour

¼ teaspoon baking powder

¼ teaspoon salt

1 egg, beaten

2 tablespoons milk

2 tablespoons water

1. In medium bowl, combine flours with salt and baking powder and mix well. In small bowl, combine egg, milk, and water and mix well. Add to flour mixture and stir until a dough forms. Knead the dough right in the bowl, adding more all-purpose flour if necessary, until smooth and elastic, about 5–6 minutes.

2. Cover dough with towel and let rest for 15 minutes. Then roll dough out onto floured surface into ⅛" thickness. Roll dough and cut into ¼" slices. Unroll slices and let air dry for 20–30 minutes before cooking.

3. To cook pasta, bring a large pot of salted water to a boil. Add pasta and cook for 1–2 minutes or until al dente; drain and serve.

Freezing Homemade Pasta Homemade pasta can be frozen after it is rolled, cut, and dried. Be sure it's not moist or sticky to the touch. You might want to toss it with a spoonful of flour so it will not stick together. Place in large freezer bag and seal, sealing in some air along with the pasta. Label and freeze for up to 3 months. Cook for a minute or two longer than normal.

Spaghetti Pizza

This hearty meatless casserole serves a crowd for very little money. For a splurge, add cooked sausage or pepperoni to the tomato sauce.

1 tablespoon olive oil

1 onion, chopped

3 cloves garlic, minced

2 (4-ounce) cans mushroom pieces

1 (8-ounce) can tomato sauce

1 teaspoon dried Italian seasoning

½ teaspoon salt

⅛ teaspoon cayenne pepper

1 pound spaghetti pasta

3 eggs

½ cup milk

1 cup shredded mozzarella cheese

1 cup shredded sharp Cheddar cheese

1. Preheat oven to 350°F. Spray a 13" x 9" glass baking dish with nonstick cooking spray and set aside. Bring a large pot of salted water to a boil.

2. In medium saucepan, heat olive oil over medium heat. Add onion, garlic, and drained mushrooms; cook and stir until crisp-tender, about 5 minutes. Add tomato sauce, Italian seasoning, salt, and pepper; cook for 15 minutes, stirring occasionally.

3. When water boils, cook pasta until al dente according to package directions. In large bowl, combine eggs and milk and beat well. When pasta is done, drain and immediately add to bowl with egg mixture; toss with tongs to coat.

4. Pour spaghetti mixture into prepared dish and spread evenly. Spoon tomato sauce over all, then sprinkle with cheeses. Bake 30–40 minutes or until casserole is hot and cheeses are melted and beginning to brown. Let stand for 5 minutes, then cut into squares to serve.

Penne with Squash

COST PER SERVING $1.23

Penne, which means "quill" in Italian, is a tubular pasta cut on an angle into short sections. It's delicious in this creamy and sweet sauce.

SERVES ▶ 6

1. Bring a large pot of salted water to a boil. Peel squash and cut into ½" cubes. Place in medium saucepan along with milk, basil, salt, and pepper. Bring to a boil over high heat. Reduce heat to medium, cover, and simmer until squash is tender, about 8–10 minutes.

2. Meanwhile, in large saucepan, cook bacon until crisp. Remove bacon, crumble, and set aside. Cook onion and garlic in bacon drippings until tender, about 5 minutes.

3. Cook pasta until al dente according to package directions. When squash is tender, cut cream cheese into cubes and add to squash mixture; cover and remove from heat.

4. Drain pasta and add to large saucepan with onions. Stir squash mixture and add to saucepan along with bacon. Toss with tongs over medium heat until mixture blends and sauce thickens. Sprinkle with Parmesan and serve immediately.

1 butternut squash

1 cup milk

1 teaspoon dried basil leaves

½ teaspoon salt

⅛ teaspoon pepper

4 slices bacon

1 onion, chopped

2 cloves garlic, minced

1 (16-ounce) package penne pasta

1 (3-ounce) package cream cheese

½ cup grated Parmesan cheese

About Squash There are two basic kinds of squash: summer and winter. Summer squash has a thin skin and cooks quickly; vegetables in this category include yellow squash and zucchini. Winter squash is very hard, with a thick skin; vegetables in this category include butternut, pumpkin, and acorn squash. To prepare winter squash, first peel the skin, then cut in half. Scrape out the seeds and cube the flesh.

Greek Pasta

SERVES ► 6

2 tablespoons olive oil

1 tablespoon butter

2 onions, chopped

3 cloves garlic, minced

2 cups frozen chopped spinach, thawed

1 (14-ounce) can diced tomatoes, undrained

½ teaspoon salt

⅛ teaspoon pepper

1 (16-ounce) package linguine

½ cup crumbled feta cheese

You can turn pasta into any ethnic cuisine just with the ingredients you choose. This Greek pasta is flavorful and delicious.

1. Bring a large pot of salted water to a boil. Meanwhile, in large saucepan combine olive oil and butter over medium heat. When butter melts, add onion and garlic; cook and stir until crisp-tender, about 4 minutes.

2. Add spinach to pan; cook and stir until water evaporates. Add undrained tomatoes, salt, and pepper and bring to a simmer. Reduce heat and cover.

3. Cook pasta until al dente according to package directions. Drain pasta, reserving ¼ cup cooking water. Add pasta to saucepan and toss gently, adding some of the reserved cooking water if necessary. Sprinkle with feta and serve immediately.

Al Dente Al Dente is the Italian term that translates literally as "to the tooth." This means that the pasta is tender to the bite, but still has a slightly give in the center. It's important to not overcook pasta or it will become gummy. Start testing the pasta a couple of minutes before the package says it is done to be sure it's perfect.

Pasta with Fresh Tomatoes

COST PER SERVING
67¢

This is the perfect dish to make in summer when your garden is lush. The cost per serving, if you use your own tomatoes and basil, is about 15¢.

SERVES ▶ 4

1. Bring a large pot of salted water to a boil. Meanwhile, in medium bowl combine olive oil, tomatoes, garlic, basil, and cheese and mix well.

2. Cook pasta until al dente, about 1–2 minutes. Immediately drain and toss with tomato mixture; serve immediately.

2 tablespoon olive oil

3 tomatoes, chopped

2 cloves garlic, minced

2 tablespoons chopped fresh basil

⅓ cup shredded Parmesan cheese

1 batch Homemade Pasta (page 213)

Spaghetti and Meatballs

COST PER SERVING
$1⁵⁷

Adding flavor to a plain tomato sauce costs half as much as buying a jar of flavored pasta sauce. And it makes your kitchen smell terrific!

SERVES ▶ 6

1. In large pot, heat olive oil over medium heat. Add onion and garlic; cook and stir until crisp-tender, about 3 minutes. Add tomato paste. Cook, without stirring, until the tomato paste begins to brown in spots. Then stir in water, scraping up brown bits from pan. Add tomato sauce, Italian seasoning, salt, and pepper and bring to a simmer. Simmer for 30 minutes.

2. Bring a large pot of salted water to a boil. Meanwhile, add the cooked meatballs to the sauce along with ¼ cup Parmesan cheese; continue simmering. Cook pasta until al dente according to package directions. Drain and return to pot.

3. Stir 1 cup of the sauce into the drained pasta and arrange on serving plate. Top with remaining sauce, meatballs, and sprinkle with remaining ¼ cup Parmesan cheese. Serve immediately.

1 tablespoon olive oil

1 onion, chopped

3 cloves garlic, minced

2 tablespoons tomato paste

¼ cup water

1 (29-ounce) can tomato sauce

1 teaspoon dried Italian seasoning

½ teaspoon salt

⅛ teaspoon pepper

½ cup grated Parmesan cheese, divided

1 batch Sicilian Meatballs (page 135)

1 (16-ounce) package spaghetti

The Best Macaroni and Cheese

SERVES ► 6

Macaroni and cheese is such delicious comfort food. Use any type of cheese you'd like; Fontina and Colby would also be a nice combination.

3 tablespoons butter, divided

1 onion, chopped

2 cups macaroni pasta

1 (12-ounce) can evaporated milk

¼ cup all-purpose flour

1 tablespoon mustard

½ teaspoon salt

⅛ teaspoon pepper

½ cup water

1 cup shredded Cheddar cheese

1 cup shredded American cheese

2 slices Oatmeal Bread (page 53), crumbled

1. Preheat oven to 375°F. Bring a large pot of salted water to a boil. Meanwhile, in large saucepan melt 1 tablespoon butter over medium heat. Add onion; cook and stir until tender, about 5 minutes.

2. Cook pasta as directed on package until al dente; drain, rinse with cold water, and drain again. In small bowl, combine milk, flour, mustard, salt, and pepper; whisk until smooth. Add to onions along with water and bring to a simmer; simmer for 3–5 minutes until thickened.

3. Remove saucepan from heat and add cheeses and pasta. Pour into 2-quart baking dish. In small microwave-safe bowl, melt remaining 2 tablespoons butter. Add bread crumbs and toss to coat. Sprinkle on pasta mixture in casserole. Bake for 30–35 minutes or until casserole bubbles and bread crumb topping is browned. Serve immediately.

Melting Cheese Cheese should generally be melted over low heat or it might separate or become tough and stringy. Pasteurized process cheeses, like American cheese or some presliced cheeses, melts perfectly every time, but natural cheeses can still make a smooth sauce. Be sure to melt the cheese into the sauce off the heat and stir constantly.

Pasta with Spinach Pesto

COST PER SERVING $1^{16}

Serve this simple, yet elegant, dish with some cooked salmon and a simple fruit salad.

SERVES ► 4

1 tablespoon olive oil

1 onion, chopped

3 cloves garlic, minced

1 (12-ounce) package spaghetti

1 cup Spinach Pesto (page 28)

½ cup chopped toasted walnuts

¼ cup grated Parmesan cheese

1. Bring a large pot of salted water to a boil. Meanwhile, in large saucepan heat olive oil over medium heat. Add onion and garlic; cook and stir until crisp-tender, about 4 minutes. Remove from heat.

2. Cook pasta according to package directions until almost al dente. Drain, reserving ½ cup pasta cooking water.

3. Return saucepan with onions to medium heat. Add drained pasta and pesto, with a few tablespoons cooking water; toss to form a sauce. Add more cooking water if necessary.

4. Sprinkle with walnuts and cheese and serve immediately.

Toasting Nuts Toasting nuts enhances the flavor, meaning you can use less. To toast nuts, spread in a single layer on a cookie sheet. Toast in a preheated 350°F oven for 8–10 minutes, stirring once, until nuts are fragrant and turn a darker color. Let cool completely before chopping or grinding; if the nuts are still warm, they will become oily.

Country Lasagna

Using macaroni instead of lasagna noodles helps reduce the cost and also makes this hearty dish easier to prepare.

SERVES ▶ 8–10

½ pound ground pork sausage

½ pound 80 percent lean ground beef

1 onion, chopped

3 cloves garlic, minced

1 green bell pepper, chopped

2 (4-ounce) cans mushroom pieces, undrained

1 (14-ounce) can diced tomatoes, undrained

1 (6-ounce) can tomato paste

1 tablespoon Worcestershire sauce

1 teaspoon dried Italian seasoning

½ teaspoon salt

½ cup water

⅛ teaspoon cayenne pepper

1 pound macaroni

3 tablespoons butter

1 cup diced Cheddar cheese

1 cup shredded mozzarella cheese

⅓ cup grated Parmesan cheese

1. Bring a large pot of salted water to a boil. Meanwhile, in large saucepan, combine sausage, ground beef, onion, and garlic over medium heat. Cook, stirring to break up meat, until meat is cooked. Drain thoroughly.

2. Add bell pepper to saucepan; cook and stir for 2–3 minutes. Then add mushrooms and their liquid, tomatoes, tomato paste, Worcestershire sauce, Italian seasoning, salt, water, and cayenne pepper; bring to a simmer and let simmer for 10 minutes.

3. Cook macaroni until al dente according to package directions. Drain and return to pot; add butter and let melt.

4. Preheat oven to 350°F. Spray a 13" x 9" glass baking dish with nonstick cooking spray. Put ½ cup of the meat sauce in the bottom, then top with ⅓ of the macaroni. Dot with ⅓ of the Cheddar cheese. Repeat layers, ending with meat sauce. Sprinkle with mozzarella and Parmesan cheese.

5. Bake for 35–45 minutes or until casserole is bubbling and cheese is melted and beginning to brown.

▶ CHAPTER 16 ◀

Side Dishes on Sale

Roasted Scalloped Corn

COST PER SERVING
64¢

Scalloped corn is an old-fashioned recipe that is excellent served with ham or pork. Add a green salad for a nice dinner.

1 (10-ounce) package frozen corn, thawed

2 tablespoons olive oil, divided

1 tablespoon butter

1 onion, finely chopped

2 cloves garlic, minced

2 slices Oatmeal Bread (page 53), toasted

1 (15-ounce) can creamed corn

2 eggs, beaten

½ teaspoon salt

⅛ teaspoon pepper

¾ cup shredded Cheddar cheese

¼ cup grated Parmesan cheese

1. Preheat oven to 425°F. Spray a 9" casserole dish with nonstick cooking spray and set aside. Drain thawed corn and place on cookie sheet. Drizzle with 1 tablespoon olive oil and toss to coat. Roast for 10–20 minutes or until corn just starts to turn color. Remove from oven and set aside. Reduce oven temperature to 350°F.

2. In large saucepan, heat remaining 1 tablespoon olive oil with butter over medium heat. Add onion and garlic; cook and stir until tender, about 5 minutes. Remove from heat and set aside.

3. Crumble the toasted bread to make fine crumbs; reserve ¼ cup. Stir crumbs into onion mixture along with roasted corn and creamed corn; mix well. Add eggs, salt, and pepper, beating well to combine. Stir in Cheddar cheese.

4. Pour into prepared casserole dish. In small bowl, combine reserved crumbs with the Parmesan cheese and sprinkle over the top of the corn mixture. Bake for 20–30 minutes or until casserole is set and beginning to brown.

Scalloped Vegetables Scalloped means to cook in a cream sauce or a white sauce. You can achieve the same effect without making a white sauce; just beat together eggs and milk and stir that into cooked vegetables, then pour into a casserole and bake. This is a great way to turn leftover vegetables into another dish.

Black and White Bean Stir-Fry

This colorful side dish can also be served as a vegetarian main dish, along with Double Corn Bread (page 41) and some fresh fruit.

1. In small bowl, combine soy sauce, cornstarch, water, honey, and pepper; mix well and set aside.

2. In large skillet, heat olive oil over medium heat. Add onion and bell pepper; stir-fry until crisp-tender, about 4 minutes. Add carrots; stir-fry for another minute.

3. Meanwhile, drain and rinse black beans and navy beans; drain thoroughly. Add to skillet; stir-fry gently for 2 minutes.

4. Stir sauce and add to skillet; stir-fry until sauce bubbles and thickens, about 3 minutes. Sprinkle with chives and serve immediately.

SERVES ► 6

1 tablespoon soy sauce
1 tablespoon cornstarch
2 tablespoons water
1 tablespoon honey
⅛ teaspoon pepper
2 tablespoons olive oil
1 onion, chopped
1 green bell pepper, chopped
1 cup shredded carrots
1 (15-ounce) can black beans
1 (15-ounce) can navy beans
¼ cup chopped chives

Sautéed Peas and Radishes

Frozen sweet peas are a great value. Unless you're picking the peas directly from your garden, frozen peas are actually the freshest because they're processed right after picking.

Melt butter in saucepan over medium heat. Add radishes; cook and stir until the radish skins turn light pink. Add peas and water and bring to a simmer. Simmer for 2–3 minutes or until peas are hot. Sprinkle with salt and pepper and serve.

SERVES ► 4

2 tablespoons butter
2 radishes, thinly sliced
2 cups frozen sweet peas
¼ cup water
½ teaspoon salt
⅛ teaspoon pepper

Creamy Mashed Potatoes

COST PER SERVING 22¢

Dried potato flakes are made from 100 percent potatoes, and they are delicious and nutritious. These additions make them taste even better.

2 cups water

⅓ cup milk

3 tablespoons butter

2 cups potato flakes

⅓ cup sour cream

¼ cup grated Parmesan cheese

1. In large saucepan, combine water, milk, and butter over high heat. Bring to a rolling boil, then add potatoes flakes and remove from heat.

2. Let stand for 1 minute, then whip with a fork. Stir in sour cream and Parmesan cheese, cover, and let stand for 2 minutes, then serve.

Dried Potato Handling Make sure that you handle potatoes made from dried potato flakes just as carefully as any other perishable food. Refrigerate leftovers promptly, and be sure never to leave the prepared potatoes at room temperature for more than 2 hours. Store the flakes in a cool, dry, dark place and obey the use-by dates.

Honey Carrots

COST PER SERVING 28¢

SERVES ▶ 6

Remember, whole carrots are the best value, but if you're pressed for time, you could substitute prepared sliced carrots or frozen sliced carrots.

8 carrots, peeled and sliced

2 cups water

3 tablespoons butter

2 cloves garlic, minced

3 tablespoons honey

½ teaspoon salt

⅛ teaspoon pepper

1. In large saucepan, combine carrots and water and bring to a boil. Reduce heat, cover, and simmer for 4–5 minutes or until carrots are just barely tender. Drain and place carrots in serving bowl.

2. Return pan to heat and add butter and garlic. Cook and stir over medium heat until garlic is fragrant. Return carrots to pot and add honey, salt, and pepper. Cook and stir for 2–3 minutes until carrots are glazed. Serve immediately.

Zucchini Picadillo

COST PER SERVING
96¢

Picadillo is a Latin dish typically made of ground beef, tomatoes, raisins, and olives. This complex side dish is great with a broiled steak, or for a vegetarian lunch dish.

1. In large saucepan, heat olive oil over medium heat. Add onion and garlic; cook and stir until crisp-tender, about 4 minutes. Add zucchini and tomatoes; bring to a simmer. Cover and simmer for 5 minutes.

2. Stir in rice, raisins, olives, salt, and pepper and bring to a simmer. Simmer, stirring frequently, until mixture is hot and well blended. Serve immediately.

> *Hearty Side Dishes* Many hearty side dishes can be served as vegetarian main dishes. For instance, Zucchini Picadillo can be served with warmed flour tortillas and some grated cheese to let diners make their own burritos. Or serve them with Double Corn Bread (page 41) or even spooned into split Popovers (page 49).

SERVES ▶ 6

2 tablespoons olive oil

1 onion, chopped

3 cloves garlic, minced

2 zucchini, sliced

1 (14-ounce) can diced tomatoes, undrained

2 cups cooked rice

¼ cup raisins

¼ cup sliced green olives

½ teaspoon salt

⅛ teaspoon pepper

Old-Fashioned Apples and Onions

SERVES ▶ 4

This sweet and tart side dish is perfect served with a grilled steak or some sautéed chicken breasts.

2 tablespoons butter
1 tablespoon olive oil
2 onions, chopped
2 cloves garlic, minced
2 Granny Smith apples, sliced
2 tablespoons brown sugar
1 tablespoon apple cider vinegar
½ teaspoon salt
⅛ teaspoon pepper

1. In saucepan, combine butter and olive oil over medium heat. When butter melts, add onions and garlic. Cook and stir for 5–6 minutes until soft. Add apples; cook and stir for 1 minute.

2. Sprinkle with brown sugar, vinegar, salt, and pepper. Cover saucepan and cook for 5–7 minutes, shaking pan occasionally, until apples are just tender. Stir gently and serve.

Apples for Cooking For recipes like this one, you need firm tart apples to contrast with the sweet onions. Granny Smith apples are not only inexpensive, but they are tart and crisp and keep their shape when cooked. Don't peel the apples unless the recipe tells you to; the peel adds fiber and nutrition.

Roasted Vegetables

SERVES ▶ 6

By roasting in stages, each vegetable is cooked to perfection in this delicious medley. Be sure to save some to make Sicilian Bread Salad (page 111).

2 russet potatoes, cubed
1 onion, chopped
3 cloves garlic, minced
3 tablespoons olive oil
1 teaspoon salt
⅛ teaspoon pepper
1 (14-ounce) package whole frozen green beans
1 (10-ounce) package frozen corn
1 green bell pepper, chopped
1 cup frozen peas

1. Preheat oven to 400°F. In large roasting pan, combine potatoes, onions, and garlic and toss. Drizzle with olive oil and sprinkle with salt and pepper; toss to coat. Roast for 30 minutes, then remove from oven.

2. Add green beans along with corn to pan; turn vegetables with a large spatula. Return to oven and roast for 20 minutes longer. Remove from oven.

3. Add bell pepper and peas and turn with spatula again. Return to oven and roast for 10–20 minutes longer or until potatoes and all vegetables are hot and tender. Serve immediately.

COST PER SERVING **79¢**

COST PER SERVING **99¢**

Polenta—Two Ways

COST PER SERVING **21¢**

You can serve this polenta immediately, or chill it, slice it, and fry it to crisp perfection to be used in recipes like Beef Ragout with Polenta (page 127).

(page 127)

1. In large saucepan, combine stock, water, and salt and bring to a rolling boil. Add cornmeal slowly, stirring constantly with a wire whisk. Cook, stirring constantly, over medium heat until the cornmeal thickens, about 12–17 minutes. Remove from heat and add cheese and butter, stirring until mixture is smooth.

2. You can now serve the polenta immediately, or chill it to fry the next day.

3. To chill, butter a 9" × 13" pan and spread polenta in an even layer. Cover and chill until very firm, at least 8 hours.

4. The next day, cut polenta into 3" squares. Heat olive oil in a large skillet over medium heat. Fry polenta squares until crisp and golden brown, turning once, about 2–3 minutes per side. Serve immediately.

Polenta Polenta, also known as cornmeal mush, has been nourishing populations for centuries. Its mild flavor means you can flavor it a thousand different ways. And, if you serve it with beans, wheat, or legumes, you're serving foods that can be used by your body as complete proteins, making it the ideal vegetarian main dish idea.

SERVES ► 12

3 cups Chicken Stock (page 79) or water

4 cups water

2 cups yellow cornmeal

1 teaspoon salt

⅓ cup grated Parmesan cheese

2 tablespoons butter

2 tablespoons olive oil

Roasted Potatoes

COST PER SERVING 57¢

SERVES ▶ 8

5 pounds russet potatoes

3 tablespoons olive oil

2 onions, chopped

4 cloves garlic, minced

1 teaspoon salt

⅛ teaspoon pepper

If you don't peel the potatoes you won't have any waste, and the dish will have more vitamins and fiber.

1. Preheat oven to 400°F. Scrub potatoes and cut into 1" pieces. Place in large roasting pan and drizzle with olive oil. Sprinkle with onion, garlic, salt, and pepper and toss with hands until vegetables are coated with oil.

2. Bake, uncovered, for 30 minutes. Using a spatula, turn the vegetables; arrange in even layer. Bake for 35 minutes longer or until potatoes are tender and beginning to brown. Serve immediately.

> **Storing Potatoes** Potatoes need to be stored in a cool, dark place. Do not store them in the refrigerator; the cool temperatures will cause the starches to turn to sugars and the potatoes will taste sweet when cooked. Also, be sure to store potatoes and onions far away from each other; they emit gasses that cause the others to over ripen.

Garlic-Parmesan Green Beans

COST PER SERVING 73¢

SERVES ▶ 4

1 (14-ounce) package frozen whole green beans

3 cloves garlic, minced

2 tablespoons olive oil

¼ teaspoon salt

⅛ teaspoon pepper

⅓ cup grated Parmesan cheese

Frozen whole green beans are a bit more expensive than cut green beans, but the result when roasted is so much better it's worth the extra 50 cents.

1. Preheat oven to 450°F. Place frozen beans on a cookie sheet with sides. Roast for 10 minutes, stirring once, until beans are thawed and liquid has evaporated. Remove beans from oven and reduce temperature to 400°F.

2. Sprinkle beans with garlic, olive oil, salt, and pepper and toss with tongs to coat. Sprinkle with cheese and return to oven. Roast for 10–15 minutes longer or until beans are tender and cheese has melted. Serve immediately.

Classic Sweet Potatoes

COST PER SERVING
52¢

*Double this delicious casserole to serve eight at Thanksgiving.
The crunchy sweet topping is the perfect complement to the
smooth potatoes.*

SERVES ► 4

1. Preheat oven to 350°F. Spray a 1-quart baking dish with nonstick cooking spray and set aside. In small bowl, combine 2 tablespoons butter, brown sugar, flour, and mix well. Stir in granola and set aside.

2. Place sweet potatoes in large bowl and mash with potato masher. Beat in egg, milk, and remaining 1 tablespoon butter. Place in prepared dish and sprinkle with granola mixture.

3. Bake for 20–30 minutes or until potatoes are hot and topping is crunchy and brown. Serve immediately.

3 tablespoons butter, melted, divided

¼ cup brown sugar

2 tablespoons all-purpose flour

½ cup Whole Grain Granola (page 62)

1 (17-ounce) can vacuum-pack sweet potatoes

1 egg

2 tablespoons milk

> *Old-Fashioned Recipes* There's a reason that old-fashioned, or classic, recipes have been around a while. They always taste good, are nutritious, and are usually quite inexpensive to make. After all, grape tomatoes, filet mignon, and marinated salmon steaks have been available for only a short time in the timeline of food history.

Two Potato Gratin

Serve this creamy and crunchy dish alongside some grilled hamburgers or with the roasted Thanksgiving turkey.

SERVES ▶ 6

2 slices Hearty White Bread (page 48)

4 tablespoons butter, divided

2 tablespoons grated Parmesan cheese

1 onion, chopped

2 tablespoons all-purpose flour

1 teaspoon salt

⅛ teaspoon white pepper

1¼ cups milk

2 tablespoons mustard

½ teaspoon dried dill weed

1 sweet potato

2 russet potatoes

1. Crumble bread into tiny pieces with fingers and place in small bowl. In small microwave-safe dish, melt 2 tablespoons butter. Drizzle over bread crumbs and add Parmesan cheese; toss and set aside.

2. Preheat oven to 350°F. In medium saucepan, combine 2 tablespoons butter and the onion; cook and stir until onion is tender, about 5 minutes. Sprinkle with flour, salt, and pepper; cook until bubbly, about 3 minutes. Add milk; cook and stir until thickened, about 5 minutes. Stir in mustard and dill weed.

3. Grease a 2-quart baking dish with butter. Peel potatoes and grate directly into the baking dish. Top with milk mixture, stirring gently to coat. Sprinkle top with bread crumb mixture. Bake for 40–50 minutes or until potatoes are tender and top is golden brown and crusty.

Garlic Lemon Broccoli

COST PER SERVING **60¢**

Frozen florets cost a little bit more than chopped broccoli, but the presentation is so much nicer it's worth the extra 12¢ per serving.

1. In large saucepan, combine olive oil and butter over medium heat. Add garlic; cook and stir until fragrant, about 2–3 minutes. Then add thawed but not drained broccoli and bring to a boil.

2. Reduce heat and cook until most of the liquid evaporates. Remove pan from heat and sprinkle with salt, lemon zest, and pepper. Drizzle lemon juice over, toss, and serve immediately.

Lemon in Vegetables Lemon juice not only adds fabulous flavor to fresh or frozen vegetables, it also helps preserve the color and adds a bit of nutrition. Fresh lemon juice tastes so much better than bottled that it's worth the small extra cost. To squeeze a lemon, first roll it firmly on the counter with the palm of your hand, then slice and squeeze. Juice freezes well too.

SERVES ► 4

1 tablespoon olive oil

1 tablespoon butter

3 cloves garlic, minced

1 (13-ounce) package frozen broccoli florets, thawed

½ teaspoon salt

½ teaspoon lemon zest

2 tablespoons lemon juice

⅛ teaspoon pepper

Mushroom Rice Pilaf

COST PER SERVING **24¢**

Mushrooms add a rich earthy flavor to this simple pilaf. Use it for any recipe that calls for hot cooked rice.

1. In large saucepan, melt butter over medium heat. Add onion; cook and stir until crisp-tender, about 4 minutes. Meanwhile, drain mushrooms, reserving juice, and cut mushrooms into smaller pieces. Add mushrooms to saucepan.

2. Stir in rice; cook and stir for 2–3 minutes or until rice becomes opaque. Add reserved mushroom liquid, water or stock, and salt. Bring to a boil, then reduce heat, cover, and simmer for 20–25 minutes or until liquid is absorbed and rice is tender.

3. Add parsley, remove from heat, cover pan, and let stand for 5 minutes. Fluff rice with a fork and serve.

SERVES ► 6

2 tablespoons butter

1 onion, finely chopped

1 (4-ounce) can mushroom pieces

1½ cups long grain white rice

2½ cups water or Chicken Stock (page 79)

½ teaspoon salt

¼ cup chopped fresh parsley

Vegetable Rice

COST PER SERVING
27¢

SERVES ▶ 6

1 tablespoon butter
1 tablespoon olive oil
½ onion, chopped
½ cup shredded carrots
1½ cups long grain rice
3 cups water
½ teaspoon salt
⅛ teaspoon pepper

Adding some vegetables to rice makes them a heartier accompaniment. Serve this dish with any main dish with sauce.

1. In large saucepan, heat butter and olive oil over medium heat. Add onion; cook and stir until crisp-tender, about 4 minutes. Add carrot and rice; cook and stir for 2–3 minutes longer.

2. Add water, salt, and pepper. Bring to a boil, then cover, reduce heat to low, and simmer for 20–25 minutes or until rice is tender. Remove from heat and let stand for 5 minutes, then fluff rice with fork and serve.

Cooking Rice Different types of rice cook at different times. White rice, which has had the bran and endosperm removed, cooks the quickest. Brown and wild rice take the longest to cook. For fool proof rice, cook in a large amount of water like you do pasta, testing until it's tender, then draining thoroughly.

Zucchini Medley

COST PER SERVING
78¢

SERVES ▶ 4

2 tablespoons butter
1 tablespoon olive oil
1 onion, chopped
1 zucchini, chopped
1 cup frozen corn
1 cup frozen peas
½ teaspoon salt
⅛ teaspoon pepper
⅓ cup grated Parmesan cheese

This will serve 4–6 people, depending on the size of the zucchini! At the end of the harvest, some zucchini can get very large.

1. In large skillet, combine butter and olive oil over medium heat. Add onion; cook and stir for 2 minutes.

2. Add zucchini, corn, and peas. Cook and stir for 2 minutes, then cover skillet and cook for 3 minutes. Uncover and stir again; sprinkle with salt and pepper and cook for 1–2 minutes longer until vegetables are tender and hot. Sprinkle with cheese and serve.

CHAPTER 17

Sate Your Sweet Tooth: Cookies and Candy

Chocolate Marshmallow Balls

COST PER COOKIE 10¢

YIELDS ▶ 48 BALLS

Let the chocolate mixture cool until it's lukewarm; then the marshmallows won't melt when mixed in with the graham cracker crumbs. For a splurge, use cashews.

¼ cup butter

1¼ cups sugar

1 (14-ounce) can sweetened condensed milk

1 (1-ounce) square unsweetened chocolate

¼ cup cocoa powder

1 teaspoon vanilla

30 individual graham crackers, crushed

1 (8-ounce) package miniature marshmallows

1 cup chopped walnuts

1. In large saucepan, combine butter, sugar, condensed milk, chocolate, and cocoa powder. Cook over low heat, stirring frequently, until chocolate melts. Continue cooking, stirring constantly, until the sugar dissolves and mixture is smooth. Remove from heat and add vanilla. Let cool for 30 minutes.

2. Reserve 1 cup of the graham cracker crumbs. Add remaining crumbs, marshmallows, and walnuts to chocolate mixture in saucepan and mix well. Chill for 30 minutes. Then form into 1" balls. Roll balls in reserved graham cracker crumbs. Chill until firm; store covered at room temperature.

No-Bake Cookies   There are some secrets to making the best no-bake cookies. They're almost always cooked on the stovetop or in the microwave. Be absolutely sure that the sugar is dissolved before you stop cooking. If you don't, the finished cookies will be grainy. Also follow cooling and shaping instructions carefully.

Potato Chip Cookies

COST PER SERVING 9¢

Leftover potato chips (plain variety only, please!) make a crisp and crunchy cookie that's slightly salty. You'll need about 1-1/4 cups of chips to make the fine crumbs.

1. Preheat the oven to 350°F. Make sure that potato chips are crushed very fine. In large bowl, combine butter, margarine, sugar, brown sugar, and powdered sugar and beat until smooth. Add vanilla and mix well. Stir in flour, then work in potato chip crumbs and chopped chocolate chips.

2. Press dough into 1" balls and place on ungreased cookie sheets. Dip the bottom of a drinking glass in granulated sugar and press down on cookies to flatten to ¼" thickness. Bake for 8–12 minutes or until cookies are light golden brown around the edges and on the bottom. Cool on pans for 3 minutes, then remove to wire racks to cool.

YIELDS ► 36 COOKIES

⅔ cup finely crushed plain, salted potato chips

½ cup butter, softened

¼ cup margarine

½ cup sugar

¼ cup brown sugar

¼ cup powdered sugar

1½ teaspoons vanilla

1¾ cups all-purpose flour

½ cup semisweet chocolate chips, chopped

Brown Sugar Shortbread

COST PER COOKIE 17¢

These bar cookies taste a lot like a popular name-brand candy bar, but they are tender and chewy rather than ultra crunchy. For a splurge, use all butter and cashews in place of walnuts.

1. Preheat oven to 325°F. In large bowl, combine butter and margarine along with brown sugar; beat until blended. Add egg and beat well. Stir in vanilla, then oatmeal, flour, whole wheat flour, and salt. Spread mixture into 10" x 15" jelly roll pan. Bake 15–25 minutes or until bars are set.

2. In small microwave-safe bowl, combine both kinds of chocolate chips. Melt at 50 percent power for 2 minutes, then remove from microwave and stir until melted and smooth. Pour over warm bars and spread carefully. Sprinkle with nuts, then cool completely and cut into bars.

YIELDS ► 36 BARS

½ cup butter, softened

½ cup margarine

1 cup brown sugar

1 egg

2 teaspoons vanilla

1 cup oatmeal, ground

1½ cups all-purpose flour

¼ cup whole wheat flour

½ teaspoon salt

1 cup semisweet chocolate chips

1 cup milk chocolate chips

1 cup chopped walnuts

Casserole Cookies

Purchase whole dates for this recipe. You can find them in the bulk section of the supermarket. The precut dates are too hard and won't dissolve as the mixture bakes.

YIELDS ► 36 COOKIES

3 eggs

½ cup sugar

½ cup brown sugar

1 cup finely chopped dates

1 cup chopped walnuts

1 cup regular oatmeal

1 teaspoon vanilla

½ cup white chocolate chips, chopped

Powdered sugar

1. Preheat oven to 350°F. In large bowl, beat eggs until light yellow. Gradually add sugar and beat until fluffy. Then add brown sugar and beat well. Stir in dates, walnuts, and oatmeal and mix well. Place mixture in a 2-quart casserole dish. Bake for 30–40 minutes, stirring once during baking, until light golden brown.

2. Remove casserole from oven and beat mixture for 3 minutes. Then let cool until lukewarm. Stir in vanilla and white chocolate chips. Form mixture into 1" balls and roll in powdered sugar. Let cool completely; store covered at room temperature.

Vanilla Pure vanilla extract can be very expensive. In fact, you can buy gourmet extract, made from premium vanilla beans. Imitation extract is much less expensive. You can use the imitation when the flavor isn't as important, or when the recipe already has many different flavors, as in this recipe.

Filled Peanut Butter Cookies

COST PER SERVING **7¢**

These cookies are reminiscent of a popular name-brand candy.

1. In large bowl, combine flour, brown sugar, baking soda, and salt and mix with wire whisk until sugar is evenly distributed. Cut in margarine until small crumbs form. Add peanut butter and corn syrup and mix well. Form dough into 2 rolls, about 2" in diameter. Wrap in waxed paper and chill for at least 2 hours.

2. Preheat oven to 350°F. In small bowl, combine 6 tablespoons peanut butter and powdered sugar and beat until smooth. Slice dough ⅛" thick and place half the slices on ungreased cookie sheets. Top each with about ½ teaspoon of the peanut butter filling and sprinkle with some of the chocolate chips.

3. Top with remaining slices of dough and press edges to seal. Bake 10–12 minutes or until cookies are set and light golden brown on bottom. Let cool on cookie sheets for 4 minutes, then remove to wire racks to cool completely.

YIELDS ► 36 COOKIES

1½ cups all-purpose flour

½ cup brown sugar

½ teaspoon baking soda

¼ teaspoon salt

½ cup margarine or butter

½ cup chunky peanut butter

¼ cup light corn syrup

6 tablespoons peanut butter

2 tablespoons powdered sugar

6 tablespoons milk chocolate chips, chopped

Coconut Chews

COST PER BAR **18¢**

These chewy bars are rolled in powdered sugar when cooled to seal in the moistness. For a splurge, use macadamia nuts in place of the walnuts.

1. Preheat oven to 350°F. In 9" x 13" pan, combine graham cracker crumbs, butter, and ½ cup chopped coconut and mix well. Press into pan. Bake for 10 minutes, then remove from oven.

2. In large bowl, beat egg yolks until light colored. Add brown sugar, 1 cup coconut, and nuts and beat well. In small bowl, beat egg whites until stiff. Fold into the egg yolk mixture. Pour on top of crust and bake 25–30 minutes or until set. Cool completely, then cut into bars and roll bars in powdered sugar to coat.

YIELDS ► 36 BARS

2 cups graham cracker crumbs

½ cup butter, melted

½ cup flaked coconut, finely chopped

3 eggs, separated

2 cups brown sugar

1 cup flaked coconut

1 cup chopped walnuts

Powdered sugar

Caramel Tea Cakes

COST PER COOKIE **10¢**

These cookies are a variation on traditional tea cakes, but with a bit of brown sugar and caramel sauce added for more flavor. For a splurge, use pecans instead of walnuts.

YIELDS ► 36 COOKIES

⅓ cup margarine

½ cup butter, softened

⅓ cup brown sugar

2 tablespoons powdered sugar

2 tablespoons caramel ice-cream topping

1 teaspoon vanilla extract

2½ cups all-purpose flour

¼ teaspoon salt

1 cup finely chopped walnuts

Extra powdered sugar

1. In large bowl, combine margarine, butter, brown sugar, powdered sugar, ice-cream topping, and vanilla and beat until smooth. Stir in flour, salt, and walnuts and mix until a dough forms. Cover and chill dough for at least 2 hours.

2. When ready to bake, preheat oven to 400°F. Form dough into 1" balls and place 1" apart on ungreased cookie sheets. Place more powdered sugar in a shallow bowl. Bake cookies 9–12 minutes until they are set and light golden brown on the bottom.

3. Remove cookies from cookie sheet and drop into powdered sugar. Roll to coat, then set on wire racks to cool. When cookies are cool, re-roll in powdered sugar. Store covered at room temperature.

Storing Cookies Most cookies are stored at room temperature. Soft cookies should be tightly covered so they don't dry out. You can add an apple slice to the container to keep the cookies soft. Crisp cookies can be stored in looser containers, like cookie jars. Line your cookie jar with a plastic food storage bag for easiest cleanup.

Fudge Frosted Brownies

COST PER SERVING 25¢

What's a cookie plate without brownies? These are fudgy and creamy, and less expensive because they use cocoa powder instead of baking chocolate.

YIELDS ► 36 BARS

1. Preheat oven to 325°F. Spray a 9" x 13" baking pan with nonstick cooking spray and set aside. In large microwave-safe bowl, combine butter and margarine with brown sugar and cocoa; microwave on high for 1 minute. Remove from oven and stir; return and microwave on high for 1–2 minutes longer until butter is melted.

2. Add sugar and beat well. Then add eggs and vanilla and beat until blended. Fold in flour, salt, and baking powder until mixed; add walnuts. Pour into prepared pan and bake for 25–35 minutes or until brownies are just set. Cool for 30 minutes.

3. In small microwave-safe bowl, combine condensed milk with both kinds of chocolate chips. Microwave on medium power for 2 minutes, then remove and stir. Return to microwave and cook for 30–second intervals on high until chips are melted. Stir until smooth, then pour over warm brownies. Cool completely and cut into bars.

½ cup butter

½ cup margarine

1 cup brown sugar

⅔ cup cocoa

1 cup sugar

3 eggs

2 teaspoons vanilla

1½ cups all-purpose flour

½ teaspoon salt

1 teaspoon baking powder

1 cup chopped walnuts

1 (14-ounce) can sweetened condensed milk

1 cup semisweet chocolate chips

1 cup milk chocolate chips

About Cocoa There are many varieties of cocoa powder, from the gourmet to the generic. For baking, the cheapest will work just fine. Dutch cocoa powder has been neutralized to a pH of about 7, which makes a milder flavor, but it is more expensive. Most recipes are based on regular cocoa powder.

Cinnamon Cookies

Graham crackers and brown sugar combine to create a crunchy crust on these tender little cookies. Pack them into lunchboxes for a nice surprise.

YIELDS ► 48 COOKIES

½ cup butter, softened

½ cup margarine

1 cup sugar

1½ cups brown sugar, divided

2 eggs

1 teaspoon vanilla

2⅓ cups all-purpose flour

1 teaspoon baking powder

1 teaspoon baking soda

½ teaspoon salt

2 teaspoons cinnamon, divided

½ cup crushed graham cracker crumbs

1. Preheat oven to 350°F. In large bowl, combine butter, margarine, sugar, and 1 cup brown sugar and beat until fluffy. Add eggs and vanilla and beat until combined. Then stir in flour, baking powder, baking soda, salt, and 1 teaspoon cinnamon.

2. On shallow plate, combine ½ cup brown sugar, graham cracker crumbs, and 1 teaspoon cinnamon and mix well. Form dough into ¾" balls and roll in graham cracker mixture to coat; gently press graham cracker mixture into cookies so it doesn't fall off. Place on ungreased cookie sheets. Bake 10–14 minutes or until cookies are set and light golden brown. Cool on wire racks; store at room temperature.

Replace Your Spices Dried spices (and herbs too) only retain their flavor for about a year. When you buy fresh spices, mark the purchase date on the bottle or jar with a grease pencil. After they are about six months old, smell them before using. If the spice doesn't smell intense and flavorful, chances are it won't add flavor to the recipe. Discard and buy new spices.

Homemade Caramels

COST PER CARAMEL 4¢

Homemade caramels are a fabulous treat. They're so inexpensive to make compared to candy shop caramels. And so much better!

YIELDS ► 81 CARAMELS

1. Grease 9" x 9" square pan with unsalted butter and set aside. In large heavy saucepan, combine all ingredients except vanilla. Bring to a boil over high heat, then cover and let boil for 2 minutes to let steam wash down sugar crystals on sides of pan. Uncover, reduce heat to medium, and cook until mixture reaches 248°F or hard ball stage.

2. Remove from heat and add vanilla. Immediately pour into prepared pan and let stand. When firm cut into small squares and wrap individually in waxed paper.

1 cup sugar

½ cup brown sugar

½ cup light corn syrup

½ cup heavy cream

½ cup butter

½ cup whole milk

2 teaspoons vanilla

Hard Ball Stage When making crystalline candy like caramels, a sugar syrup is cooked until some of the liquid evaporates. As the mixture concentrates, it will form shapes in cold water. Caramels are cooked to hard ball stage, or 248°F. Use a candy thermometer, or drop a bit of the candy in cold water. If it forms a ball that is hard but not brittle, the candy is done.

Kit 'n Cat Bars

YIELDS ► 36 BARS

2 sleeves rectangular salted crackers, divided

1¼ cups brown sugar

½ cup butter

½ cup milk

1 cup peanut butter, divided

1 (12-ounce) package semisweet chocolate chips

The candy that these cookies are based upon is one of the most popular name-brands in the world. You can use any kind of plain cracker you'd like in this easy recipe.

1. Remove ¼ of the crackers from one sleeve and crush finely. Put a layer of the whole crackers in the bottom of a 9" x 13" pan and set aside.

2. In large saucepan, combine cracker crumbs, brown sugar, butter, and milk and bring to a boil over medium-high heat. Boil, stirring constantly, for 5 minutes. Remove from heat and stir in ½ cup peanut butter until melted. Pour over the crackers in pan. Top with a layer of crackers.

3. In medium microwave-safe bowl, combine chocolate chips with ½ cup peanut butter. Microwave for 2 minutes at 50 percent power; remove from microwave and stir. Return to microwave for another 30 seconds at 50 percent power. Remove and stir until smooth. Pour over bars and spread gently to cover. Cool completely and cut into bars.

Peanut Butter There are many brands and varieties of peanut butter on the market. You can spend a lot of money for "natural" brands and even the name brands, but, especially in baking, the generic brands are just fine. Try a couple of generic varieties and you'll probably find one that your kids love spread on toast or crackers for snacks.

Caramel Coconut Bars

COST PER BAR **14¢**

*These chewy bar cookies are so good and so easy to make.
They keep well, if you have any left to store!*

YIELDS ▶ 36 BARS

1. Preheat oven to 325°F. Grease a 9" x 13" pan with solid shortening and dust with flour; set aside. In large bowl, combine margarine, 1 cup brown sugar, and eggs and beat well. Add flour and mix until a dough forms. Spread into prepared pan.

2. In small bowl, combine condensed milk, coconut, and vanilla and mix well. Spoon and spread over crust. Bake 15–25 minutes or until bars are light golden brown. Cool completely.

3. In small saucepan, combine butter with ¼ cup brown sugar; cook and stir over medium heat until mixture blends and comes to a boil. Remove from heat and add 2 tablespoons milk. Beat in powdered sugar, then add enough additional milk for spreading consistency. Frost bars, let stand until firm, then cut into squares.

1 cup margarine or butter, softened

1¼ cups brown sugar, divided

2 eggs

1½ cups all-purpose flour

1 (14-ounce) can sweetened condensed milk

2 cups coconut

1 teaspoon vanilla

¼ cup butter

3 cups powdered sugar

3–4 tablespoons milk

Oatmeal No-Bake Bars

YIELDS ▶ 36 BARS

This easy bar cookie is perfect for summer because you don't have to bake them. The chewy chocolate and peanut butter mixture is layered over a buttery crumb crust.

2 cups crushed graham cracker crumbs

¼ cup brown sugar

½ cup finely chopped peanuts

½ cup butter, melted

2 cups sugar

½ cup milk

½ cup butter

1 cup peanut butter

3 cups quick-cooking oatmeal

1 (11-ounce) package milk chocolate chips

1. In large bowl, combine graham cracker crumbs, brown sugar, and peanuts and mix well. Stir in ½ cup melted butter until crumbs are coated. Press into a 9" × 13" pan and set aside.

2. In heavy saucepan, combine sugar, milk, and ½ cup butter and cook over medium heat, stirring frequently, until mixture boils. Boil, stirring constantly, for 2 minutes. Remove from heat and stir in peanut butter until smooth. Then stir in oatmeal until blended.

3. Pour over graham cracker crust. Chill until firm. In heavy saucepan, melt chocolate chips over very low heat, stirring until smooth. Spoon and spread over bars, then chill again until firm. Store covered in the refrigerator.

Graham Cracker Crumbs You can purchase graham cracker crumbs already crushed, but they are much more expensive. Thirty square graham crackers, crushed, will yield about 2 cups. To crush the crackers, break them into pieces and place them in a heavy duty plastic bag. Using a rolling pin, crush the crackers into fine crumbs, turning the bag as you work.

Raisin Bars

COST PER BAR
14¢

These old-fashioned bars have the best flavor; the combination of soft raisins and spices with the tender cookie is really wonderful.

1. Preheat oven to 350°F. Spray a 10" x 15" jelly roll pan with baking spray containing flour and set aside. In large saucepan, combine raisins with water and bring to a boil. Remove from heat and stir in margarine, sugar, brown sugar, lemon juice, and ¼ cup milk; stir until margarine is melted. Add eggs and 1 teaspoon vanilla and beat well.

2. Stir in flour, whole wheat flour, spices, salt, and baking soda and mix well. Pour into prepared pan. Bake 20–35 minutes or until bars are light golden brown and spring back when lightly touched with finger. Let cool until warm.

3. While bars are still warm, combine powdered sugar, ¼ cup milk, and 1 teaspoon vanilla in small bowl and beat until smooth. Spoon and spread over warm bars. Let cool completely, then cut into squares. Store covered at room temperature.

YIELDS ► 48 BARS

1½ cups dark raisins

1½ cups water

¾ cup margarine

¾ cup sugar

¼ cup brown sugar

1 tablespoon lemon juice

½ cup milk, divided

2 eggs

2 teaspoons vanilla, divided

2 cups all-purpose flour

½ cup whole wheat flour

1 teaspoon cinnamon

½ teaspoon cloves

¼ teaspoon allspice

¼ teaspoon nutmeg

½ teaspoon salt

½ teaspoon baking soda

2 cups powdered sugar

Chocolate Tassies

YIELDS ▶ 48 COOKIES

1 (12-ounce) package semisweet chocolate chips, divided

2½ cups finely crushed graham crackers

1 cup finely chopped walnuts

¼ cup butter

¼ cup margarine

1 (13-ounce) can evaporated milk

1 cup brown sugar

1 cup milk chocolate chips

Tassies are little cakes and cookies that are baked in muffin tins. It's essential that you use mini muffin tins in this recipe; in regular tins, the mixture will not bake through.

1. Preheat oven to 375°F. Spray mini muffin cups with nonstick baking spray containing flour and set aside. In medium microwave-safe bowl, melt 1 cup of the semisweet chocolate chips at 50 percent power; stir until smooth; set aside. In large bowl, combine remaining semisweet chocolate chips, graham crackers, and walnuts.

2. In medium bowl, combine butter, margarine, and brown sugar and mix until fluffy. Gradually add melted chocolate, then evaporated milk, beating thoroughly. Pour over graham cracker mixture; stir until combined. Fill each muffin tin about ⅔ full. Bake 8–12 minutes or until set. Let cool in muffin tins for 3 minutes, then carefully remove and cool completely on wire rack.

3. In microwave-safe small bowl, heat milk chocolate chips at 50 percent power for 1 minute; remove and stir until smooth. Frost tassies; let stand until firm.

> *Chocolate Chips* There are many new varieties of chocolate chips that appear (and unfortunately disappear) on the market. Current favorites include dark chocolate/white chocolate swirl as well as a caramel filled milk chocolate chip. As long as the label says "100 percent real" you can substitute generic brands of chocolate chips for the name brands and save quite a bit of money.

Chocolate Cream Bars

COST PER SERVING **10¢**

This recipe makes two jelly roll pans of bars, which are frosted and put together. Refrigerate half of the batter while you're baking the first pan.

1. Preheat oven to 350°F. Line two 10" × 15" jelly roll pans with foil; grease foil and set aside. In large bowl, combine cake mix, pudding mix, eggs, and 1½ cups milk. Beat until combined, then beat at medium speed for 2 minutes. Divide into prepared pans. Bake for 15–20 minutes or until set.

2. Let cool in pans for 30 minutes, then invert onto kitchen towels sprinkled with powdered sugar. Let cool completely.

3. In saucepan, combine flour, cocoa powder, and ½ cup milk; mix with wire whisk. Cook over medium heat until thick, then stir in vanilla and chill until cold. In bowl, beat together sugar and margarine until sugar dissolves. Gradually beat in the chilled flour mixture until very fluffy. Spread on one bar, top with the second. Let stand until set, then slice bars and wrap in plastic wrap.

YIELDS ► 48 BARS

1 (18-ounce) package chocolate cake mix

1 (3-ounce) package instant chocolate pudding mix

4 eggs

2 cups milk, divided

3 tablespoons all-purpose flour

3 tablespoons cocoa powder

1 teaspoon vanilla

1 cup sugar

1 cup margarine

Butterscotch Brownies

COST PER BAR **15¢**

The ground oatmeal adds chewiness to this updated brownie recipe.

1. Preheat oven to 350°F. Spray a 9" × 13" pan with baking spray containing flour and set aside. In heavy saucepan, melt butter over medium heat. Cook butter, stirring constantly, until brown flecks appear. Remove from heat and stir in brown sugar. Beat in eggs and corn syrup. Add ground oatmeal and butterscotch chips.

2. Stir in vanilla, flour, and baking powder and mix well. Spoon batter into prepared pan. Bake 25–35 minutes or until just set. Do not overbake. Let cool on wire rack.

3. For frosting, combine sugar, milk, and 2 tablespoons butter in heavy saucepan. Cook over medium heat until mixture comes to a rolling boil. Remove from heat and stir in chocolate chips, beating until frosting is smooth. Pour over cooled brownies and let stand until firm. Cut into bars and store at room temperature.

YIELDS ► 36 BARS

½ cup butter

1½ cups brown sugar

2 eggs

2 tablespoons corn syrup

½ cup ground oatmeal

½ cup butterscotch chips, ground

1½ teaspoons vanilla

1½ cups all-purpose flour

1½ teaspoons baking powder

1 cup sugar

¼ cup milk

2 tablespoons butter

1 (12-ounce) package semisweet chocolate chips

Frosted Ginger Cookies

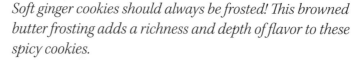

Soft ginger cookies should always be frosted! This browned butter frosting adds a richness and depth of flavor to these spicy cookies.

YIELDS ► 48 COOKIES

½ cup butter, softened

1 cup brown sugar

½ cup sour cream

½ cup buttermilk

½ cup molasses

2½ cups all-purpose flour

¼ teaspoon salt

1 teaspoon ground ginger

½ teaspoon cinnamon

¼ teaspoon nutmeg

2 teaspoons baking soda

¼ cup butter

⅓ cup brown sugar

¼ cup milk

1 teaspoon vanilla

2–3 cups powdered sugar

1. In large bowl, combine ½ cup butter with brown sugar and beat well. Then add sour cream, buttermilk, and molasses and beat again. Stir in flour, salt, ginger, cinnamon, nutmeg, and baking soda until a dough forms. Cover dough and chill for at least 1 hour in the fridge.

2. Preheat oven to 375°F. Roll dough into 1" balls and place on ungreased cookie sheets. Flatten slightly with palm of hand. Bake 8–13 minutes or until cookies are puffed and set. Let cool on baking sheet 2–3 minutes, then remove to wire racks to cool.

3. For frosting, in heavy saucepan melt ¼ cup butter over medium heat. Continue cooking butter, stirring frequently, until butter just begins to brown, about 7–9 minutes. Remove from heat and add brown sugar and milk; stir with wire whisk. Then add vanilla. Stir in enough powdered sugar until spreading consistency. Frost cooled cookies.

Browned Butter Browned butter adds great flavor to any recipe, but it can be tricky to make. The milk proteins in butter turn brown when they reach a certain temperature. The proteins break down and recombine to form the complex flavors and the brown color. Watch the butter carefully as it's cooking, because it goes very quickly from brown to black.

Oatmeal Raisin Cookies

 COST PER COOKIE **7¢**

Three kinds of oatmeal make these cookies nice and chewy.
Toasting the uncooked oatmeal adds nice flavor and crunch.

1. Preheat oven to 350°F. Place the quick cooking oatmeal and rolled oatmeal on a cookie sheet and bake 5–10 minutes, stirring frequently, until oatmeal is fragrant and light golden brown around the edges. Remove from cookie sheet and cool.

2. In large bowl, combine margarine, oil, brown sugar, and sugar and beat until smooth. Stir in honey, eggs, and leftover oatmeal and mix well. Add flour and baking soda and mix. Then stir in toasted and cooled oatmeal, walnuts, and raisins.

3. Drop by teaspoons onto greased cookie sheets. Bake 10–13 minutes or until cookies are set and golden brown around the edges. Cool on pans for 3 minutes, then remove to wire racks to cool. Store covered at room temperature.

> **Oatmeal: Quick or Regular?** Regular oatmeal is made from groats, or whole oat kernels, which have been hulled. Quick oatmeal is a more finely cut version. It does make a difference which type you use. The regular oatmeal will be more separate and discrete in cookies, while the quick oatmeal will blend more with the batter.

YIELDS ▶ 48 COOKIES

½ cup quick-cooking oatmeal

½ cup rolled oatmeal

½ cup margarine

¼ cup oil

1 cup brown sugar

½ cup sugar

2 tablespoons honey

2 eggs

1 cup leftover Nutty Slow Cooker Oatmeal (page 57)

2 cups all-purpose flour

1½ teaspoons baking soda

½ cup chopped walnuts

1 cup chopped raisins

Chocolate Crunch Bars

COST PER BAR 13¢

Two kinds of cereal and walnuts add crunch to this delicious bar cookie. And cream cheese in the frosting adds body with less fat than butter or margarine.

YIELDS ► 36 BARS

½ cup margarine

¾ cup brown sugar

¼ cup sugar

1 egg

1 teaspoon vanilla

1 cup all-purpose flour

½ teaspoon baking soda

1 cup crushed corn flakes cereal

1 cup quick-cooking oatmeal

½ cup chopped walnuts

1½ cups semisweet chocolate chips

3 tablespoons milk

1 (3-ounce) package cream cheese

1 cup powdered sugar

1. Preheat oven to 350°F. In large bowl, combine margarine with sugars and beat well. Add egg and vanilla and beat until blended. Stir in flour and baking soda. Then add cereal, oatmeal, and nuts. Pour into ungreased 9" x 13" pan. Bake for 25–35 minutes or until bars are set and light golden brown (do not overbake). Cool on wire rack.

2. In medium saucepan, combine chocolate chips, milk and cream cheese. Cook and stir over medium low heat until chips are melted and mixture is smooth. Remove from heat and stir in powdered sugar until smooth. Frost cooled bars.

Using Stale Cereal If the leftover cereal at the bottom of the box has lost its crunch, you can bring it back to life. Just put the cereal on a pan and place in a 350°F oven for 3–6 minutes until crisp. Watch carefully, because the cereal can burn easily. Let the cereal cool and use it immediately in the recipe.

What a
Deal Desserts

18

Cinnamon Crusted Apple Pie

SERVES ▶ 8

A classic apple pie just gets better when cinnamon is added to every layer.

½ cup solid shortening

⅓ cup butter, softened

2¼ cups all-purpose flour

½ teaspoon cinnamon

¼ teaspoon salt

¼ cup sugar

6 tablespoons apple juice, divided

3 pounds apples, peeled and sliced

1 tablespoon lemon juice

2 tablespoons all-purpose flour

1 teaspoon cinnamon

½ teaspoon nutmeg

⅔ cup brown sugar

3 tablespoons butter, divided

2 tablespoons sugar

½ teaspoon cinnamon

1. In small bowl, combine shortening and ⅓ cup butter and mix well. Place in refrigerator for 1 hour to chill. In large bowl, combine 2¼ cups flour, ½ teaspoon cinnamon, ¼ cup sugar, and ¼ teaspoon salt and mix well. Cut in chilled shortening mixture until particles are fine. Drizzle 4 tablespoons apple juice over mixture and work together until a dough forms. Form into a ball, wrap in plastic wrap, and chill for 1 hour.

2. Divide dough in half and roll each into a 12" circle on lightly floured surface. Fit one circle into a 9" pie plate, letting edges hang over.

3. Prepare apples and place in large bowl, sprinkling with 2 tablespoons apple juice and lemon juice as you work. Sprinkle with 2 tablespoons flour, 1 teaspoon cinnamon, nutmeg, and brown sugar and toss to coat. Pile into pie crust and dot with 2 tablespoons butter.

4. Preheat oven to 425°F. Top pie with second pie crust. Roll edges together to seal, then flute. Cut decorative holes in top to release steam. Melt 1 tablespoon butter and brush over pie. In small bowl, combine 2 tablespoons sugar and ½ teaspoon cinnamon; sprinkle over pie.

5. Bake pie for 15 minutes, then reduce heat to 350°F and bake for 35–45 minutes longer or until crust is browned and crisp and juices are bubbling in center of pie. Cool for at least one hour before serving.

Creamy Melon Parfaits

COST PER SERVING **72¢**

This elegant dessert is perfect for company. If the gelatin mixture sets before you're ready, reheat it over low heat, then chill again until syrupy.

SERVES ▶ 8

1. In small bowl, sprinkle gelatin over cold water and set aside. In large saucepan, combine sugar and nectar. Place over medium-high heat and cook until mixture simmers and sugar is completely dissolved.

2. Remove from heat and stir in softened gelatin; stir until gelatin is completely dissolved. Let cool for 30 minutes. Chill until mixture is syrupy, about 1 hour.

3. Fold in melon and chill while preparing cream mixture. In medium bowl, beat cream cheese until fluffy; beat in powdered sugar and vanilla. In small bowl, beat whipping cream until stiff; beat into cream cheese mixture. In 8 wine goblets, layer melon mixture and cream cheese mixture. Sprinkle with coconut and chill until firm, at least 4 hours.

1 (0.25 ounce) package unflavored gelatin

½ cup cold water

½ cup sugar

1½ cups apricot nectar

1½ cups diced melon

1 (8-ounce) package cream cheese, softened

¼ cup powdered sugar

1 teaspoon vanilla

½ cup whipping cream

¼ cup chopped, toasted coconut

Chopping Coconut There are a few ways to chop coconut. Combine the coconut with a teaspoon of flour in a food processor and process until finely chopped. Or put the coconut on a cutting board and cut with a chef's knife, stopping occasionally to gather coconut back into a mound. Continue until desired consistency is reached.

Grape and Lemon Frozen Pie

Lemon and grape is a refreshing flavor combination that's delicious in this easy frozen pie.

SERVES ▶ 8

1½ cups graham cracker crumbs (about 20 crackers)

¼ cup butter or margarine, melted

1 (14-ounce) can sweetened condensed milk

½ cup lemon juice

1 (6-ounce) container lemon yogurt

1½ cups frozen whipped topping, thawed

1½ cups grapes, cut in half

1. In medium bowl, combine crumbs and melted butter and mix well. Press into bottom and up sides of 9" pie plate; set aside.

2. In another medium bowl, combine sweetened condensed milk, lemon juice, and lemon yogurt and blend well with wire whisk. Fold in whipped topping until combined.

3. Fold grapes into lemon mixture and spoon into prepared crumb crust. Cover and freeze for at least 4 hours before serving.

Peach Crisp

COST PER SERVING
62¢

Try this easy recipe with other flavors of cake mix and other types of canned fruit. Cherries would be wonderful, as would apricots.

1. Preheat oven to 325°F. In large bowl, combine cake mix with coconut. Cut in butter until crumbs form. Add walnuts and mix well.

2. In small bowl, combine brown sugar with cinnamon and nutmeg and mix well.

3. Place drained peaches in glass 9" × 13" baking pan and sprinkle with brown sugar mixture. Sprinkle cake mix mixture over all. Using a straw or chopstick, poke holes in the topping down to the peaches. Bake for 50–60 minutes or until peach juices are bubbling and crumbs are golden brown. Let cool for 30 minutes, then serve.

> *Serving Crisps*   Crisps, crumbles, grunts, and cobblers are all made of a fruit filling topped with a crunchy or cake-like topping. Serve them warm, placed in dessert dishes with whipped cream, ice cream, or hard sauce to melt onto the crisp. To make hard sauce, combine ½ cup butter with 1 cup powdered sugar, 1 teaspoon vanilla, and 2 tablespoons cream or rum, and beat well.

SERVES ▶ 8–10

1 (18-ounce) box spice cake mix

½ cup coconut

½ cup butter or margarine, softened

½ cup chopped walnuts

¼ cup brown sugar

1 teaspoon cinnamon

¼ teaspoon nutmeg

2 (15-ounce) cans sliced peaches, drained

Grandma's Banana Fruit Pudding

Fruit cocktail adds flavor to the homemade pudding and the banana mixture in this classic old-fashioned recipe.

SERVES ▶ 8

1 (15-ounce) can fruit cocktail

1 cup sugar, divided

¼ cup all-purpose flour

¼ teaspoon salt

3 eggs, separated

1 cup milk

1 tablespoon butter or margarine

2 teaspoons vanilla

2 cups vanilla wafer cookies

1 large banana

⅓ cup toffee bits

1. Preheat oven to 350°F. Spray a 2-quart baking dish with cooking spray and set aside.

2. Drain fruit cocktail, reserving juice. Place fruit in a small mixing bowl and set aside. In medium saucepan, combine 1 cup reserved fruit juice, ¾ cup sugar, flour, salt, and egg yolks and beat well. Gradually add milk, stirring until combined. Cook pudding over medium heat until mixture thickens and boils, stirring constantly, about 8 minutes.

3. Remove pudding from heat and stir in butter and vanilla. Put a layer of vanilla wafer cookies in the bottom of prepared baking dish. Slice banana and combine with reserved fruit and toffee bits in small bowl. Spoon half of banana mixture over cookies in dish.

4. Top with half of pudding mixture; repeat layers, ending with pudding. Refrigerate while preparing meringue.

5. In medium bowl, beat egg whites until foamy. Gradually beat in remaining ¼ cup sugar until stiff peaks form. Top pudding with meringue mixture, spreading to cover and sealing meringue to sides of dish. Bake for 15–20 minutes or until meringue is browned. Remove from oven and chill for at least 4 hours before serving.

> *Meringues* For the best meringue, be sure to beat the egg white and sugar mixture until the sugar completely dissolves. With this much sugar, it's difficult to overbeat the egg whites. Place on top of the dessert and gently spread with the back of a spoon, being sure to seal the meringue to the edge of the dish or pan to prevent shrinking.

Lemon White Chocolate Cake

COST PER SERVING 54¢

This fabulous layered cake is a great choice for a celebration.
It's sweet and tart, with a wonderful velvety texture.

SERVES ▶ 12

1 (12-ounce) package white chocolate chips, divided

1 (18-ounce) package white cake mix

1 cup water

½ cup lemon juice, divided

⅓ cup oil

3 egg whites

1 (3-ounce) package cream cheese, softened

¼ cup butter, softened

2 tablespoons corn syrup

3 cups powdered sugar, divided

¼ cup heavy whipping cream

3 tablespoons milk

1. Preheat oven to 350°F. Spray a 9" x 13" cake pan with nonstick cooking spray containing flour and set aside. Measure out 1 cup of the white chocolate chips and grind in a blender or food processor; set aside.

2. In large bowl, combine cake mix, water, ¼ cup lemon juice, oil, and egg whites and beat until combined. Beat for two minutes on high speed. Fold in the reserved ground white chocolate chips. Spoon into prepared pan. Bake for 35–40 minutes or until cake is light golden brown and pulls away from edges of cake pan. Place on wire rack to cool completely.

3. In small bowl, combine cream cheese, butter, ¼ cup lemon juice, and corn syrup and beat until fluffy. Alternately add powdered sugar and heavy cream, beating until fluffy.

4. In small microwave-safe bowl, combine remaining 1 cup white chocolate chips with 3 tablespoons milk. Microwave on medium power for 1 minute, then remove and stir. Continue microwaving on medium for 30 second intervals, stirring after each time, until mixture is blended and smooth.

5. To assemble cake, pour melted white chocolate chip mixture over cake, spreading to cover. Let stand for 15 minutes, then frost with cream cheese mixture.

Easy Dessert Crepes

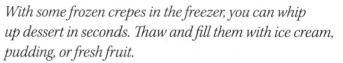

COST PER SERVING 12¢

YIELDS ► 8 CREPES

With some frozen crepes in the freezer, you can whip up dessert in seconds. Thaw and fill them with ice cream, pudding, or fresh fruit.

1¼ cups all-purpose flour

2 eggs

1 cup milk

¼ cup orange juice

½ teaspoon grated orange zest

1 teaspoon vanilla

2 tablespoons sugar

3 tablespoons butter, melted

1. In medium bowl, combine all ingredients. Beat at low speed until batter is smooth, about 1 minute. Cover and let stand for 30 minutes.

2. Heat a 6" nonstick skillet over medium heat for 1 minute. Lightly brush with oil, then pour in 3 tablespoons of batter, using a ¼ cup measure so you add the batter all at once. Swirl and tilt the pan so the batter evenly covers the bottom.

3. Cook crepe for 2–3 minutes or until bottom turns light golden brown. Using a fork, loosen the crepe from the pan and flip over; cook for 30 seconds on second side. Let cool on kitchen towels.

4. When crepes are completely cool, stack them with waxed paper or parchment paper between each crepe. Place in heavy duty freezer bags, label, and freeze up to 3 months. To use, unwrap crepes and separate. Let stand at room temperature for 20–30 minutes.

Making Crepes Making crepes takes some practice, but after one or two tries you'll be an expert. The tricks are to use a nonstick skillet, quickly rotate the pan once the batter has been added, and to adjust the batter as necessary. The batter should be about as thick as heavy cream; any thicker and it will be difficult to manipulate.

Cocoa Nut Crumble Cheesecake

COST PER SERVING **74¢**

A buttery crumbly topping on top of creamy cocoa cheesecake makes a spectacular dessert.

1. Preheat oven to 350°F. In medium bowl, combine graham cracker crumbs, ⅓ cup melted butter, and walnuts and mix well. Press into bottom and up sides of a 9" springform pan and set aside.

2. In large bowl, combine cream cheese with sugar and ½ cup brown sugar and beat until smooth. Add cocoa powder and beat just until combined. Then add eggs and vanilla and beat until smooth. Pour into crust.

3. In small bowl, combine flour, oatmeal, and ⅓ cup brown sugar and mix well. Add ¼ cup melted butter and mix until crumbly. Stir in chocolate chips and sprinkle over cheesecake, pressing in slightly.

4. Bake for 30–40 minutes or until filling is just set and crumbly topping is brown. Cool for 1 hour, then chill in refrigerator for at least 3 hours before serving.

> ***About Cheesecakes*** Cheesecakes aren't light and airy; they are creamy and dense. So when you make the filling, do not beat until fluffy; beat just until the ingredients are combined and the mixture is smooth. Too much air in the cheesecake will make the batter rise and fall, which creates cracks. But even if it cracks, it will still be good!

SERVES ▶ 10

1½ cups graham cracker crumbs

⅓ cup butter or margarine, melted

¼ cup finely chopped walnuts

2 (8-ounce) packages cream cheese, softened

½ cup sugar

½ cup brown sugar

⅓ cup cocoa powder

2 eggs

1 teaspoon vanilla

½ cup all-purpose flour

½ cup quick-cooking oatmeal

⅓ cup brown sugar

¼ cup butter, melted

½ cup semisweet chocolate chips

Orange Cranberry Sorbet

SERVES ► 6

This sorbet is for grownups! If you want to make it for kids, just omit the liqueur. The sorbet will freeze harder without it.

1½ cups orange juice
1 cup cranberry juice
¾ cup sugar
1 teaspoon orange zest
2 tablespoons orange liqueur

1. In medium saucepan, combine 1 cup of the orange juice with the sugar over medium heat. Cook and stir until sugar dissolves completely.

2. Remove pan from heat and stir in remaining orange juice, cranberry juice, and orange zest. Then blend in orange liqueur.

3. Pour mixture into a freezer-proof bowl and place in freezer. Freeze until firm, about 2 hours. Remove from freezer and beat with electric beater until smooth. Return to freezer and repeat process. Then transfer sorbet to a freezer container and freeze for at least 3 hours before serving.

> *Nips* Liqueurs are expensive! If you need just a little bit for cooking or baking, save money by purchasing "nips," or small presentation bottles that contain about 1 ounce, or 2 tablespoons, each. They are also a good way to try liqueur to see if you like it before investing in a larger bottle.

Caramel Mandarin Orange Cake

COST PER SERVING 34¢

Adding fruit to cake mix not only adds flavor, but moistness too. The caramel topping is the perfect finishing touch.

1. Preheat oven to 350°F. Spray a 9" x 13" cake pan with cooking spray containing flour and set aside.

2. In large bowl, combine cake mix, eggs, oil, and undrained oranges. Beat on low speed until combined, then beat at medium speed for 3 minutes. Fold in coconut. Pour into pan. Bake for 25–35 minutes or until cake pulls away from sides of pan and top springs back when lightly touched. Place on wire rack.

3. While cake is cooling, make caramel topping. In medium saucepan, combine brown sugar, dark corn syrup, butter, and milk. Bring to a boil, stirring constantly with wire whisk. Boil for 3 minutes.

4. Using a chopstick, poke about 20 holes evenly in the warm cake. Add vanilla to caramel topping and slowly pour over cake, spreading evenly if necessary. Cool completely before serving.

SERVES ▶ 16

1 (18-ounce) box yellow cake mix

4 eggs

¾ cup vegetable oil

1 (11-ounce) can mandarin oranges, undrained

½ cup coconut

1¼ cups brown sugar

2 tablespoons dark corn syrup

6 tablespoons butter

6 tablespoons milk

2 teaspoons vanilla

Apple Meringue Cake

COST PER SERVING

44¢

2 apples, peeled and diced

2 tablespoons lemon juice

⅓ cup butter or margarine, softened

½ cup brown sugar

¾ cup sugar, divided

2 eggs, separated

¼ cup milk

1 cup all-purpose flour

½ teaspoon baking powder

½ teaspoon baking soda

1 teaspoon cinnamon

¼ teaspoon salt

½ teaspoon nutmeg

½ cup chopped walnuts

A crisp nut-studded meringue tops a tender and velvety apple cake in this simple yet elegant recipe.

1. Preheat oven to 350°F. Spray a 9" square pan with cooking spray containing flour and set aside.

2. Prepare apples, sprinkling with lemon juice as you work; set aside. In large bowl, combine butter, brown sugar, and ½ cup sugar and beat until fluffy. Add egg yolks and milk and beat well.

3. Stir in flour, baking powder, baking soda, cinnamon, salt, and nutmeg until combined. Stir in apples and spread into prepared pan.

4. In small bowl, beat egg whites until foamy. Gradually add ¼ cup sugar, beating until stiff peaks form. Fold in nuts and spread over batter in pan. Bake for 30–40 minutes or until meringue is light brown and crisp. Cool for 30 minutes, then serve.

Apples for Baking The best apples for baking are those that are firm and rather tart. Granny Smith apples are the best choice because they also turn brown less slowly than other varieties. Haralson, McIntosh, and Cortland are also good choices for baking apples. Do not use Gala, Jonathan, or Fuji apples in baking, because they will fall apart during baking.

Honey Double Gingerbread

COST PER SERVING **31¢**

Gingerbread should be served warm from the oven. Top it with hard sauce (see recipe on page 255) or vanilla ice cream.

1. Preheat oven to 350°F. Spray a 9" x 13" pan with nonstick cooking spray containing flour and set aside.

2. In large bowl, combine butter, brown sugar, sugar, and honey and beat well. Add eggs, one at a time, beating well after each addition. Stir in flour, ginger, salt, cinnamon, nutmeg, baking soda, and baking powder. Then add the candied ginger, milk, and cream, stirring until batter is smooth.

3. Pour batter into prepared pan and bake for 45–55 minutes or until gingerbread springs back when lightly touched in center and begins to pull away from sides of pan. Cool for 30 minutes, then serve.

> *Candied Ginger* You can make your own candied ginger; it's much less expensive than store-bought. Ginger root is found in the produce aisle of the supermarket. To candy it, combine ½ cup sugar with ½ cup water and 1 tablespoon lemon juice. Bring to a simmer, then add ⅓ cup chopped fresh ginger root. Simmer for 20 minutes, then cool, drain, and roll the ginger pieces in sugar.

SERVES ► 16

⅔ cup butter or margarine, softened

¾ cup brown sugar

½ cup sugar

¾ cup honey

3 eggs

2 cups all-purpose flour

2 teaspoons ground ginger

¼ teaspoon salt

1 teaspoon cinnamon

½ teaspoon nutmeg

1 teaspoon baking soda

1 teaspoon baking powder

1 tablespoon minced candied ginger

¾ cup milk

¼ cup heavy cream

Best Cranberry Bread Pudding

Bread pudding is not only economical, it is the ultimate comfort food. Two kinds of chocolate chips add a sweet touch to the tart cranberries in the bread.

SERVES ▶ 8

3 tablespoons butter

6 slices Cranberry-Walnut Loaf (page 51)

3 eggs

¾ cup brown sugar

½ teaspoon cinnamon

2 teaspoons vanilla

1½ cups milk

1 cup semisweet chocolate chips

1 cup white chocolate chips

1. Preheat oven to 350°F. Butter both sides of the bread and cut into ½" cubes. Place in a 9" square baking pan and set aside.

2. In medium bowl, combine eggs, brown sugar, cinnamon, and vanilla and beat until fluffy. Gradually add milk, stirring until smooth.

3. Sprinkle both kinds of chips over the bread in the baking pan. Pour egg mixture over all and let stand for 15 minutes, pressing bread down into the custard with a fork as necessary.

4. Bake for 40–45 minutes or until pudding is set and golden brown. Let cool for 30 minutes, then serve with hard sauce (see page 255).

Vary the Recipe   Instead of cranberry bread, use raisin swirl bread or just plain white bread in any bread pudding recipe. Use white sugar or honey instead of brown sugar, and add dried fruits instead of the chocolate chips. It's easy to vary a recipe like this one, which doesn't rely on precise measurements.

Peach Foster Crepes

COST PER SERVING 56¢

You could make this recipe with sliced pears or apricots too.
For a splurge, sprinkle the crepes with some pistachio nuts.

1. Drain peach slices, reserving juice. In medium saucepan, combine butter with brown sugar and sugar. Bring to a boil over medium heat, stirring constantly, until mixture combines and forms a sauce. Add ½ cup reserved peach juice and bring back to a simmer. Add cinnamon and peach slices; simmer for 1–2 minutes or until peaches are hot; remove from heat.

2. In small bowl, combine cream with powdered sugar and beat until stiff peaks form. Stir in sour cream until blended.

3. Place crepes, light side up, on work surface. Using a slotted spoon, arrange a few peach slices on crepes. Roll up crepes and place, seam side down, on serving plate. Drizzle with syrup remaining in pan, and top with sour cream mixture.

SERVES ▶ 8

1 (16-ounce) can peach slices

¼ cup butter or margarine

½ cup brown sugar

⅓ cup sugar

½ cup reserved peach juice

½ teaspoon cinnamon

½ cup heavy whipping cream

2 tablespoons powdered sugar

½ cup sour cream

1 recipe Easy Dessert Crepes (page 258)

Lemon Chocolate Pie

COST PER SERVING 54¢

Lemon and chocolate is a fabulous combination. This pie is
perfect for a birthday celebration or anniversary.

1. In small saucepan, combine ¼ cup sweetened condensed milk with ½ cup chocolate chips. Melt over very low heat, stirring constantly, until chocolate is melted and mixture is smooth. Spread into bottom of pie crust.

2. In medium bowl, combine remaining sweetened condensed milk with the lemon juice and beat until smooth. Fold whipped topping into lemon mixture and spoon over chocolate mixture in pie shell.

3. Using a chef's knife, finely chop 2 tablespoons chocolate chips and sprinkle over the pie. Chill for at least 4 hours before serving.

SERVES ▶ 8

1 Pie Crust (page 270), baked and cooled

1 (14-ounce) can sweetened condensed milk

½ cup semisweet chocolate chips

⅓ cup lemon juice

1½ cups frozen whipped topping, thawed

2 tablespoons semisweet chocolate chips

Cocoa Peach Parfaits

Beating a boiling hot sugar syrup into egg whites is how divinity is made. These parfaits are creamy and sweet, with a bit of crunch from the almonds. Yum.

SERVES ▶ 6

1 (16-ounce) can sliced peaches
½ cup reserved peach juice
¾ cup sugar
1 tablespoon water
2 egg whites
¾ cup heavy whipping cream
¼ cup cocoa powder
2 tablespoons powdered sugar
1 teaspoon vanilla
½ cup sliced almonds, toasted

1. Drain peaches, reserving juice. Chop peaches and set aside.

2. In small saucepan, combine ½ cup reserved juice, sugar, and water and bring to a boil. Boil, stirring, until sugar dissolves, then boil for 5 minutes. Meanwhile, in medium bowl place egg whites. Beat until soft peaks form, then slowly drizzle in the hot sugar syrup, beating constantly. The egg whites will thicken as the syrup is added. Set aside to cool for 20 minutes.

3. In small bowl, combine cream, cocoa, powdered sugar, and vanilla and beat until stiff peaks form. Fold into egg white mixture.

4. In stemmed goblets, layer egg white mixture with peaches, ending with egg white mixture. Sprinkle with almonds, cover, and chill for at least 2 hours.

Parfaits Parfaits are fabulous inexpensive and last-minute desserts. You can use pudding, mousse, ice cream, or flavored whipped cream as the base, and everything from chocolate chips to chopped candy to fruit, nuts, or granola for layering. They're also ideal for entertaining because they can be made ahead of time. Top with a dollop of whipped cream.

Chocolate Butterscotch Pudding

COST PER SERVING 52¢

For the smoothest pudding, you need to dissolve the cornstarch in liquid before adding it to the rest of the ingredients, and be sure to stir constantly with a wire whisk.

1. In medium saucepan, place milk and heat over medium heat until it begins to steam. Meanwhile, in small bowl combine cream with cornstarch and mix well until perfectly smooth.

2. Remove hot milk from heat and stir in brown sugar and salt, then add cornstarch mixture, stirring constantly with wire whisk. Then beat in eggs. Return saucepan to heat and cook over medium-low heat until pudding thickens and coats the back of a spoon.

3. Remove from heat and add vanilla and butter, stirring until smooth. Divide half of this mixture among four 6-ounce custard cups. Add chocolate to mixture remaining in saucepan and stir until chocolate melts and mixture is smooth (you may need to return the pan to the heat briefly to completely melt the chocolate). Spoon carefully over pudding in custard cups and chill for 2–4 hours before serving.

SERVES ► 4

1½ cups milk

½ cup heavy cream

2 tablespoons cornstarch

1 cup brown sugar

½ teaspoon salt

2 eggs

1½ teaspoons vanilla

3 tablespoons butter

½ cup semisweet chocolate chips

Orange Cranberry Crepes

SERVES ▶ 8

This mousse can also be served on its own; just spoon it into dessert glasses and chill for several hours. Drizzle with chocolate syrup before serving.

½ cup cranberry juice

½ cup orange juice

1 (3-ounce) package orange gelatin

1 (16-ounce) can whole berry cranberry sauce

1½ cups frozen whipped topping, thawed

1 recipe Easy Dessert Crepes (page 258)

½ cup chocolate syrup

1. In microwave-safe measuring glass, combine cranberry juice and orange juice. Microwave on high for 2–4 minutes until boiling. Meanwhile, place gelatin in a large bowl. Add boiling juice mixture and stir until gelatin dissolves completely. Add cranberry sauce, stirring well. Cover and chill until mixture is almost set, about 1 hour.

2. Remove cranberry mixture from refrigerator and beat for 1 minute. Fold whipped topping into cranberry mixture. Cover and chill until firm, about 3 hours.

3. When ready to serve, place crepes on serving plates. Fill with cranberry mixture and roll up. Drizzle each with some chocolate syrup and serve immediately.

Changing Flavors It's easy to change the flavor of desserts. For instance, in Orange Cranberry Dessert Crepes, use apple juice, lemon gelatin, and applesauce in place of the cranberry and orange juices, orange gelatin, and cranberry sauce. Or peach nectar, peach gelatin, and puréed peaches. It's easy once you use your imagination!

Chocolate Soufflé

COST PER SERVING 44¢

Soufflés aren't difficult as long as you follow a few rules.
Make the chocolate mixture ahead of time and refrigerate it to
save time.

SERVES ► 4

1. Up to 1 day ahead of time, make the chocolate mixture. In medium saucepan, melt butter over medium heat. Add flour and salt; cook and stir until bubbly, about 3 minutes. Then stir in chocolate milk and cook, stirring constantly with wire whisk, until mixture thickens.

2. Remove from heat and stir in cocoa, chocolate syrup, and brown sugar until blended. Then beat in egg yolks, cover, and refrigerate until cold. Place egg whites in medium bowl, cover, and keep refrigerated.

3. When ready to eat, preheat oven to 350°F. Grease a 6-cup soufflé dish with unsalted butter and set aside. Let egg whites stand at room temperature for 20 minutes. Add lemon juice and beat until foamy. Gradually add sugar and beat until egg whites are stiff but not dry.

4. With same beaters, beat chocolate mixture until smooth. Add a spoonful of egg whites and mix until combined. Then add remaining egg whites and fold together just until blended. Pour into prepared dish.

5. Bake for 30–40 minutes or until soufflé is puffed and just set. Serve immediately with ice cream.

¼ cup butter or margarine

3 tablespoons all-purpose flour

⅛ teaspoon salt

¾ cup chocolate milk

⅓ cup cocoa powder

⅓ cup chocolate syrup

⅓ cup brown sugar

4 eggs, separated

2 teaspoons lemon juice

2 tablespoons sugar

Soufflé Rules Be sure that the sauce that contains the egg yolks is cold before you fold in the egg whites. To fold, use a spatula and bring it down one side of the bowl, scrape the bottom, and up the other side, turning the mixtures together. And be sure to serve the soufflé as soon as possible. If it falls, it will still taste wonderful!

Pie Crust

COST PER SERVING
8¢

Making your own pie crusts saves you more than 50 percent than buying premade crusts. Plus they taste so much better!

YIELDS ► 1 CRUST
SERVES ► 8

¼ cup solid vegetable shortening

3 tablespoons cream cheese, softened

1¼ cups all-purpose flour

½ teaspoon salt

2 tablespoons water

1 tablespoon milk

1. In small bowl, combine shortening and cream cheese and beat until combined. Cover and chill in refrigerator for 2 hours.

2. In medium bowl, combine flour and salt and mix well. Add shortening mixture and cut in, using pastry blender or two knives, until mixture looks like cornmeal. Sprinkle water and milk over all, tossing with fork until combined. Form into ball.

3. Wrap ball in plastic wrap and chill for at least 4 hours. When ready to bake, preheat oven to 400°F. Roll out dough between two sheets of waxed paper.

4. Remove top sheet of paper and flip into pie pan. Ease dough into pan. Turn edges under and flute. Prick bottom and sides of dough with fork. Bake for 10–15 minutes, pricking once during baking time, until crust is light golden brown.

Freezing Pie Crusts You can make a large batch of pie crusts and freeze them so they're as easy to use as the purchased prepared kind. Just roll out each crust between two layers of waxed paper, then place in large freezer bags, label, seal, and freeze for up to 3 months. To use, just let each crust stand at room temperature for 30–40 minutes to thaw.

Price Difference for Equivalent Foods

One of the surprising things about budget cooking is that some prepared ingredients are cheaper than homemade, and vice versa. It all comes down to unit pricing and doing your homework, and of course these comparisons change when coupons and sales are factored into the price.

These foods are compared by cups, ounces, pounds, or servings. When compared by servings, the calorie counts are approximately equal. So, for instance, the frozen pizza you purchase will only serve four people at 300 calories each, while the homemade pizza will serve six people at 380 calories each.

Prices of Equivalent Grocery and Fresh Foods

Canned or Boxed Food	Price	Homemade Food	Price
Canned Alfredo Sauce	$1.82/cup	Homemade Alfredo Sauce	$1.18/cup
Canned Pasta Sauce	73¢/cup	Homemade Pasta Sauce	51¢/cup
Jarred Salsa	$3.80/lb	Homemade Salsa	$2.00/lb
Chicken Stock	56¢/cup	Homemade Stock	42¢/cup
Beef Stock	56¢/cup	Homemade Stock	41¢/cup
Chicken Bouillon Cubes	9¢/cup	Homemade	42¢/cup
Whole Grain Pasta	$3.00/lb	Plain Pasta	99¢/lb
Canned Soup	$1.10/cup	Homemade Soup	62¢/cup
Canned Baked Beans	60¢/serving	Homemade Baked Beans	37¢/serving
BBQ Sauce	$1.50/cup	Homemade BBQ Sauce	60¢/cup

Prices of Equivalent Frozen and Prepared Foods

Value-Added Food	Price	Homemade Food	Price
Whipped Topping	32¢/cup	Whipped Cream	74¢/cup
Frozen Carrots	$1.79/lb	Fresh Carrots	99¢/lb
Frozen Potatoes	$1.37/lb	Fresh Potatoes	59¢/lb
Frozen Strawberries	$2.99/lb	Fresh Strawberries	$4.00/lb
Frozen Mashed Potatoes	$1.89/lb	Homemade Mashed Potatoes	$1.20/lb
Frozen Blueberries	$3.99/lb	Fresh Blueberries	$11.20/lb
Frozen Hash Browns	$1.79/pound	Fresh Potatoes	49¢/pound
Prepared Stuffed Chicken	$4.33/each	Homemade Stuffed Chicken	$1.89/each
Guacamole	58¢/serving	Homemade Guacamole	33¢/serving
Frozen Pizza	97¢/slice	Homemade Pizza	51¢/slice

Prices of Equivalent Produce Foods

Value-Added Food	Price	Plain Food	Price
Canned Mushrooms	64¢/4 oz	Fresh Mushrooms	$1.10/4 oz
Bagged Salad	40¢/cup	Lettuce	22¢/cup
Baby Carrots	$1.60/12 oz	Carrots	99¢/lb
Shredded Carrots	$1.99/10 oz	Carrots	99¢/lb
Sliced Carrots	$1.99/lb	Carrots	99¢/lb
Celery Heart	$3.99/lb	Celery	$2.19/lb
Cauliflower Florets	$3.99/lb	Whole Cauliflower	$1.12/lb
Prepared Polenta	$3.49/4 servings	Homemade Polenta	$2.57/12 servings
Refrigerated Alfredo Sauce	$3.39/cup	Homemade Alfredo Sauce	$1.18/cup
Refrigerated Pasta Sauce	$1.93/cup	Homemade Pasta Sauce	51¢/cup

Prices of Equivalent Baking and Homemade Foods

Value-Added Food	Price	Plain Food	Price
Cake Mix	94¢	Cake Ingredients	$1.44
Unsweetened Chocolate	33¢/oz	Cocoa Powder	19¢/3 Tbsp
Artificial Vanilla	$1.99/8 oz	Real Vanilla	$6.49/2 oz
Prepared Pesto	$3.99/12 oz	Homemade Pesto	$2.76/12 oz
Bakery Bread	$3.29/loaf	Homemade Bread	$1.40/loaf
Crackers	3¢/each	Homemade Crackers	8¢/each
Corn Bread Mix	49¢	Dry Ingredients	89¢
Pie Crust	$1.52	Homemade Crust	64¢
Muffin Mix	49¢	Muffin Ingredients	88¢

Prices of Equivalent Dairy Foods

Value-Added Food	Price	Plain Food	Price
Butter	$3.49/lb	Margarine	$1.09/lb
Powdered Milk	23¢/cup	Fresh Milk	25¢/cup
Prepared Pesto	67¢/serving	Homemade Pesto	33¢/serving
Crescent Dough	31¢/roll	Homemade Crescent Rolls	12¢/roll
Shredded Cheese	$2.79/8 oz	Cheese Block	$2.79/8 oz
Parmigiano-Reggiano	$9.00/8 oz	Canned Cheese	$3.29/8 oz
Jumbo Eggs	$1.69/12	Large Eggs	$1.49/12
Name Brand Cream Cheese	$1.89/8 oz	Generic Cream Cheese	$1.49/8 oz

Suggested Menus

When planning the menu, cost is an important factor, but nutrition, taste, and satisfaction are also important. Be sure to balance your meals by selecting foods that are nutrient dense and by building the most colorful plate possible.

Lunch *for* Eight Bucks

NOTES

date

----

shopping list

date

....

shopping list

....

....

....

....

....

....

....

....

....

....

....

....

....

....

Dinner *for the* Boss

notes

Breakfast *for* Four, *for* Five

notes

date

shopping list

date

....

shopping list

....

....

....

....

....

....

....

....

....

....

....

....

....

....

....

....

....

Christmas Dinner

NOTES

Sunday Brunch

NOTES

date

shopping list

date

....

shopping list

....	....
....	....
....	....
....	....
....	....
....	....
....	....
....	....
....	....
....	....
....	....
....	....
....	....
....	....
....	....
....	....
....	....

Picnic *in the* Park

NOTES

Special Birthday Celebration

NOTES

date

shopping list

date

----

shopping list

-----------------	-----------------
-----------------	-----------------
-----------------	-----------------
-----------------	-----------------
-----------------	-----------------
-----------------	-----------------
-----------------	-----------------
-----------------	-----------------
-----------------	-----------------
-----------------	-----------------
-----------------	-----------------
-----------------	-----------------
-----------------	-----------------
-----------------	-----------------
-----------------	-----------------
-----------------	-----------------

Brown Bag It *for* Two Dollars

NOTES

Kid's Birthday Party

NOTES

date

shopping list

date

....

shopping list

....	....
....	....
....	....
....	....
....	....
....	....
....	....
....	....
....	....
....	....
....	....
....	....
....	....
....	....
....	....
....	....

Cozy Night *with* Friends

NOTES

Family Dinner *for* Ten

NOTES

date

shopping list

date

....

shopping list

....	....
....	....
....	....
....	....
....	....
....	....
....	....
....	....
....	....
....	....
....	....
....	....
....	....
....	....
....	....
....	....
....	....

Appetizer Party

NOTES

When *the* Cupboard's Bare

NOTES

date

shopping list

date

....

shopping list

....

....

....

....

....

....

....

....

....

....

....

....

....

....

....

....

Feed Four *for* Ten

NOTES

Index

THE EVERYTHING SERIES!

BUSINESS & PERSONAL FINANCE

Everything® Accounting Book
Everything® Budgeting Book, 2nd Ed.
Everything® Business Planning Book
Everything® Coaching and Mentoring Book, 2nd Ed.
Everything® Fundraising Book
Everything® Get Out of Debt Book
Everything® Grant Writing Book, 2nd Ed.
Everything® Guide to Buying Foreclosures
Everything® Guide to Mortgages
Everything® Guide to Personal Finance for Single Mothers
Everything® Home-Based Business Book, 2nd Ed.
Everything® Homebuying Book, 2nd Ed.
Everything® Homeselling Book, 2nd Ed.
Everything® Human Resource Management Book
Everything® Improve Your Credit Book
Everything® Investing Book, 2nd Ed.
Everything® Landlording Book
Everything® Leadership Book, 2nd Ed.
Everything® Managing People Book, 2nd Ed.
Everything® Negotiating Book
Everything® Online Auctions Book
Everything® Online Business Book
Everything® Personal Finance Book
Everything® Personal Finance in Your 20s & 30s Book, 2nd Ed.
Everything® Project Management Book, 2nd Ed.
Everything® Real Estate Investing Book
Everything® Retirement Planning Book
Everything® Robert's Rules Book, $7.95
Everything® Selling Book
Everything® Start Your Own Business Book, 2nd Ed.
Everything® Wills & Estate Planning Book

COOKING

Everything® Barbecue Cookbook
Everything® Bartender's Book, 2nd Ed., $9.95
Everything® Calorie Counting Cookbook
Everything® Cheese Book
Everything® Chinese Cookbook
Everything® Classic Recipes Book
Everything® Cocktail Parties & Drinks Book
Everything® College Cookbook
Everything® Cooking for Baby and Toddler Book
Everything® Cooking for Two Cookbook
Everything® Diabetes Cookbook
Everything® Easy Gourmet Cookbook
Everything® Fondue Cookbook
Everything® Fondue Party Book
Everything® Gluten-Free Cookbook
Everything® Glycemic Index Cookbook
Everything® Grilling Cookbook
Everything® Healthy Meals in Minutes Cookbook
Everything® Holiday Cookbook
Everything® Indian Cookbook
Everything® Italian Cookbook

Everything® Lactose-Free Cookbook
Everything® Low-Carb Cookbook
Everything® Low-Cholesterol Cookbook
Everything® Low-Fat High-Flavor Cookbook
Everything® Low-Salt Cookbook
Everything® Meals for a Month Cookbook
Everything® Meals on a Budget Cookbook
Everything® Mediterranean Cookbook
Everything® Mexican Cookbook
Everything® No Trans Fat Cookbook
Everything® One-Pot Cookbook
Everything® Pizza Cookbook
Everything® Quick and Easy 30-Minute, 5-Ingredient Cookbook
Everything® Quick Meals Cookbook
Everything® Slow Cooker Cookbook
Everything® Slow Cooking for a Crowd Cookbook
Everything® Soup Cookbook
Everything® Stir-Fry Cookbook
Everything® Sugar-Free Cookbook
Everything® Tapas and Small Plates Cookbook
Everything® Tex-Mex Cookbook
Everything® Thai Cookbook
Everything® Vegetarian Cookbook
Everything® Whole-Grain, High-Fiber Cookbook
Everything® Wild Game Cookbook
Everything® Wine Book, 2nd Ed.

GAMES

Everything® 15-Minute Sudoku Book, $9.95
Everything® 30-Minute Sudoku Book, $9.95
Everything® Bible Crosswords Book, $9.95
Everything® Blackjack Strategy Book
Everything® Brain Strain Book, $9.95
Everything® Bridge Book
Everything® Card Games Book
Everything® Card Tricks Book, $9.95
Everything® Casino Gambling Book, 2nd Ed.
Everything® Chess Basics Book
Everything® Craps Strategy Book
Everything® Crossword and Puzzle Book
Everything® Crossword Challenge Book
Everything® Crosswords for the Beach Book, $9.95
Everything® Cryptic Crosswords Book, $9.95
Everything® Cryptograms Book, $9.95
Everything® Easy Crosswords Book
Everything® Easy Kakuro Book, $9.95
Everything® Easy Large-Print Crosswords Book
Everything® Games Book, 2nd Ed.
Everything® Giant Sudoku Book, $9.95
Everything® Giant Word Search Book
Everything® Kakuro Challenge Book, $9.95
Everything® Large-Print Crossword Challenge Book
Everything® Large-Print Crosswords Book
Everything® Lateral Thinking Puzzles Book, $9.95
Everything® Literary Crosswords Book, $9.95
Everything® Mazes Book
Everything® Memory Booster Puzzles Book, $9.95
Everything® Movie Crosswords Book, $9.95

Everything® Music Crosswords Book, $9.95
Everything® Online Poker Book
Everything® Pencil Puzzles Book, $9.95
Everything® Poker Strategy Book
Everything® Pool & Billiards Book
Everything® Puzzles for Commuters Book, $9.95
Everything® Puzzles for Dog Lovers Book, $9.95
Everything® Sports Crosswords Book, $9.95
Everything® Test Your IQ Book, $9.95
Everything® Texas Hold 'Em Book, $9.95
Everything® Travel Crosswords Book, $9.95
Everything® TV Crosswords Book, $9.95
Everything® Word Games Challenge Book
Everything® Word Scramble Book
Everything® Word Search Book

HEALTH

Everything® Alzheimer's Book
Everything® Diabetes Book
Everything® First Aid Book, $9.95
Everything® Health Guide to Adult Bipolar Disorder
Everything® Health Guide to Arthritis
Everything® Health Guide to Controlling Anxiety
Everything® Health Guide to Depression
Everything® Health Guide to Fibromyalgia
Everything® Health Guide to Menopause, 2nd Ed.
Everything® Health Guide to Migraines
Everything® Health Guide to OCD
Everything® Health Guide to PMS
Everything® Health Guide to Postpartum Care
Everything® Health Guide to Thyroid Disease
Everything® Hypnosis Book
Everything® Low Cholesterol Book
Everything® Menopause Book
Everything® Nutrition Book
Everything® Reflexology Book
Everything® Stress Management Book

HISTORY

Everything® American Government Book
Everything® American History Book, 2nd Ed.
Everything® Civil War Book
Everything® Freemasons Book
Everything® Irish History & Heritage Book
Everything® Middle East Book
Everything® World War II Book, 2nd Ed.

HOBBIES

Everything® Candlemaking Book
Everything® Cartooning Book
Everything® Coin Collecting Book
Everything® Digital Photography Book, 2nd Ed.
Everything® Drawing Book
Everything® Family Tree Book, 2nd Ed.
Everything® Knitting Book
Everything® Knots Book
Everything® Photography Book
Everything® Quilting Book

Everything® Sewing Book
Everything® Soapmaking Book, 2nd Ed.
Everything® Woodworking Book

HOME IMPROVEMENT

Everything® Feng Shui Book
Everything® Feng Shui Decluttering Book, $9.95
Everything® Fix-It Book
Everything® Green Living Book
Everything® Home Decorating Book
Everything® Home Storage Solutions Book
Everything® Homebuilding Book
Everything® Organize Your Home Book, 2nd Ed.

KIDS' BOOKS

All titles are $7.95
Everything® Fairy Tales Book, $14.95
Everything® Kids' Animal Puzzle & Activity Book
Everything® Kids' Astronomy Book
Everything® Kids' Baseball Book, 5th Ed.
Everything® Kids' Bible Trivia Book
Everything® Kids' Bugs Book
Everything® Kids' Cars and Trucks Puzzle and Activity Book
Everything® Kids' Christmas Puzzle & Activity Book
Everything® Kids' Connect the Dots
Puzzle and Activity Book
Everything® Kids' Cookbook
Everything® Kids' Crazy Puzzles Book
Everything® Kids' Dinosaurs Book
Everything® Kids' Environment Book
Everything® Kids' Fairies Puzzle and Activity Book
Everything® Kids' First Spanish Puzzle and Activity Book
Everything® Kids' Football Book
Everything® Kids' Gross Cookbook
Everything® Kids' Gross Hidden Pictures Book
Everything® Kids' Gross Jokes Book
Everything® Kids' Gross Mazes Book
Everything® Kids' Gross Puzzle & Activity Book
Everything® Kids' Halloween Puzzle & Activity Book
Everything® Kids' Hidden Pictures Book
Everything® Kids' Horses Book
Everything® Kids' Joke Book
Everything® Kids' Knock Knock Book
Everything® Kids' Learning French Book
Everything® Kids' Learning Spanish Book
Everything® Kids' Magical Science Experiments Book
Everything® Kids' Math Puzzles Book
Everything® Kids' Mazes Book
Everything® Kids' Money Book
Everything® Kids' Nature Book
Everything® Kids' Pirates Puzzle and Activity Book
Everything® Kids' Presidents Book
Everything® Kids' Princess Puzzle and Activity Book
Everything® Kids' Puzzle Book
Everything® Kids' Racecars Puzzle and Activity Book
Everything® Kids' Riddles & Brain Teasers Book
Everything® Kids' Science Experiments Book
Everything® Kids' Sharks Book
Everything® Kids' Soccer Book
Everything® Kids' Spies Puzzle and Activity Book
Everything® Kids' States Book
Everything® Kids' Travel Activity Book
Everything® Kids' Word Search Puzzle and Activity Book

LANGUAGE

Everything® Conversational Japanese Book with CD, $19.95
Everything® French Grammar Book
Everything® French Phrase Book, $9.95
Everything® French Verb Book, $9.95
Everything® German Practice Book with CD, $19.95
Everything® Inglés Book
Everything® Intermediate Spanish Book with CD, $19.95
Everything® Italian Practice Book with CD, $19.95
Everything® Learning Brazilian Portuguese Book with CD, $19.95
Everything® Learning French Book with CD, 2nd Ed., $19.95
Everything® Learning German Book
Everything® Learning Italian Book
Everything® Learning Latin Book
Everything® Learning Russian Book with CD, $19.95
Everything® Learning Spanish Book
Everything® Learning Spanish Book with CD, 2nd Ed., $19.95
Everything® Russian Practice Book with CD, $19.95
Everything® Sign Language Book
Everything® Spanish Grammar Book
Everything® Spanish Phrase Book, $9.95
Everything® Spanish Practice Book with CD, $19.95
Everything® Spanish Verb Book, $9.95
Everything® Speaking Mandarin Chinese Book with CD, $19.95

MUSIC

Everything® Bass Guitar Book with CD, $19.95
Everything® Drums Book with CD, $19.95
Everything® Guitar Book with CD, 2nd Ed., $19.95
Everything® Guitar Chords Book with CD, $19.95
Everything® Harmonica Book with CD, $15.95
Everything® Home Recording Book
Everything® Music Theory Book with CD, $19.95
Everything® Reading Music Book with CD, $19.95
Everything® Rock & Blues Guitar Book with CD, $19.95
Everything® Rock & Blues Piano Book with CD, $19.95
Everything® Songwriting Book

NEW AGE

Everything® Astrology Book, 2nd Ed.
Everything® Birthday Personology Book
Everything® Dreams Book, 2nd Ed.
Everything® Love Signs Book, $9.95
Everything® Love Spells Book, $9.95
Everything® Paganism Book
Everything® Palmistry Book
Everything® Psychic Book
Everything® Reiki Book
Everything® Sex Signs Book, $9.95
Everything® Spells & Charms Book, 2nd Ed.
Everything® Tarot Book, 2nd Ed.
Everything® Toltec Wisdom Book
Everything® Wicca & Witchcraft Book, 2nd Ed.

PARENTING

Everything® Baby Names Book, 2nd Ed.
Everything® Baby Shower Book, 2nd Ed.
Everything® Baby Sign Language Book with DVD
Everything® Baby's First Year Book
Everything® Birthing Book

Everything® Breastfeeding Book
Everything® Father-to-Be Book
Everything® Father's First Year Book
Everything® Get Ready for Baby Book, 2nd Ed.
Everything® Get Your Baby to Sleep Book, $9.95
Everything® Getting Pregnant Book
Everything® Guide to Pregnancy Over 35
Everything® Guide to Raising a One-Year-Old
Everything® Guide to Raising a Two-Year-Old
Everything® Guide to Raising Adolescent Boys
Everything® Guide to Raising Adolescent Girls
Everything® Mother's First Year Book
Everything® Parent's Guide to Childhood Illnesses
Everything® Parent's Guide to Children and Divorce
Everything® Parent's Guide to Children with ADD/ADHD
Everything® Parent's Guide to Children with Asperger's Syndrome
Everything® Parent's Guide to Children with Asthma
Everything® Parent's Guide to Children with Autism
Everything® Parent's Guide to Children with Bipolar Disorder
Everything® Parent's Guide to Children with Depression
Everything® Parent's Guide to Children with Dyslexia
Everything® Parent's Guide to Children with Juvenile Diabetes
Everything® Parent's Guide to Positive Discipline
Everything® Parent's Guide to Raising a Successful Child
Everything® Parent's Guide to Raising Boys
Everything® Parent's Guide to Raising Girls
Everything® Parent's Guide to Raising Siblings
Everything® Parent's Guide to Sensory Integration Disorder
Everything® Parent's Guide to Tantrums
Everything® Parent's Guide to the Strong-Willed Child
Everything® Parenting a Teenager Book
Everything® Potty Training Book, $9.95
Everything® Pregnancy Book, 3rd Ed.
Everything® Pregnancy Fitness Book
Everything® Pregnancy Nutrition Book
Everything® Pregnancy Organizer, 2nd Ed., $16.95
Everything® Toddler Activities Book
Everything® Toddler Book
Everything® Tween Book
Everything® Twins, Triplets, and More Book

PETS

Everything® Aquarium Book
Everything® Boxer Book
Everything® Cat Book, 2nd Ed.
Everything® Chihuahua Book
Everything® Cooking for Dogs Book
Everything® Dachshund Book
Everything® Dog Book, 2nd Ed.
Everything® Dog Grooming Book
Everything® Dog Health Book
Everything® Dog Obedience Book
Everything® Dog Owner's Organizer, $16.95
Everything® Dog Training and Tricks Book
Everything® German Shepherd Book
Everything® Golden Retriever Book
Everything® Horse Book
Everything® Horse Care Book
Everything® Horseback Riding Book
Everything® Labrador Retriever Book
Everything® Poodle Book
Everything® Pug Book

Everything® Puppy Book
Everything® Rottweiler Book
Everything® Small Dogs Book
Everything® Tropical Fish Book
Everything® Yorkshire Terrier Book

REFERENCE

Everything® American Presidents Book
Everything® Blogging Book
Everything® Build Your Vocabulary Book, $9.95
Everything® Car Care Book
Everything® Classical Mythology Book
Everything® Da Vinci Book
Everything® Divorce Book
Everything® Einstein Book
Everything® Enneagram Book
Everything® Etiquette Book, 2nd Ed.
Everything® Guide to C. S. Lewis & Narnia
Everything® Guide to Edgar Allan Poe
Everything® Guide to Understanding Philosophy
Everything® Inventions and Patents Book
Everything® Jacqueline Kennedy Onassis Book
Everything® John F. Kennedy Book
Everything® Mafia Book
Everything® Martin Luther King Jr. Book
Everything® Philosophy Book
Everything® Pirates Book
Everything® Private Investigation Book
Everything® Psychology Book
Everything® Public Speaking Book, $9.95
Everything® Shakespeare Book, 2nd Ed.

RELIGION

Everything® Angels Book
Everything® Bible Book
Everything® Bible Study Book with CD, $19.95
Everything® Buddhism Book
Everything® Catholicism Book
Everything® Christianity Book
Everything® Gnostic Gospels Book
Everything® History of the Bible Book
Everything® Jesus Book
Everything® Jewish History & Heritage Book
Everything® Judaism Book
Everything® Kabbalah Book
Everything® Koran Book
Everything® Mary Book
Everything® Mary Magdalene Book
Everything® Prayer Book
Everything® Saints Book, 2nd Ed.
Everything® Torah Book
Everything® Understanding Islam Book
Everything® Women of the Bible Book
Everything® World's Religions Book

SCHOOL & CAREERS

Everything® Career Tests Book
Everything® College Major Test Book
Everything® College Survival Book, 2nd Ed.
Everything® Cover Letter Book, 2nd Ed.
Everything® Filmmaking Book
Everything® Get-a-Job Book, 2nd Ed.
Everything® Guide to Being a Paralegal
Everything® Guide to Being a Personal Trainer
Everything® Guide to Being a Real Estate Agent
Everything® Guide to Being a Sales Rep
Everything® Guide to Being an Event Planner
Everything® Guide to Careers in Health Care
Everything® Guide to Careers in Law Enforcement
Everything® Guide to Government Jobs
Everything® Guide to Starting and Running a Catering
    Business
Everything® Guide to Starting and Running a Restaurant
Everything® Job Interview Book, 2nd Ed.
Everything® New Nurse Book
Everything® New Teacher Book
Everything® Paying for College Book
Everything® Practice Interview Book
Everything® Resume Book, 3rd Ed.
Everything® Study Book

SELF-HELP

Everything® Body Language Book
Everything® Dating Book, 2nd Ed.
Everything® Great Sex Book
Everything® Self-Esteem Book
Everything® Tantric Sex Book

SPORTS & FITNESS

Everything® Easy Fitness Book
Everything® Fishing Book
Everything® Krav Maga for Fitness Book
Everything® Running Book, 2nd Ed.

TRAVEL

Everything® Family Guide to Coastal Florida
Everything® Family Guide to Cruise Vacations
Everything® Family Guide to Hawaii
Everything® Family Guide to Las Vegas, 2nd Ed.
Everything® Family Guide to Mexico
Everything® Family Guide to New England, 2nd Ed.
Everything® Family Guide to New York City, 3rd Ed.
Everything® Family Guide to RV Travel & Campgrounds
Everything® Family Guide to the Caribbean
Everything® Family Guide to the Disneyland® Resort, California
    Adventure®, Universal Studios®, and the Anaheim
    Area, 2nd Ed.
Everything® Family Guide to the Walt Disney World Resort®,
    Universal Studios®, and Greater Orlando, 5th Ed.
Everything® Family Guide to Timeshares
Everything® Family Guide to Washington D.C., 2nd Ed.

WEDDINGS

Everything® Bachelorette Party Book, $9.95
Everything® Bridesmaid Book, $9.95
Everything® Destination Wedding Book
Everything® Father of the Bride Book, $9.95
Everything® Groom Book, $9.95
Everything® Mother of the Bride Book, $9.95
Everything® Outdoor Wedding Book
Everything® Wedding Book, 3rd Ed.
Everything® Wedding Checklist, $9.95
Everything® Wedding Etiquette Book, $9.95
Everything® Wedding Organizer, 2nd Ed., $16.95
Everything® Wedding Shower Book, $9.95
Everything® Wedding Vows Book, $9.95
Everything® Wedding Workout Book
Everything® Weddings on a Budget Book, 2nd Ed., $9.95

WRITING

Everything® Creative Writing Book
Everything® Get Published Book, 2nd Ed.
Everything® Grammar and Style Book, 2nd Ed.
Everything® Guide to Magazine Writing
Everything® Guide to Writing a Book Proposal
Everything® Guide to Writing a Novel
Everything® Guide to Writing Children's Books
Everything® Guide to Writing Copy
Everything® Guide to Writing Graphic Novels
Everything® Guide to Writing Research Papers
Everything® Improve Your Writing Book, 2nd Ed.
Everything® Writing Poetry Book